MOROCCO

MOROCCO

Land of the Farthest West

ROBIN BRYANS

FABER AND FABER
24 Russell Square
London

First published in mcmlxv
by Faber and Faber Limited
24 Russell Square, London, WC1
Printed in Great Britain by
W. & J. Mackay & Co Ltd, Chatham

For
MARY AND RANDOLPH CHETWYND

Illustrations

ILLUSTRATIONS

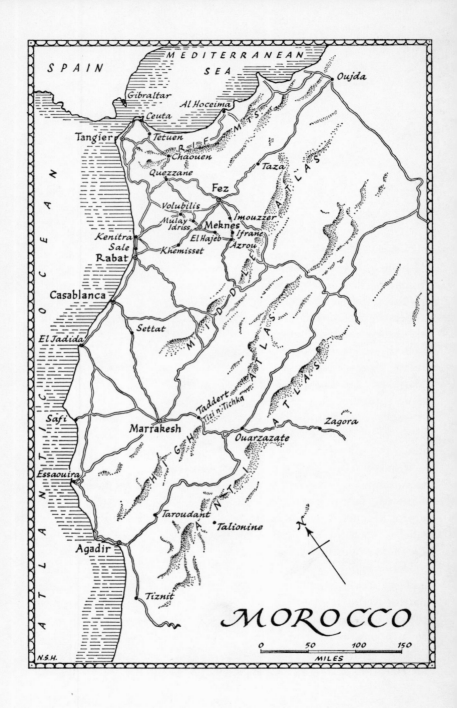

Preliminaries

The first thing a visitor learns in Morocco is not to be suspicious of friendliness. The second is not to be surprised.

Not to be suspicious is easy. Not to be surprised is difficult. You expect and get date palms and camels, but oak and cedar forests and ski resorts and mountain-trout fishing come as a surprise—like the sacred storks everywhere or the vast acreage of wheatfields, or the intact beauty of the four walled imperial cities of Fez, Meknes, Marrakesh and Rabat, the present capital. And nothing perhaps is more surprising than the once-remote Berber south with its quasi-deserts and mud-walled houses and fantastic fortified kasbahs, or the chain of trade wind-cooled sea towns and fabled golden beaches down the Atlantic coast.

Unexpected, too, is the splendour of Morocco's Moorish architecture hidden behind the walls and great gates of the ancient cities. Extensive Roman remains and Emmanueline fortresses surprise the visitor as much as the richness of gardens like those of Chaouen or Chella. Not least unexpected are the birds in a wide variety from Eleonora's falcon to alpine accentor.

And besides the superb landscapes of plain and mountain, desert and sea-shore and the scent of mint tea and the clamour of the narrow Arab streets and the endless music of drums and strings and the call of *mouddhins* from minarets, there is Moroccan friendliness, so surprising as to cause suspicion—groundlessly.

I met many students delighting to speak English who taught me a lot about their country of twelve million people whose productive area alone is larger than France. Many bus drivers helped me and some slowed down so that I could look at bee-eaters and gardens, country fairs and historic landmarks. Fishermen talked to me about their catch and often shared it with me over charcoal braziers on the quayside. And the Berber horsemen's tent at Tetuan was not the only one I slept in.

Moroccans love to talk and to laugh, and the stranger is welcome who does the same. Friendship is sacred. Under those blue skies it is simple. It also imposes an obligation to return to their sun one day.

So many people made my journey possible and pleasurable. But special thanks are due to members of the British Embassy and British Council in Rabat, particularly Mr. A. F. Ward and his secretary. Their stoic patience with my questions about fauna and flora and their kindness in getting photographs from the Moroccan National Tourist Office for the illustrations deserve citations.

The only thing not surprising about Morocco is that I am going again, to explore more of this golden country bordered by silent deserts on the east and south and by warm blue seas on the west and north. After all, my Moroccan friends expect me to.

ROBIN BRYANS

London,
December 1964

1

And So to Tangier

'Hi! What do you want?'

Always difficult to answer, that question seemed unusually so, asked within one minute of my stepping on to the quay at Tangier. What indeed did I want? I looked at the questioner. His face was a sultry colour, the skin dark on top with endless days of sunshine and dark beneath with the reddish mahogany of his Arab and negro forebears. A hood of thick brown wool framed the long, strong-boned face. The lips were broad and, in their smile, held partly open to show white and perfect teeth. From the Gothic friar's hood I looked down at his enveloping gown. The *djellaba* fell about him in graceful folds like sculpture. And though ragged, half-heartedly mended with alien patches, it was a dignified dress, ending just above two large brown feet clasped in ancient leather sandals.

'You want good hotel?' he insisted from the deep shadow of the pointed hood.

I looked from the quay across the tranquil water of Tangier harbour. Ripples and white foam scored its surface where water-skiers ploughed swift furrows in the wake of motor-boats. In the briefest and brightest of swim-briefs the young bucks fled past us in their flashy, exhibitionist sport. *They* would be staying at the good hotels, I reflected. The cool marble hotels I knew well from other tropical travels. Such hotels peppered the Atlantic and Pacific and Mediterranean coasts. They resembled each other so closely that being in Brazil was no different from being in Biarritz or Bombay.

'Me know good hotel.' The earnest, friendly face smiled again from the monkish *djellaba*. His world was so different from the smart, air-conditioned world of the water-skiers. I sensed that Morocco was going to be real and immediate.

I only had a small worn bag with me. It looked pathetic compared with the luxury trappings of other passengers. They were streaming now down the gangway of the Bland Line ferry from Gibraltar like the animals leaving Noah's ark after the flood. Sensing my hesitation and seeing my scruffy bag, the youth in the *djellaba* left me. Experience of other tourists on other summer afternoons had taught him where the fattest tips for his services as guide would come from. Moving in his heavy robe, he made off to where the holiday-makers stood pausing, wondering which way to go. English voices came from little groups with tennis rackets and National Health spectacles. French laughter came from under plain straw hats bought specially for the holiday in the Galeries Lafayette. And big Germans loaded with photographic outfits mingled with sparse Scandinavians come south to worship the sun. They all, no doubt, would want good hotels such as the brown-faced boy had offered.

When the customs man had scrawled a secret sign in green chalk on my bag, I wandered along the quay. Hotels could wait. I wanted to savour my first taste of Tangier. The city tumbled about its seven hills above me and looked down on a scimitar of sand, curving round the turquoise water of the bay. Sand and sea and the seven hills had been there when Roman soldiers patrolled the waterfront 2,000 years before. Perhaps the city, in those days the capital of Mauretania Tingitania, had reminded them of Rome's seven hills, as the straight classical nose of my would-be guide in the *djellaba* had reminded me of Roman noses on bronze busts.

A short distance along the quay I sat in the shadow thrown by the hull of the *Hurrying Angel*, pulled out of the water for a refit. Several Moroccans slept their way through the two-o'clock sun beneath the bows, curled up in *djellabas*, sandals beneath their heads for pillows.

Hurrying Angel seemed a good name for a boat, suggestive of Sir Wilfred Grenfell's mission to the Eskimos. But there was nothing arctic about Tangier, except perhaps the whiteness of the sun. Tall houses jostled dangerously on escarpments near the dock gateway.

Shutters kept out the sun which lit on the waterfalls of bougain-villaea gushing over high garden walls.

The ferry from Gibraltar, the pleasure liners from New York and Valencia had emptied their own flood of colour. But tomato-red convertible cars and emerald-green headscarves paled beside the brilliance of the bougainvillaea which burst the dams of old stone walls and flowed in waves of intense magenta over the wastelands to the warehouses and the burnished sea. And if the colours of the tourists' clothes clashed shockingly, their violence to the eye was nothing beside the collision of the magenta and crimson creeper against the radiant blue of the sky.

I could not believe this was Africa. Morocco, I thought, should have been a blasted heath of burnt-up rock, yet here everything was green and prolific. Morning glory spread as a royal mantle over back-yards and cloistered alleyways. Even the dock warehouses were smothered under a lemon and white dustsheet of honeysuckle that weighted the air already heavy with oleander.

Fig trees and the feathery asterisks of palms punctuated the after-noon's pulsating air which, in the warmth of high summer, was re-puted to be too fierce for the English season.

But beyond the docks, up in the heart of the old city, stood an aged fig tree under which Samuel Pepys was said to have written many pages of his Tangier journals in similar high summers and fashionable winters. Mr. Pepys, however, was hardly on holiday. Not one among all the twenty-three years of British rule in Tangier was conducive to holidays. Moulay Ismail saw to that. Even when the forces of this Moroccan king allowed a lull in their perpetual siege of the city, English soldiers guarded Mr. Pepys as he sat writing under the fig tree.

The spry Samuel Pepys of the English journals is, alas, absent from those written in Tangier. Perhaps the strain of knowing that Moulay Ismail was encamped just outside the city wall, ready to pounce, deprived the diarist of his accustomed gaiety. In Tangier he wrote almost entirely of tedious governmental affairs, of mismanage-ment by the various British governors of the colony and the incon-veniences occasioned by Whitehall's reluctance to spend money on its African possession. Mr. Pepys's account of Tangier makes dull reading compared with an earlier one written by a Moorish author, Leo Africanus, who became Giovanni Leone after his conversion to Christianity. He wrote a history of Africa, and this, with several others of his works, was translated into English in 1600. Whereas poor Pepys's pages were unrelievedly weary, Leo Africanus had most imaginative things to say about the origin of Tangier: 'The great and ancient citie of Tangia called by the Portugals Tangiara, according to the fond opinion of some historiographers, was founded by one *Sedded* the son of *Had*, who (as they say) was emporour ouer the whole world. This man (say they) determined to build a citie, which for beautie might match the earthly paradise. Wherefore he compassed the same with walles of brasse, and the roofes of the houses he couered with gold and siluer, for the building whereof he exacted great tributes of all the cities of the world. But the classicall and approued authors affirme that it was built by the Romanes upon the Ocean shore, at the same time when they subdued the kingdomes of Granada.'

It must have seemed to the redoubtable Pepys that the story of Tangier was already old. The Portuguese drove the Moors out of their own country and were mad with missionary zeal to set the Cross against the Crescent on African soil. To this end, they captured Tangier in 1471. And long afterwards, for less pious purposes, they conceded the city to England. Catherine of Braganza appeared on the royal marriage market. Despite the fact that she carried a dowry twice as large as any other previous royal dowry, she lacked admirers. The solid weights in gold and silver tempted no suitors, even though the bridal offer included the much-coveted trading rights with Brazil, as well as possession of Bombay and Tangier.

Louis XIV could afford to disdain both Catherine and her dowry. But the Sun King's cousin, Charles II of England, could not. He married the Portuguese princess, and as one result of this expedient union Tangier became British in 1661, Samuel Pepys being appointed Secretary to the Committee for the Affairs of Tangier.

In those days the strong king, Moulay Ismail, ruled Morocco. He dominated the country as Louis XIV dominated France. Indeed, Moulay Ismail was known as the Sun King of Africa. He lived in a blaze of splendour and extravagance no less than the French Sun

18

King's. The difference was of style rather than intensity. Like many powerful men, Moulay Ismail suffered from a passion for building on a megalomaniac scale. He had palaces constructed which, in size at least, were not inferior to Louis XIV's operation at Versailles.

As though the two royal Suns were to combine by some gravitation of history, Moulay Ismail had a matrimonial interest in Louis's Court. In 1699 he sent an ambassador to France to sign an alliance. This was to be confirmed by the hand of Louis's daughter Marie-Anne, the Princess de Conti. But the 'most beautiful widow in all France' did not respond to the African Sun King's overtures, even though untold luxury would be hers, besides complete freedom to keep her Catholic faith. Since courtiers sought novelty as an antidote against the ennui of life at Versailles, it was surprising that the Princess declined the prospects of excitement in Morocco. She may, however, have been disinclined to accept Moulay Ismail in view of the fact that he already had a thousand women in his harem. Nor could the Princess de Conti have been much encouraged to reflect that first among the wives was a buxom negress reputed to be a witch, who always carried a sword and even made the Sultan Moulay Ismail himself afraid. The French princess's foresight in refusing the Moroccan king's offer perhaps can best be seen in the fate of a 15-year-old English girl. Braving the dangers of witchcraft and other rivalries within the Sultan's harem, she was his favourite for a time, and even became a Moslem when her white feet were plunged into boiling oil.

The great Sun King of Morocco did not like the British occupation of Tangier, for he was attempting to unify his vast empire. Being a man of many parts, diplomatist as well as bloodthirsty conqueror, in 1682 he sent a special emissary to the Court of St. James's. The colourful party, bearing gifts of lions, ostriches, Barbary apes and other exotic animals, was the most extraordinary spectacle London had ever seen. Later history was to give tit-for-tat, because Queen Victoria presented an Indian elephant to the Sultan Moulay Hassan in 1891. This animal caused a similar consternation in Morocco as the lions and ostriches had done in London two centuries earlier. The elephant was used for years as an army mascot and proved to be most effective in clearing the way through mobs.

Although Moulay Ismail's unthinking extravagance matched Louis XIV's, the Moroccan king could, on occasion, display a petulant concern over trifling things. He sent a letter to the British Governor of Tangier, Colonel Kirk, better known as the famous commander of Kirk's Lambs. The Sultan wrote, 'Know that there came to us from your master three coach horses with our servants which were there. Now a coach wants four horses to draw it, wherefore you must needs send us another horse of the same likeness, sort and size that they may draw it with four. Oblige us in this. We depend upon it.' And this seems a curious request when it is borne in mind that not only had Moulay Ismail built stables specially for 12,000 horses, but that he also preferred to have his coach drawn by women or negro eunuchs.

There never was, of course, any accounting for taste, nor indeed for the whims of the powerful. It is not known whether Moulay Ismail got his fourth horse from London, but it may well have been a fit of pique at its non-delivery which led him to drive the British out of Tangier by force shortly afterwards. Although the British departure was somewhat ignominious, some tenancy of Tangier, however shortlived, was probably better than none. At least the British were able to join the long list of occupiers of the ancient city, which, if documentary evidence is to be believed, had been established as long ago as 1450 B.C. as a Phoenician town with the name of Tingis.

Like the European Sun King, Moulay Ismail enjoyed a long reign. But the empire he carefully built up during his fifty-five years on the Sherifian throne crumbled after his death, though his own royal house of the Alaouites continued unbroken, so that today one of his descendants is Morocco's king. Nevertheless, anarchy beset the country, and early in our own century France and Spain were called in to restore law and order. By 1956, however, they reluctantly left Morocco to its own devices again, a unified country once more, under Moulay Ismail's descendant.

Photographs of King Hassan II greeted me throughout my stay in Morocco, every time I went into a café, drank at a bar or boarded a bus. Sharing the position of honour in many places with the present king's picture was that of Moulay Ismail himself. The reproduced engravings of the African Sun King had been left up since the enthusiastic celebrations in 1962 which marked the tricentenary of his ascension to the throne. The Moslem calendar being lunar rather than Gregorian, in three centuries a difference of ten years had accrued. The eleven or twelve days' difference in each year meant that Moulay Ismail's anniversary of 1672 arrived in the Western 1962.

The present king's portrait also hung over the reception desk at the Hotel Madrid where I finally checked in some hours after the eager youth in brown *djellaba* had given me up as useless to his purposes. Entirely without his aid I had found what, to my mind, was a good hotel, though without mention among the starred hotels in my guide-book lists.

The Hotel Madrid fronted on to the narrow Calle de la Playa. Beach Street sounds unromantic in English. But the Calle was as romantic as its Spanish name suggested. At one end it gave on to the palm-lined promenade, and at the other, after climbing up one of Tangier's seven hills, led to the intricate and even more romantic old city. Behind the Hotel Madrid's narrow street front lay a pleasant patio, cool with tiles and shade and hung high with pots of flowers and ferns. My room, also with a tiled floor, had a window which, when I opened the shutters, overlooked the patio.

My worst fears about Tangier were now finally removed. I had been afraid that the city would be big and brash and shiny with international sin. But not a bit of it was like that. Tangier could in no way be mistaken for any other city in the world, and that is no mean achievement in these days when anonymity spreads like a fungus, unchecked by ocean or climate or history or race, disguised meanwhile as 'progress'. Tangier was itself. It was neither a cheap nor an expensive imitation of other famous resorts. And this, I was to find, was Morocco's hall-mark. I fell in love at first sight with Tangier's intimate, carefree atmosphere, a city full of delight and incident.

Now that I was in the city proper, away from the twittering flocks of tourists on the quayside, I could see how handsome a race the Moroccans were. There seemed to be more good-looking people, more potential film-star material per head of population than any other place I had ever been in. And the heads of the population were even more attractive because of their extreme animation. Black eyes laughed or smiled. Voices sounded rich with strange Arabic consonants as traders bantered and bartered, or as passers-by called out 'Hullo. You English?' or 'I spik English.' In a few yards I was offered an incredible variety of things for sale, besides drinks in bars, sight-seeing trips in cars, all with an easy friendliness. It would be, I thought, quite impossible ever to be lonely in Tangier. For one thing, as in all warm climates, life was lived in the open. The city's streets teemed. A thousand and one vendors were there with a thousand and one wares to sell, from shoe-shines to sunshine tours, though they were not the cringing apologetic importuners I had encountered in other countries. These sellers in Tangier had pride and independence.

Around the market-place outside the old city's wall at the top of Calle de la Playa a bustle and buzz of activity was going on, probably much unaltered since the Phoenicians traded there three thousand years ago. No doubt the Phoenicians were swarthy, but perhaps they did not have the modern Moroccan's fine features, compounded as they are of so many Moorish and African elements. The long, flowing *djellabas* emphasized their noble bearing, especially in the old men, who strode about like prophets, their tall sparse figures concealed by the folds of their gowns, their ancient faces ringed by a crescent of snow-white beard. The *djellaba* was not so popular with the younger generation. Like teenagers the world over, they crammed themselves into tight, washed-out jeans and black or white tee-shirts, and this was almost a second national dress.

I stopped to buy cactus fruit, the prickly pear, from a seller who looked about 8 years old. 'Good,' he said with a cheerful smile. 'Very good.' He took a knife from a tin of water and with swift slashes cut the two ends from the lemon-shaped fruit. A deft incision down one side of the green skin and then it was off, revealing the bright yellow fruit inside. I took a wary bite, watched anxiously by the young seller. 'Good,' he repeated, slightly less enthusiastically. I was not sure. The prickly pear was Morocco's most popular fruit. Trays and piles of them could be seen everywhere and the vendors were as familiar a sight at bus stops and on beaches as the water-sellers. But prickly pears possessed neither the luscious richness of the mango nor the distinctive, scented flavour of guavas, both fruits which the cactus pear resembled in a pale sort of way. They had a pappy texture with the mango's touch of turpentine and the guava's gunshot-sized hard pips. But perhaps the prickly pears demanded acquired taste. The Moroccans swallowed them like oysters. I watched a man at a bus stop one day eat two dozen, one after the other.

Where the prickly pear stands in relation to Moroccan eating, so mint tea stands to drinking. The clean fresh scent of mint floated everywhere on the air, surprisingly fragrant. Even the sales pressure behind Coca-Cola has not ousted mint tea from its position as the national drink. In some of the hot southern regions Coca-Cola became a necessity of life to me. But mint tea was always a luxury for the Moroccan people in the sense that the steaming glass of straw-pale tea filled with sprigs of mint was taken whenever two people sat down to talk.

Mint sold in enormous quantities. Bunches of the dark-green leaves lined the booths of mint-vendors or lay on the ground like heaps of mown grass beside the country women who sold it as they squatted, enveloped in their voluminous white *haiks*. Wrapped cunningly around them, the *haik* was like a toga which somehow contrived to conceal their arms and heads as well. This loose garment was extremely graceful and feminine—much more so than the tailored *djellaba* which town women tended to wear. The *djellabas* worn by women were fashioned generally from dark or sober material like cloth for suits. But the *haik* was gleaming white or was formed simply from a huge coloured bath towel. The country women concealed the lower half of their faces by drawing a part of the *haik* across. If they forgot this convention of modesty or wanted to gesticulate to their neighbours by the hand that held the *haik*, then the solid country faces would emerge. The chins were often blue, not with the stubble of beards but with tattooed patterns. Similar designs could be glimpsed occasionally when bare feet peeped from under the *haik*'s lower folds. Herring-bone patterns seemed to be popular as well as the good-luck sign used on the jacket of Somerset Maugham's books.

A separate veil was worn with the *djellaba*, a fine square often of silk tied under the hood behind the head like a handkerchief. This veil, the *negab*, varied in design from extravaganzas resembling anti-macassars to others like old-fashioned milk-jug covers complete with bobbles and glass beads.

The narrow streets of old Tangier carried a pungent smell, not only of the mint, but of verbena and thyme, also used for flavouring the sweet green tea. There was a myriad selection of spices available in scores of the market's stalls and tiny booths. I looked for camomile, which abounds in Morocco, as does the ox-eye daisy. But although camomile makes excellent tea, and can be used for shampoos and poultices, and is still listed in the *British Pharmaceutical Codex*, I could find none among the market's stalls.

When the market began to close towards the end of each afternoon the herb- and fruit-sellers made an exodus from Tangier. They left in groups strung out along the roads leading from the city to their farms in the country. Those whose affairs were comparatively thriving rode asses. The tiny frail-looking animals appeared overburdened, and almost smothered not only by the women in their *haiks* but by loaded panniers strung either side like the tympani of a mounted military band.

The women without donkeys had to walk home, perhaps many miles. Some of them did this in bare feet, though wearing leather leggings against the thorn-scrub of the dusty tracks home. But whether riding or on foot, mothers carried the youngest child on their backs, the baby being secured in yet another swaddling band round the mother's shoulders. All the country wives wore straw hats with immense brims on top of their *haiks*. The brims were so wide that thick strands of wool fixed between the crown of the hat and the edge of the brim held them up. These great sunshades made the women most attractive and distinctive. They also wore red and white towels striped like candy as a kind of apron. And so, dressed like an opera chorus, they wended their way slowly through Tangier, riding unprotesting asses or tramping shoes in hand out towards the mountains and their farms.

But though the sugar-rock-candy-striped and sombreroed women made a spectacle on their homeward pilgrimage, even they looked quite plain beside the baroque splendour of the water-sellers. Nothing in Morocco could compare with the marvels of their paraphernalia. Selling water was strictly a man's job. The richness of their garb contrasted strangely with their obvious poverty. Water did not make the same profits as Coca-Cola, even though in some instances it might have been the scarcer commodity of the two. Water-sellers were as ubiquitous as the prickly-pear boys or the shoe-shiners, though unlike them they were usually old men with cadaverous cheeks and naked spindly legs. An uncanny air hung about them as of itinerant witch-doctors. They carried brass bells which rang out constantly. Around their necks brightly polished brass cups hung as though they were fetishes of some pagan sun rites. On their heads sat big straw hats highly decorated and hung with baubles. As the men walked about they jingled and jangled, for they wore amulets and anklets and armlets studded with brass and glass and small fragments of mirror. Slung like bagpipes on their left sides were goatskins taut with water. An untrained-puppy trail dripped behind the water-sellers as water leaked from brass taps inserted into the shaggy goatskins.

I never drank their water. Fear of infection made me cautious. Yet, illogically, I ate fruit at the old city stalls. My mornings in Tangier began with peaches in the market. I had never tasted such luscious peaches before. They melted succulently in my mouth and I consumed so many that intestinal troubles were certainly courted. But how could I *not* eat them? But if the peaches drugged me, making me a kind of lotus-eater, the bustle in the market and the narrow twisting streets within the old city's walls acted like sirens, seducing me from my course. Several times I set out determinedly to visit specific places in the city. But the sirens lured me and I never ever reached my goal. I could not walk by and ignore the country women setting out their herbs and spices, peppers and eggs on the pavements under the banana trees which peeped over the garden walls of high, shuttered houses. I stood and stared like an imbecile at old men stooping to choose the choicest of green pine cones roasting there and then over charcoal braziers in a score of refreshment stalls. Some of these old men, long past active participation in this swarming life, were too-perfectly dressed. In their long, too-clean robes they looked like English Sunday-school children dressed up as the Wise Men in a Christmas play.

And just beyond the roasting pine cones a pair of cocks would be fighting over a rotten pomegranate on the main road leading to the Sultan's palace. Here small girls hurried by with enormous trays on their heads to bakehouses. Children clustered at the doors of these cave-like rooms which had glowing, sweet-smelling ovens at one end. Looking down into the bakeries, I could see the bakers themselves and the flat round cakes of dough, stamped with star shapes, being fed on long wooden spades into the deep charcoal ovens. Next door to the baker's there might be a melon shop, selling nothing but melons, huge melons heaped up like blocks of green marble in a quarry. Then I would stop again, fascinated by the orderly rows of sacks at the shop beyond the melon specialist. The sacks were rolled down at the top to reveal an astonishing variety of flour, rice, beans, lentils, spices, dyes, nuts and dried fruits, all waiting for housewives to feel and see and sample.

Though I had no crew to bind me to the mast, I managed to resist the market sirens one morning and found myself looking at the white walls of the Sultan's palace. Nothing more than a madman had detained me as, clad in dreadful rags, he cried aloud, like John the Baptist in the wilderness, except that he was surrounded by French and American cars. The Sultan's palace was not difficult to find, for at least a score of tiny boys attached themselves to me like a retinue, all wanting to act as guides and certainly speaking sufficient English to do so. One of them gave a marvellous mime to illustrate that the Bab el Assa we were passing was the Flogging Gate.

The palace crowned a maze of twisting streets on one of the seven hills. But the climb was rewarded with a panorama of the city's beaches. Even up there, far from the sands down below, droves of young boys with shaved heads wore nothing but swimming-trunks. They seemed permanently ready to plunge into the sea under the hill while they took the family goats out to graze on wastelands. The noise of boys' shouts as they played together filled the old city's narrow streets.

Outside the palace snake-charmers performed before a battery of tourist cameras. They put the snakes in their mouths and wrapped them round their necks to the low, vibrant sounds of a Bendir drum played by a bored-looking man in the background. The snakes also looked bored. Although the snakes seemed to have been milked of their poison, or drugged, I was not willing to have them placed around my own neck by the charmer for photographs I did not want.

A snake entwined itself lasciviously about a large and over-exposed blonde German bosom. I left the group of charmed tourists and went into the palace. Part of the building still contained a prison, but the rest was open to inspection as an architectural monument. Arab invaders of Europe had already evolved a style of building by the ninth century A.D. This architecture was distinctive and quite different from Moslem building of the East. It flourished in Spain particularly and was brought back again to Morocco when a million Moslems fled from Spain after the fall of Cordova in 1236.

Cordova itself was the site of a splendid and still famous mosque (now cathedral) whose great beams were made of thuya wood imported by the Moslems in Spain from their African homeland. Seville, too, had works of this school, notably the great Giralda tower. The centuries of Moorish domination in southern Spain remain curiously alive. Moroccans nostalgically recall the golden age when the Crescent was raised over the Giralda and when El Andalus was Moslem. I found that 'Andalusian' was still a word much in use. Any village boy in the Rif mountains of northern Morocco knew the word, for it was used almost as a synonym for 'music'. Although Moroccan music was Arab and had respectable origins in Medina and Mecca, its association with Moorish Spain still lingered on.

Moroccan architecture also remained linked with the Moors in Spain. The distinctive Western style which the Moors evolved in the Iberian peninsula continued virtually unchanged after their return to Morocco. The formulas of design and material conceived in Spain so long before were perpetuated, the skills of the craftsmen being passed from father to son. The Sultan's palace at Tangier was one such building. It was not old when compared with the original models built in Spain, yet old enough to be one of Tangier's historic sights.

Tangier might indeed have had more monuments to offer the modern visitor had it not been for the British of Mr. Pepys's day.

Their own contribution to building in their neglected North African possession amounted to little more than the construction of a mole by which warships could anchor safely in the bay. But when maladministration and Whitehall's continued parsimony led to the British abandonment of the city they destroyed the mole before leaving. They were not going to let Moulay Ismail get his hands on that.

I sat in the cool, arched entrance chamber of the Sultan's palace, trying to remember the long story of art and religion and wars which lay behind the use of horseshoe arches and coloured wall and floor tiles and coloured faience with restless, involved geometrical designs, projecting cornices of elaborately carved cedarwood, the stucco panels sinuously carved in Arabic script with quotations from the Koran.

Compared with the wonders of Cordova, the Sultan's palace at Tangier could not be called great architecture, nor could the slender minaret near by be measured against the Giralda in Seville or its sister towers elsewhere in Morocco. Yet the palace gave a good impression of how princes lived—and, indeed, continue to live, though nowadays their palaces evoke nineteenth-century Rhineland castles rather than ninth-century Spanish mosques.

The old palace formed a charming museum, yet lost none of its palace-like quality. In one of the rooms a collection had been assembled of pottery and stone fragments and figures from Roman sites in Morocco. It was odd to see classical sculpture within the palace, for in the past representation of the human figure or of animals or birds was strictly forbidden to Islamic artists. The palace walls were decorated by beautiful tiles of white with subtle grey-blues and gold-tawny yellows and duck-egg greens; and, unlike their counterparts and original models in Spain, consisted only of geometric patterns. The elaborate mural decorations of blue and white tiles, the *azulejos*, which the Portuguese developed, originated from the Moorish practice of covering walls and floors with glazed tiles. But the *azulejos*, reaching their peak in baroque and rococo times, rioted with figures and animals and realistic plants in a manner which would have been unthinkable to the Moslem craftsmen of Morocco.

Relics of one sort and another were displayed in other rooms in the old palace. Samuel Pepys would hardly have needed the six-foot-long Treasury door-keys for locking up the slender resources of Whitehall. Among the long rifles with silver inlay, the powder horns, lamps made of stone, wedding dresses and enamelled jewellery from the southern provinces, there was a trumpet, still sounded to herald the beginning of Ramadan. Despite extravagant stories of Tangier during and after the Second World War, tales of international smugglers and war contraband and spies, male and female prostitution, and of staggering gold and dollar transactions, 'markets of death' and the dope pedlars, and all the goings-on of a romantic, international city, no voice was more insistent nor more heeded than that of the *mouddhin* on his minaret. Tangier observed Ramadan as strictly as the remotest village in the Rif mountains. For the whole month of Ramadan, between dawn and sunset, eating, drinking, smoking, the use of perfume and sexual intercourse were given up in a strenuous fast, though the nights were given over to equally strenuous indulgences.

Although Islam resembled Christianity in some of its more ascetic aspects, the Moslem faith never had the horror of fleshly sensuality which, at any rate on paper and in prayer, distinguished the Christian Church. Fast they might at Ramadan and bow to Mecca five times a day. Yet the old palace throne had a dual view of minaret and harem. The throne room opened with considerable architectural pomp from the main palace courtyard, a cool tiled place with a fountain in the centre where I saw a solitary sparrow drinking. Between marble columns of the colonnade, whose capitals were a curious combination of both the Corinthian and Ionic Orders, the throne room showed its three domed compartments. Below the central one of these was a niche most elaborately worked with rows of miniature vaulting corbelled out to make a complex solid geometry, made richer by dark-red colouring touched with gilding. From here the Sultan could command a view of all the other doors opening from the courtyard.

One of the official palace guides was talking to a woman tourist.

'This taroona,' he said, pointing at the rich niche. Taroona was the nearest he could twist his tongue to the English word 'throne'.

'Taroona,' he repeated, savouring the strange foreign word. 'And from taroona Sultan see harem.'

He waved his arm to indicate that the courtyard was the harem.

'Was it for walking about in?' asked the woman innocently.

The guide looked at her to see if he had heard correctly. Then he lowered his voice and in the tone of a melodrama's villain said, 'In this place he had three hundred women.'

The lady tourist gave an involuntary 'Oh!' as though she had in some way been fooled into becoming No. 301.

Perhaps faintly aware of her embarrassment the guide added in mitigation, 'When Sultan on taroona he also see house of Allah above harem.' He pointed again. The woman and I followed his finger and there sure enough was the outline of a near-by minaret.

The gangsters and cigarette pirates who gave Tangier its postwar fame did not live in the old city, the *medina*, clustered round the whitewashed, battlemented walls of the palace. They and their brothers in organized crime may have fled to lose themselves within the *medina*'s mesh of alleyways when the International Police picked up their scents. But they set up house with their mistresses or boy-friends in the wider avenues and bigger buildings of the modern city which occupied the arm on the farther side of the bay and covered the high ground inland. Tall upended-shoe-box blocks of luxury flats climbed uphill from the waterfront to the high fashionable Boulevard Pasteur overlooking the city below and the bay beyond. 'The Boulevard', as it was affectionately called, boasted a garden on the wide-open side facing the view of ships in the harbour and bathers on the sandy beach. The beds held a flood of brilliant red canna lilies with a flame-like intensity which hypnotized the toddlers. Their mothers brought them there in the cool hours between the decline of the afternoon heat and sundown. For the women of the *medina* came up to the Boulevard in a cloud of white *haiks* to sit by the flowers and admire the view, and to gossip and praise each other's children.

The late-afternoon promenade up at the Boulevard had its counterpart in the day-long meetings at the famous Café de Paris. The Boulevard was terminated at one end by the Place de France, which was regarded as the modern city's centre. On one side, standing amid impressive grounds, was the French Consulate-General, bowered at that time of the year amid masses of blue agapanthus. On the opposite corner of the Place stood the Café de Paris.

Tangier earned itself an image of wickedness once reserved in the Press and bad novels for Far Eastern ports like Shanghai and Yokohama. Tangier became associated with arms deals and white slavery, secret agents and sexual excesses. Certainly during the last war the place was rife with Gestapo agents and Japanese diplomats and young men from the Italian Fascist Centre. They went to sip *café au lait* at the Café de Paris, watched by British Intelligence officers on the alert for any note slipped by a shoe-shine into a proffered foot. The spy network was principally concerned with the destiny of countless human beings. Swiss watches and nylon stockings were not in fashion as bartering material. The contents of ghettoes and concentration camps and war prisons were.

A friend of mine was head of the Swiss Section of the British Ministry of Information during the Second World War, and it was she who told me about the Café de Paris. She had known Tangier since the early 'thirties. When I went to Morocco she gave me letters of introduction to some of her wartime agents.

'Try the Café de Paris. He goes there for a *café solo* around noon,' their maids invariably said when I called at the addresses only to find them out.

Although intrigued to some extent by Tangier's cloak-and-dagger reputation, I was reluctant to waste time drinking in bars of a type to be found anywhere in the world. I wanted to see as much as possible of Morocco rather than expatriate European wide-boys and one-time diplomats. Nevertheless, my friend in London had been most anxious for me to try and pick up a particular trail of mystery which she had herself once stumbled upon. This trail belonged to a man believed by the world at large to have been dead for thirty years. My friend believed he was, in fact, still alive. Her mystery man was Lawrence of Arabia.

Nor was my friend alone in thinking Lawrence still alive. I was surprised by the number of people who had known Lawrence before his famous fatal motor-cycle crash in 1935, and who thought, crash notwithstanding, he still lived. His pathological hatred of fame, once satisfied by his quest for anonymity in the 'other ranks' of the Air Force, had led him, they said, to the deserts of Morocco. Though unwilling to offer explanations about the deception following the motor-bike crash which their theories necessitated, they maintained that Lawrence had been seen since in Morocco. My friend in London insisted she had herself met Lawrence in Tangier towards the end of the war.

I was sitting at the pavement tables of the Café de Paris one morning talking to some English residents about Lawrence. A young man at the next table was smiling and nodding and beckoning to me. I supposed he was a male prostitute and ignored him. But the following night he materialized again as I was having supper near the sea-front. If nothing else, Mohammed was persistent.

The restaurant was the opposite of the Café de Paris, or the Fat Black Pussy Cat on the front, which offered English tea and European cooking. For half the price I was enjoying a thick, tasty broth, followed by swordfish and lemon. The fish almost constituted a meal in itself, but while I ate the meat course was being threaded on to skewers and laid across the charcoal brazier on the pavement beside the table. The meat was lamb's liver cut into tiny pieces with fat and rolled in cummin seed, chopped parsley, salt and pepper. The delicious flavour of this miniature barbecue, especially when eaten with date-palm shoots or barley sprouts, was one of Morocco's chief culinary delights for me.

Two sailors had just passed by, wishing me '*Bon Apetit!*' when Mohammed appeared from the darkness under the palm trees across the avenue. He smiled as if we were old friends. I looked at his smart light-weight French suit and two-tone shoes, and his open smile. Why, I wondered to myself, is he keen on *me*? After all, there were foreigners about obviously more wealthy.

'I sit down, please?' smiled Mohammed. Prepared to be beaten up, abducted, robbed and abandoned by the rest of his gang whom I presumed to be hiding behind the palms, I nodded assent. Although he was a Moslem, and named after the Prophet like so many first-born sons, Mohammed ordered a brandy.

'I know all,' he began.

Drums in the sun—Tbel rhythm for Devil Dancers

Stripes in the sun—Rif country women

'All what?' I asked with redoubled suspicion.

'All about what you were saying at the Café de Paris.'

'I don't understand.'

'Yes. You do. Lawrence of Arabia. I know all.'

It was my turn for a brandy. A thousand possibilities rushed into my mind. Supposing Mohammed did not know all, but at least knew something, might he not be the means of my discovering the whereabouts of Lawrence, even if the famous man would now be 76 years old? Mohammed, of course, would want payment for his information. I wondered how much.

But Mohammed came straight to the point. There was not a mention of money.

'Lawrence, he not killed. Only another who rides in his place.'

In the warmth of the Tangier evening I felt suddenly chill. My second brandy seemed to taste like Coca-Cola. I controlled my excitement and began to question Mohammed, and discovered that we were talking about two different things. Mohammed had been speaking the truth, but he was referring to the making of the film *Lawrence of Arabia*. The accident concerned a stand-in for Lawrence who had been thrown from a camel, and not T. E. from his motor-bike.

My relief was immense. The exhumation of Lawrence, alive or dead, was a responsibility I could hardly have borne. Besides, it pleased me to know that Mohammed was completely guileless. His only crime was the ingenuous friendship I found everywhere in Morocco. Mohammed was the second person I met who claimed to have been an extra in the film. In the end, I found his chatter not only about the film but about Tangier in general much more interesting than all the talk I had indulged in about T. E. Lawrence himself. I lost interest altogether when a British Embassy official from Rabat told me that the person who was to have served as my main Lawrence contact was, in fact, 'more than a little fey'.

Tangier's beaches were ideal. The sands reached uninterrupted for miles round the bay, flat and kind to the feet, hot and soft for lying on, comfortable for swimming from. By a providential kindness, the heat of Tangier's hottest months was tempered by cooling winds from the sea. So that the yellow sandy beach, instead of being unbearably hot in July and August, was coolly refreshing.

Although bathing-beaches lay around the whole bay, Tangier sea-front occupied only a small part of it. The wide palm-lined Avenue d'Espagne extended in a straight line from the foot of the *medina* on its hill and the docks and ran to the undeveloped eastern end of the town. On the landward side were hotels and restaurants and bars, with streets leading off steeply to the upper part of the town. On the seaward side of the Avenue was a single-track railway line, then a long row of reasonably inoffensive and inexpensive beach cafés and clubs with changing-cubicles and shower-baths, and beyond them the wide sands themselves. Where the Avenue stopped, so did the beach buildings. All was neat and tidy in a manner which could well be recommended to many scruffy English resorts.

By nine in the morning the Avenue was full of people hurrying along to the beach. Not only German hitch-hikers and French Boy Scouts wolf-whistling at the beautiful Moroccan girls on the sands emerging like butterflies from the chrysalis of their *djellabas*, but hundreds of Tangier people went to the sea every day. Glimpses could be had of Argyll socks beneath the long robes of old men and little boys scrambling out of their clothes on the pavement unable to wait even till they reached the sea. Troops of girls like nuns were followed by youths and muscle-men in tee-shirts and jeans. Groups of northern Europeans still brightly pink with the first alarming sunburn contrasted comically with other foreigners tanned impossibly by weeks of Tangier sunshine. All those bent on this morning pilgrimage went to bask on the sands or thresh about in the warm sea with flailing limbs. All became eventually transmuted by the alchemy of the sun not into gold but into a rich, oiled rosewood, ranging in tone from the palest to the darkest jacaranda.

Although the single track was the main railway line in and out of Tangier, trains were infrequent and the country people commuting on foot into the city used it as a short cut. I also walked along it, for the track went by means of embankments and bridges beyond the city limits to where sea and countryside came together. Cactus and bramble hedges succeeded the half-finished new buildings of Tangier's eastern limits and then the farms began. By the sea, beyond the crowded city beaches, men loaded sand into panniers which their donkeys carted away with time-immemorial patience.

Near by, old boats had been drawn up from the sea and left to rot unmourned beside scores of slowly rusting anchors that stretched pronged arms to the sky like a stricken forest. Vacant lots and waste-lands began where the sands rose beyond the waves' reach. Ragwort and morning glory sprawled in the luxury of untamed wildness around these foreshores, and there was blue larkspur whose depth of colour made even the convolvulus insipid. Beyond this a concrete canal fed into the sea, its water copper-green. City boys used it as a swimming-pool. Their brown bodies gleamed and flashed like fishes. They screamed and shouted in happy nakedness, for none of them had the swimming costumes required for the city beaches.

I walked farther round the bay where the wind had sculptured the sand into low dunes. The sea fell lazily with scarcely a murmur at my feet. Thin piping came from waders stalking delicately over the mud-flats of a sluggish river. Wheeling sea-swallows dived like the mahogany-coloured urchins in the canal. I swam and sunbathed and swam again to cool off until the sun reached its noon elevation and hunger drove me back more quickly than I had come to a midday meal.

After food, sleep followed. The beaches emptied miraculously as though some disaster had swept the bathers away. Emptied, too, were the *medina*'s streets. Few people strolled under the palms along the Avenue d'Espagne. Barbers slept in their own chairs. Charcoal-burners under their log piles. Letter-writers put their heads in the boxes where their pens and paper were kept. Fruit-sellers stretched in the patch of shade under their barrows. And the gardens opposite the seaside railway station became a dormitory for scores of people sleeping on the springy mattress of Kikuyu grass roofed by shaggy tamarisks.

It seemed as if the city could never be waked from so much sleep. Yet by four o'clock the drift to the beach had begun again, and old men looked for fountains to wash themselves in preparation for evening prayers. By five o'clock the market women began the journey out into the country, ignoring the tourists having *real* English tea outside the Fat Black Pussy Cat. By six o'clock the shadows were long, and by seven it seemed suddenly cool.

Nightfall was protracted, yet the day started again. The bars and

cafés filled up. The Avenue d'Espagne became crowded with
strollers. The city glittered with lights and indefinite music from
unseen radios floated on the air. Tangier's celebrated night-life had
begun. Much of it was mythical, I felt sure, though I had no intention of finding out. A clip-joint is a clip-joint whether in Soho or
Tangier. The lure of night-clubs and floor-shows, the haunts of big-
time criminals and real-estate sharks, if such there were in Tangier,
had no appeal.

I lingered under the palms along the Avenue, enjoying the simple
life. It was not all that simple either. Apart from the men and youths
strolling hand in hand, and whole families with closely veiled women
and beautiful doe-eyed children, there were the vendors still persistent, anxious to sell one more rug or one more tooled-leather bag
before the evening's end. Under some of the trees on the Avenue's
benches young boys sat crocheting white woollen hats, using hooks
of wood like pencils, with amazing dexterity and speed. The hats
were good hats and I thought ruefully of the awful winter nights in
England when I should regret not buying some. The boys could not
understand why I refused. How could I explain that I did not want
to travel round Morocco loaded with woolly hats? And how could
I travel light if I bought a *guembri*?

True, the *guembri*, being a sort of small banjo, was more bulky
than white wool caps. Although I felt guilty at each refusal, I had to
be firm. Even when the peculiar delights of the home-made *guembri*
were explained it made no difference. I appreciated the skilled
carving of the eighteen-inch black and white neck and its pegs, and
the resonance given to the wire strings by the skin stretched tautly
over the large tortoise's shell that made the instrument's belly. I
fully understood that the *guembris* were traditional, though once
upon a day fashioned from apricot wood. I could even approve of
tortoises' shells being used instead of apricot wood to cope with the
tourist demand for *guembris*. It seemed a better fate for the poor tortoises, in which Morocco abounded, than that they should die
horribly in nature's way—whereby the great bearded vulture carried
the living creatures into the air and dropped them and smashed them
open on rocks, before swooping down again to consume the horrible
remains.

No woolly hats and no banjos. More difficult to explain was my strong desire *not* to buy the *Daily Express* or *The Times*. The newspaper boys had unerring instincts about nationality. They would never offer a Fleet Street product to a Dane, nor Denmark's *Politiken* to a Spaniard. Moreover, they were not so persistent as the other vendors. Perhaps their sharpened instincts also taught them how news is even more transitory than life itself.

Such profound philosophy was beyond their command of English, but often well within the range of students and schoolboys who were studying English. When the vendors of hats or rugs or chewing-gum or shoe-shines became too importunate, some such student would appear and rescue me and, with no doubt well-chosen words in Arabic, drive the assailants away. Then, extending his hand for me to grasp, indicate that he would like us to join the strollers while he asked about London's perpetual fog and whether English beaches were as good as Morocco's.

But at last after a gentle good night and a promise to renew acquaintance tomorrow I would be alone to look at the moon on the sea and walk back again to the hotel along the Avenue d'Espagne. As quickly as the beaches emptied at midday, so the Avenue would at night. For whatever antic wickedness the wealthy tourists indulged in up at Tangier's expensive night-clubs, the ordinary people were indoors if not in bed by eleven o'clock. Only a light-breasted owl which lived in the palms was wide awake, making daring forays among the neon lights. Strollers and vendors were gone. And so was the wrongly suspected Mohammed whose dreams no doubt were of another crowd part in some future, bigger and better *Lawrence of Arabia*.

2

Berber Bergamasque

Oleander bloomed along the thirty-seven miles to Tetuan. The heady, sickly but irresistibly sensuous smell of the pink blossom blew in the bus windows, from which I could see the dark-green bushes. They crowded the banks of sunken watercourses that threaded the flat burnt-up plains bordering the road. Although oleander grew from the Rif mountains in the north to the Anti-Atlas in the south, nowhere were they so profuse as on the Tetuan road.

High summer had dried the river-beds, but could not stop the full spate of the luxurious oleander foaming with sweet pink flowers. On either side the fields shone gold with stubble as though overlaid with burnished metal plates. Shepherds and their flocks wandered there, like ghosts doomed to search for ever in vain for green things. As the bus sped by the oleander beds seemed to be the only touch of green in that gold landscape. Yet ironically no beast would eat its succulent leaves, because they were poisonous. The mixed flocks of cattle, sheep and goats avoided the deceptive oleander. The sinister paradox had its expression in ancient writings when this most luscious plant had no mention as food value except for use as a snake-bite antidote.

The cloth-of-gold fields, indeterminate in extent because of a haze of dust or heat, lapped everywhere like a tawny sea against hills, either near or far. And as the landscape's peculiar beauties began to reveal themselves I saw that the herbage floor was not all arid. Between the burnt-up deserts of stubble and scrub, hummocks of dwarf palmetto formed little green oases, dotting the hills and

valleys and making excellent coverage for button-quail, and lending
its roots as a domestic vegetable. I saw that women were at work
reaping the palmetto's green fans, seemingly in lieu of hay.

With uncanny instinct the grazing herds found living things to
eat among the dry twigs. White and graceful cattle egrets accompanied the herds. Their whiteness was as startling as the green
rivers of oleander in the brown landscape. The egrets were most
sociable, walking beside the cattle and ignoring the herdsmen as
they picked out ticks and insects from the beasts. Their main food
came not from the animals' parasites but from the large insects and
grasshoppers fleeing before the animals' hoofs.

As we approached Tetuan the bordering hills became larger and
rockier, more powerful as a reminder that the Rif range was not far
away, guarding the central area of Morocco from the Mediterranean.
Somewhere in the distance was Djebel Tiziren at the Rif's highest
point of 8,229 feet. We passed the wide River Martin that emptied
itself in the Mediterranean and saw brickmakers cutting the clay
from its banks, and quite suddenly afterwards we were in Tetuan.

Mountains were to this city what the sea was to Tangier. They
surrounded the town like an ancient wall. Berbers had long ago come
out of those mountains and already had a community of some sort
on the site by A.D. 800, when Omar, son of Idris II, founder of Fez,
was made Pasha.

Tituan was an old Berber password, meaning *open eyes*. An additional suggestion as to the origin of the city's name is another Berber
word, *tituaen*, meaning *springs*. The presence of water would have
been a good enough reason for building a town there, though the
Berbers would equally have needed a site which could be adequately
watched by open eyes. The Moslem invasion of the early eighth
century showed what the cost of non-vigilance could be. But the
Berbers survived the Arab conquest. Nobody knows how long they
have occupied the fastnesses of the Rif and Atlas mountains. The
nineteenth-century Berbers may have been afraid of the elephant
sent by Queen Victoria to Sultan Moulay Hassan, but the earliest
rock drawings in the country showed elephants, rhinoceroses,
giraffes, all long since absent from Morocco.

Mountain peoples appear in history as mysterious and remote,

somehow different from the wanderers on the plains. The ancient
Greeks in their mountains, Tibetan monks in theirs, the lyrical
Welsh and the independent Swiss, seem to have been conditioned
by mountains. The Berber race always attracted notice. The Egyptians called them *Lebu*, the Greeks *Libyans*, the Romans *Numidae*,
and from *Barbarian* comes Berber—a quite unjust and most unfortunate association, for I found the Berbers intelligent and gifted
at languages and possessed of quicksilver humour.

The Berbers' own name for themselves was Imaziren, but within
this other names identify different groups and social types. A boy
with a deeply sun-tanned face and negroid lips told me about
Berbers, but insisted that he was an Imaziren, distinct from the
Chleuhs of the south and High Atlas regions. Yet ancient monuments in Egypt depicted his ancestors with the blond features which
still distinguish many Berbers. Theories have come thick and fast
about Berber origins, some of which claimed Celtic-Iberian sources.
Berber language has been shown by some to have affinities with early
Egyptian and even Welsh. Other suggestions included descent from
the Canaanites forced to flee Palestine by Joshua's army, while yet
others maintain that the Berbers, like Pathans of the North-West
Frontier, came from the Ten Lost Tribes.

Anthropogeny is an interesting science, because nothing can be
proved or disproved. One man's informed guess is as good as the
next man's. I liked to think of the Berbers' origins being shrouded in
impenetrable obscurity. People would go on talking about them, but
nobody would ever know. It is fairly certain, however, that the
Berbers were not African stock. Quite a number have negro blood
today from intermarriage with Sudanese slaves in comparatively
recent times. Fusion of one blood into another has given Morocco
some of its most handsome and virile people.

In the first century B.C. Moroccan Berbers enrolled as soldiers to
Pompey and Sertorius. And they later assisted the Arabs in the
invasion of Spain. By the eleventh century the first of the great
Berber dynasties had subjected the Arabs and become masters of
Granada.

'Sister of Granada' was one epithet attached to Tetuan by a
tourist pamphlet I read, though it was the Caliph of Cordova who

raised Tetuan to the status of a city in A.D. 961. The last, return conquest of Tetuan by Christian Spain only took place in 1913. But although everybody was speaking Spanish in the Restaurant Marina where I went for lunch after my bus journey from Tangier, the Arabs and Berbers were the city's masters once more. The High Commissioner of Spanish Morocco had packed his bags for Madrid eight years before.

Spain's modern occupation of the venerable city had left only a mongrel Latin town. The pretensions of its third-rate provincial builders fortunately stopped outside the seventeenth-century ramparts which Moulay Ismail built as his headquarters for raiding British Tangier and Portuguese Ceuta.

Tetuan was nearer to Ceuta than to Tangier. The Portuguese city had been captured in A.D. 1415 after a memorable battle in which a thousand English lances joined the Portuguese. Amongst the Christian warriors was a young prince who later became the famous Henry the Navigator. He was the son of Don Juan and Philippa of Lancaster, and consequently a grandson of John of Gaunt.

How spectacular those absurd wars of religion must have been with their lances and banners and armour and coats of arms on the one side and the Barbary splendour of the Moslems on the other. Prince Henry proved his manhood by fighting non-stop for five hours at Ceuta, for which he was knighted by his father in the mosque they had just desecrated and over which the Cross had been raised to the sound of Te Deums. The wonder and beauty of early fifteenth-century Morocco filled Henry's imagination, and he determined to find the lost kingdom of Prester John, the Earthly Paradise and the Land of the Pepper Trees. Ceuta's palaces, with their cool mosaics, playing fountains, precious stones, spices, lion cubs and tapestries from the East, appealed to the young man. He had never seen anything like it before. But he did not emulate the life lived in them. Surrounded by astronomers and old sea-dogs and young discoverers, the Prince lived like a monk in a bleak stone house at Sagres. One of the most important of these contacts in Henry's dreams of discovery was a Spanish slave they took back to Portugal after the victory at Ceuta. But though the captive's stories of shipwrecks off the Moroccan coast may have led to the discovery of

Madeira, the great name among discoverers was the extraordinary
Arab navigator Sherif Mohammed el Edrisi.

Born in Tetuan in 1099, El Edrisi helped King Roger II to make
Sicily one of the world's wonders, even surpassing Byzantium. As
well as producing his descriptive manuscript *Al Rojari*, he spent
fifteen years making a huge silver globe of the world. El Edrisi constructed it from accounts given him by seamen and travellers of every
colour and creed whom King Roger collected at his court to assist
the Moroccan. His descriptions and statistics of towns in his homeland show how civilized North Africa was compared with Europe.

Three centuries later Henry the Navigator filled his court with
similar men, trying to rediscover the lands and islands described in
El Edrisi's book. And two centuries later still Moulay Ismail was
filling El Edrisi's birthplace with troops as anxious to get the Portuguese out of Ceuta as he was to unseat Mr. Pepys from under the
fig tree in Tangier. The Moroccan Sun King built Tetuan's immense
walls as part of his plan, equipping it with castellated turrets and
giving access to and from the city only by seven gates—one of which
I entered—the Gate of Thoughts.

The Spanish armies of occupation had known it as *Puerta de los
Pensamientos*. But they had now taken the last of their thoughts with
them, leaving their barracks to the Moroccan soldiers whose green
berets, bright as billiard-tables, were familiar in the human landscape. But the army in khaki I encountered in the Rue Ibn Aazzuz
was not at all warlike. They insisted I should look inside their old,
domed building which, through its low entrance from the narrow
medina street, looked like a mosque. But it was the Boy Scouts'
headquarters, and a rehearsal was going on for a concert by the boys
that evening.

Immensely pleased with the novelty of a foreign visitor, the boys
showed me photographs of international jamborees they had attended, and then invited me to hear the lusty community singing of
French-sounding songs by the Wolf Cubs, who stood up and saluted
when I went in. There was an electric enthusiasm in the air and,
about the place, the orderliness in which Scout groups indulge. But
I had already discovered that Morocco liked cleanliness.

For inexplicable reasons, it is more difficult to keep towns unsullied in hot countries than in cool ones. Perhaps because the rain does not wash things so often, or because dust hangs in the air and because in any case so much more of life is lived in the open air and therefore leaves its litter there rather than at home. But Morocco seemed to me to be remarkably and irreproachably kempt. The narrow streets of the *medina* at Tetuan were as impeccable as the Scouts' building, the street boys themselves as spruce as the Scouts.

Compared with the terrible shanty settlements, the *favelas*, up in the hills behind Rio de Janeiro, or the similar shacks made of flattened oil drums, the *ranchitas*, that dot the hills of Caracas, the old Moroccan cities were luxurious. In Brazil the women climb long distances up- and downhill with petrol cans of water to fill their American washing machines. But though the *medina*'s streets were as narrow as the spaces between the shacks in Rio's *favelas*, they were somehow dignified and beautiful. They were paved and in many places, shaded overhead by large cane awnings. Houses and courtyards opened surprisingly from the streets. Doorways gave glimpses of spacious, cool places secluded from the narrow, jostling streets.

Much of this hygiene was due to the Koran. Like Hebrew laws in the Old Testament, the Moslem holy book prescribed not only belief but ways of daily life, of which frequent washing was one. Many tourists have the opposite impressions when they see food being prepared by women whose hands look alarmingly dirty. But the hands are, in fact, only dyed by the constant staining with certain roots and by henna.

Dyeing hands and feet and the hair was a popular form of make-up for Moroccan women, though religion and superstition lay behind it quite as much as female vanity. Little girls in the street had their hair gingered by henna. Because it had miraculous powers, newborn babies were rolled in henna powder. Later, when the baby was taken for purification on the seventh day and given its name, a sheep would be sacrificed if the child was a boy and his hands and feet painted with more henna. And when the henna-painted baby grew up he would see the green heaps of fresh henna for sale in the markets, just as I saw when I said good-bye to the Boy Scouts and tried

to find my way out of the *medina* through another of its seven gateways—the Gate of the Winds.

Tetuan's royal palace lay near the crowded *medina* and hid itself
behind the high walls of a narrow street. Only a high horseshoe door
revealed its presence. King Mohammed V, father of Morocco's
present King Hassan II, continued to use the Tetuan palace until a
few years ago. Even visitors with no sense of history could not ignore
these two monarchs, for every town in Morocco has named its main
streets and squares after them. Though I have a penchant for palaces,
my palate was not stimulated by Tetuan's particular brew of Moorish
architectural elements. A suggestion of Victoriana tainted the whole
thing. A heavy hand had somehow usurped the delicate and graceful
touch which was the peculiar genius of Arabic-Andalusian architecture. The central courtyard, for instance, was roofed in coloured
glass. Instead of the eye of heaven being overhead there were the
virulent colours found in English Victorian hall windows and front
doors. The palace's central courtyard and gallery above might have
been done in fretwork. The throne itself—green plush and gilded
carving—looked as if it had been delivered yesterday from the
Tottenham Court Road. My feeling that the palace would make a
good casino at Monte Carlo was confirmed when a guide switched
on the coloured electric bulbs in the entrance hall. They glared out
vulgarly in the shape of a crown.

Back in the street once more, guilt assailed me for not liking the
palace. After all, the Moroccans were under no obligation to let
hordes of gaping foreigners like myself into their special places,
especially for a low entrance fee of only one dirham, about 1s. 6d.
I tended to regard the coin as a shilling. The dirham was Morocco's
new currency, equal to a hundred of the old francs which were still
in circulation. During my visit the rate of exchange yielded fourteen
dirhams to the pound. In London, however, the bank had given me
sixteen, the same as the exchange rate given in Gibraltar or from the
black marketeers in Tangier.

At the end of the street lay Hassan II Square, which made me
happy again. It was Saturday afternoon and all the world, or at least
a jam of Tetuanese, were there enjoying the passing moment, the
spectacle of life. The square was large and pleasant, surrounded by

inoffensive buildings and a mosque in one corner, and was shaded by fairy-lighted plane trees and was paved and had seats for the world to sit on and watch the rest of the world sipping mint tea at pavement cafés or playing draughts with pieces home-made from bottle-tops, or eating hot broad beans sold from buckets with little charcoal braziers fixed underneath.

Children clustered like bees watched by their veiled mothers. Old men in stately *djellabas* engaged in grave discussion, their importance suggested by the long curving daggers thrust through their belts. These daggers, though rather frightening, were, in most cases, no more lethal than the umbrella carried by the respectable Englishman. The Koran does not allow Moslem men to wear jewellery, so the silver-mounted and chased, enamel and semi-precious stone inlaid daggers were a sublimation of the male desire for decoration. Such daggers, together with superbly tooled leather goods, were being sold in Hassan II Square. Like so many things in Morocco which looked as if devised for the delight of tourists, the dagger salesmen were principally catering for the Moroccans themselves.

The musicians were the same. Their strains became audible above the clamour, eventually clarifying itself into some kind of South American samba rhythm. People in the square lined the pavements to watch them go by.

'Who are they?' I asked a boy in a claret-coloured tee-shirt with EASTWOOD BAPTIST printed on it in bold white letters.

'The King's Second Band,' he said.

If these were the Second what must the First be like? The musicians looked jolly, a privilege of expression denied military bands in Britain, and were obviously happy blowing and banging away at their reed pipes and drums while making an equally jolly sight in their fezes, red monkey jackets and baggy blue pantaloons. But behind them came a band of tall negroes clad in white, and they were responsible for the percussion of the samba, for these were the Gnaoua Dancers—the Devil Dancers—I had heard so much about.

Eastwood Baptist accompanied me round the square as I followed the band and he pointed to a poster. *Feria Regional de Tetuan.* Eastwood also told me how to get to this fair being held by the River Martin outside the city, for which the Gnaoua Dancers had come to town. So many people were waiting for the green single-decker trolley-bus to the fairground that Eastwood Baptist offered me a lift down the long hill on his bicycle and I accepted gladly.

He had omitted to tell me that a seat on the handlebars had also been booked by a friend of his, and another on the carrier at the back by yet another friend. I did not decline for fear of giving offence to Eastwood and his two friends. Convinced that I was about to make the last journey of my life, the four of us spun shakily down the hill. At the bottom I got off, having made vows as to what I would do if the Almighty spared me, which I immediately forgot when a trolley-bus arrived to take me the rest of the way. As on most local buses in Morocco, only a few seats were provided, the rest being standing room. For short journeys this seemed to be more convenient than the effort needed to get in and out of seats on a crowded London bus. Belladonna lilies pushed pink-lustre spearheads up amongst the palm trees in the gardens banking the road.

Darkness had almost fallen by the time the *Feria Regional* opened. Feasts and festivities throughout the country not infrequently began with the spectacular *fantasia*. This display of horsemanship demanded a large field. When I arrived a throng already lined the field, waiting for the group of riders to show off their traditional skills. The ornamentation denied men by the Koran had been lavished on the harness as well as on the men's long rifles and daggers. The beautiful silver-grey horses, highly strung and excitable, set off perfectly the sky-blue, pink and orange silken finery of the trappings. Their riders sat proudly on the magnificent saddles, well aware of cutting fine figures in white robes and turbans, their silver-mounted rifles held upright.

At a signal the horses started forward and charged like the wind, kicking up spurts of dust as though bullets struck the dry ground. The men, still sitting upright, controlled the horses with their legs alone. With both hands free they juggled with the slender rifles, flung them high into the air like drum-majors' maces, and fired them at point-blank range, pulled up miraculously, at full speed, only two or three feet away from the children at the crowd's edge.

A number of the horses were restless, heavy stallions. Such a sight must have inflamed the Prophet's imagination when he wrote,

'By the snorting war steeds, which strike fire with their hoofs as they gallop to the raid at dawn and with a trail of dust split the foe in two.'

The fun of the fair spread to a garden beside the field of the *fantasia*, near a football stadium and an imposing house with a swimming-pool behind. Besides merry-go-rounds and sideshows, the *Feria* provided a trade fair, with booths representing many different occupations, from blind weavers to mobile medical assistants with bottles of blood plasma and jars of mercurochrome, whose red, antiseptic dye used liberally on minor wounds and even foot-rot was a rival to henna.

In addition to exhibitions of hand-bellows, essential to a nation of charcoal-burners, there were three open-air cinemas whose rapt audience sat on the ground on both sides of screens which billowed in the night breeze. The air carried delicious smells from the restaurant booths built of green palm branches, before which reed mats covered the ground for the comfort of squatting patrons absorbed with dishes of stuffed peppers or boiled locusts. The egg-heavy female locust, when cooked in salt water for half an hour, tasted rather like prawns. Several small girls in ankle-length dresses of gold damask looked as though hypnotized when I sat on the ground beside them for a bowl of stewed beef and artichoke stalks.

Our waiter was none other than the Biggest Ironmonger in Morocco. We had met earlier in the day up at the second-hand market in the *medina*. I had rarely seen such a collection as that young man spread on the market pavement—electric irons, crankshafts, coffee-mills, cycle pedals, rat traps, hoes, goldfish in jam jars, besides some very healthy caladium plants growing in bidets. The collection was too fantastic to absorb, but seeing my admiration, the young man laughed and said in English that he was the Biggest Ironmonger in Morocco. Now there he was at the fair transformed into a nimble waiter arranging me a sliced orange and radish salad.

I bolted the last of the meal when the insistent samba rhythm of the Gnaoua Dancers floated across the fairground, a penetrating noise that even the loudspeakers of the three cinemas and relayed music could not subdue. I found the Devil Dancers warming up to their ancient rites on the gravel forecourt of the big house. The

Gnaoua were negroes, with dark skins that showed like purple grapes against the white robes whose sashes were bejewelled with tiny sea-shells. The dances and the trances they induced, the rhythms and dress had all been brought from the Sudan by their ancestors, who came to Morocco as slaves.

Just as the negroes shipped by the British and Portuguese to the New World took their African gods with them to defend them against the enforced conversion to Christianity, so the Sudanese brought their own gods to worship in secret while paying lip service to Mecca. The African cults in South America grew instead of dwindling away. Today they form important and powerful religious groups, such as Candombles, Macumbas and Xangos, and in the cities have a growing number of 'white' followers. But in Morocco the Gnaouas had atrophied and become no more than groups of entertainers such as those I saw at Tetuan.

The spirit of the sensuously hypnotic rituals lived on in the Devil Dancers who clapped out their mesmerizing rhythms with the extraordinary *qaraqeb*. These were a kind of double castanet of metal, like a figure-of-eight a foot long. The crisp clashing sound mingled with the heart thump of the drum beats. With a pair of *qaraqeb* in each hand, the eleven players were accompanied by the large double-head Tbel drum, which was fairly flayed as the mounting rhythm took command of the white-robed figures and the black feet stamping and twisting on the dusty earth. The dancers formed a gyrating circle, each in turn moving to the centre to go through whirling convolutions which, after hours of dancing, would induce a trance. Perhaps in the secrecy of their own homes, or perhaps in some hidden places in the deserts, the Devil Dancers abandoned their bodies to possession by the god of the rainbow or the god of lightning and became as transformed in their possession as the hundreds of negro dancers in the streets of Rio de Janeiro during carnival. At Tetuan fair I could see that the dancers' main concern was to entertain some local bigwigs seated on cane chairs on the steps of the house.

In any case, it was too early in the evening to expect pagan gods to be abroad. Twilight still lingered over the Rio Martin, a slow trance of nature induced by murky shadows and mistiness rising

Drifts in the cedars—for skiing near Ifrane

Dunes near the palms—for caravans in the south

Fit for a king—
Rabat's Imperial
Palace

Fit for a beggar—
Fez street fountain
and gateway of
17th century
caravanserai

from the water. In the grounds behind the residence's swimming-pool I surprised a group of very young boys smoking *kif*—the hashish which their elders smoke openly in public. I saw little red points of light glowing in the dark grass and thought it must be some unusual kind of firefly. But the pulsating lights were only hashish glowing in the tiny bowls of the boys' long, thin wooden pipes. Nearer the river other boys were throwing stones at birds in euca-lyptus trees. While I watched they brought down two pigeons and caused a colony of bats to invade a camp farther down the river-bank, where the tribesmen from the *fantasia* had set up their beautiful tents.

Four tents had been erected in a corner of the river-bank field, and fourteen horses were tethered by their legs near by. I looked into one of the 16-feet-long tents and saw the orderly array of be-longings set out on straw mats—rifle-cases and pillows, elaborate silver teapots and gorgeously caparisoned harness glimmering richly in soft lamplight.

The grandson of one of the old riders beckoned me in with a smile. The patriarch, for so he looked, nodded royally, his goatish wisp of white hair being rather less astonishing than his teeth, which were the longest and biggest I had ever seen in a human being, and gave me cause to wonder disrespectfully if he had been a horse in a previous existence. He followed my every movement, delighted to have so much attention paid to his horses and their extravagant furnishings. Youssef was 16 and annoyed at his grandfather's monopoly of me, for the boy wanted me to himself, or, rather, my camera. Youssef was deeply in love with a Spanish pen-friend living in far-away La Coruna. He wanted a photograph to send his señorita. He already had a large collection of self-photography. But they had all been done by studios in the town. Like hundreds of others dis-played outside every photographer's shop in Morocco, the shots made him into a terrified criminal. Youssef wanted me to photo-graph him with a background of the family horses. He fancied himself mounted in the powder-blue silk saddle, a pose which could not fail to move the heart in La Coruna.

Youssef knew that outdoor photography was different from the rigid pose of the studio, for he had been taken four years earlier at another festivity. It had not been an occasion of crowds like the Tetuan fair, but a much more important one in Youssef's life, as it was to other village boys over the age of 8. Between that age and 12 years the elaborate ceremony of circumcision took place. The ceremony was expensive and poorer people usually arranged for several boys to be circumcised together, so sharing the cost. While Youssef was immensely proud of the photograph, showing himself in an elaborately decorated head-dress, being held in the arms of a big brother while school-friends sang hymns, he realized that it was not a suitable photograph for dispatch to the girl in Spain.

My excuse for spending the night in the tent was that I should have to wait until morning light before taking Youssef's photograph. This was true, but not the whole truth, for by now it was too late to go back into an hotel in Tetuan. Some of Youssef's friends came with the irresistible suggestion that we climb the wall and take a moonlight bath in the swimming-pool, which the soldiers on guard did not seem to mind, for they came to join us afterwards in the last supper of that evening. It was corn roasted on the cob in front of the tent door. We drained the final glass of mint tea, with grandfather looking remarkably like a parson's withered wife passing cucumber sandwiches as he presided over the silver teapot.

I woke early and puzzled, not by the strangeness of the camp and its surroundings and the sleep-noises of the eight bodies around me, but by strange morning music from the Rio Martin. The long-drawn-out bubbling trill of curlew and the nasal chorus of teal mingled with a weird, hooted shriek. I thought this extraordinary sound might mean that the Rio Martin was the haunt of purple gallinule, even though the river's reed-beds here were not extensive for so great a bird. During a later visit I met a wildfowler who confirmed my belief of that morning in the tent, though he called the purple gallinule by the French name *poule sultane*. And with its blue-purple upper parts glossed with turquoise on the breast, its pure white tail-coverts and bright red long legs and eyes, the great marsh bird ruled supreme.

A more familiar voice in that region, though none the less mystifying when first encountered, was that of the Andalusian hemipode. This quail preferred dry grasslands to the marshes, and to suit its pastoral mood had a call, heard at dusk, like the lowing of cattle waiting to be milked. I saw a shepherd flush Andalusian hemipode as his flocks moved slowly around him, when the bus took me on to Chaouen.

This little town lay less than forty miles south from the *fantasia* horsemen's camp on the bank of the Rio Martin. Youssef came into Tetuan, where I got the Chaouen bus. Though we had only met twelve hours previously, he treated me as though I were an elder brother going off to a war. His concern for my safety on the journey was as great as it had been when I woke the whole tent that morning with a terrified yell. When putting on my shoes I thought one of the dangerous small red scorpions had got into it. An unpleasant experience during my stay in Pakistan came sharply to mind and I flung the shoe away with a warning cry to the other sleepers in the tent. Only a small frog fell among the collection of silver teapots. Youssef enjoyed the joke. He laughed about it and mimicked my yell as I washed and shaved under a hydrant. And as the bus left for Chaouen he yelled after it.

Expansive landscapes simmered in the sun. We went through low dry hills, leaving a trail behind us of massacred grasshoppers who failed to jump quickly enough from our wheels. Large flocks of goats floated like shadows of clouds across a shining sea. The animals ravaged the dotted clumps of shrubs which here aided the dwarf palmetto's greenness. Water was not absent altogether. It coursed down the mountains in channels beside the road. We stopped once while the driver topped up the radiator. Most of the passengers got out to drink or plunge heads and arms and legs into the cool running water. I plunged my head into the fragrant myrtle and rosemary crowding the roadside. The strawberry tree and blue borage and rock rose grew there also, though the cistus, like the Spanish broom, had long lost its perfumed blossom.

Some people changed places and I found myself next to a serious little boy conscientiously guarding an umbrella, a large kettle and a cockerel which he fondled and talked to all the way. Alongside the road groups of shepherds sheltered under almond trees from the sun, or sat under temporary, home-made tents watching the infrequent traffic go by. Some shepherd lads, in heavy brown garments and heads shaved, sat by the roadside brooks, staff in hand, dangling their feet in the rushing water. I envied them their innocence and wished the simplicity of their life could be mine also. Though they, no doubt, were dreaming equally romantically about city life and the fast cars they would never own. I could not suppress the idyll these mountain shepherds conjured in my mind. Such an idyll haunted the poet Casimiro de Abreu who died in 1860 when scarcely more than a youth,

> *Free boy of the mountains,*
> *I was always happy*
> *with my shirt open to my chest*
> *barefooted and bare-armed,*
> *running through the fields*
> *on the way to the waterfalls.*

On we went, this time getting the feel of mountains rather than of hills. The road we climbed was the one followed by Moslem refugees from Spain centuries before to the small agricultural town belonging to the Akhmas tribe. Until the Spanish army came in 1920 few Europeans except slaves ever penetrated this part of the Rif mountains, 2,000 feet above the sea. And when Franco later established a large garrison at Chaouen he was not concerned to give the town the same air of self-importance considered desirable in the modern part of Tetuan. In consequence Chaouen's twentieth-century additions had charm where Tetuan's had none.

White walls and pantiled roofs smiled under a perfect sky and peeped over high garden walls with half-revealed gardens. It was like a stage set for *Carmen*. The extravagance of the gardens was tropical. Roses and dahlias, antirrhinums and delphiniums, chrysanthemums and montbretia, pansies and Michaelmas daisies, made up the rich, formal planting. Sprawling everywhere, like the gilded decoration trailing over medieval manuscripts, was nasturtium and honeysuckle. But even their glowing orange and lemon could not rival the milky-blue canopy of plumbago that shaded so many streets—not only at Chaouen but everywhere in the kingdom.

One garden displayed the pomp of allamanda in a screen of beaten gold petals more elaborate than gold-leaf on an ironwork screen in a Spanish church. The overfull gardens fell over walls like green waves breaking with flying spume of blossom. Overhanging shrubs gave shade to the streets, though double rows of trees on each side gave the most shade, especially the inner rows of dark, waxy orange trees loaded with bitter fruit which nobody seemed to want.

The air at Chaouen was mountain air, clear, bright and dry. Above the houses and the gardens and their trees were the flanks of a great mountain, its edge cutting the sky like a diamond cuts glass. This was a different Morocco from the one I had so far seen, and was a sure bet for the Tourist Board. Tourists are not so bad as they are sometimes made out to be. They are generally content with what they find. If they don't like it, they stay away. Their bad name comes from the sordid cashing-in done by the locals. Cheap souvenirs and touts and neon signs. So far, Chaouen had avoided that sort of vulgarity. I hoped the Tourist Board who have put the town on the travel map would keep things that way.

Some changes had, of course, occurred. The Parador Hotel had recently been modernized for all-the-year-round visitors. And boys surrounded every bus that arrived to offer their services as guides. When I sat in a leafy niche in the gardens of Mohammed V Square two such boys came to drink and wash in the fountain whose water gushed from the ever-open mouths of brass frogs. Afternoon torpor sealed Chaouen in a silent siesta. The heat was intense. The water sounded delicious. I remembered the roadside streams we had passed on the way up through the mountains. Where real thirst is concerned Coca-Cola has nothing on cool, clear water. I leaned over the fountain and let the perfect stream splash from the frog's mouth into my own and let it run down my chin and inside my shirt. The moment of temptation had made me forget the rule of hygiene about not drinking public water. Drink now, pay later, as I was to discover.

The boys came and stood in front of me, grinning and cheeky.

'Hullo, Charlie! You English? I speak English, *Español, Deutsch*.'

This was Abdullah aged 9. To prove his claim he said, 'Good-bye, *Hasta la vista, Gute Reise*.'

His friend Allal, a year younger, was not so cosmopolitan. But he knew more English than Abdullah. 'You Englishman?' he asked. 'Me drink beer. Good-bye. See you later, alligator.'

What a marvellous game to play on a Sunday afternoon! The two boys' friends decided it was, too, and they came after me like the children of Hamelin following the Pied Piper. But I was rescued by Amor Abdelaziz, who spoke English well. He belonged to the new generation of Moroccan who prefer Western clothes to the traditional *djellaba* and who have no objection to wine at table. Amor did not want to stretch his pocket by staying at the rather grand Parador, so we went together for rooms at the *pension* owned by an Arab family near the bus office. Amor was taking a few days' holiday from Rabat, where he and his wife both worked in the Ministry of the Interior. He had left his wife at home and so we spent a riotous two days in and out of Chaouen's *medina*.

The old town here was different from that of Tangier or Tetuan and, as I found, from any other in Morocco. Perhaps because of its mountain isolation the town within the walls had developed an independent way of life. As in all *medinas*, the streets were constricted and formed into tunnels here and there where houses had been built on arches that buttressed the close-spaced walls. But at Chaouen, in the blind alleys, walls of the houses curved up in one continuous surface from the paving, as though moulded in plastics. Both walls and paving were coloured in a luminous pale-blue wash, creating a weird moonscape in plaster, as the plumbago of the new town created it with blossom.

Chaouen was crowded with children, beautiful creatures with eyes like dark, precious stones and handsome faces quick with joy. They raced, shouting, lost in their games, from one archway to another, dashing through the tunnels, sending a fruit-seller's prickly pears tumbling over the street like a harvest of grotesque gooseberries. Solemn little girls sat on the moonscape doorways with baby sisters and brothers fastened in swaddling bands on their backs. They neither smiled nor scowled, but looked a misty-eyed vacant look, dreaming already perhaps of the time, not far away, when their own babies would be sleeping behind them.

We stopped to look at a baby eagle pinioned by a length of string on one foot. For all its pathetic, fledgeling appearance, the beak was vicious, and I wondered how long the captor, a boy of 7 or so, would keep it. The young eagle did not fly when the boy threw it in the air like a paper kite, though whether from obstinacy or inability I could not tell.

The boy and his fluffy prisoner followed us into the open space of the *medina*. The afternoon had come to life again and the big open square by the castle was full of people. The former fortified palace had fallen into ruin. Only its outer walls and corner towers and gateways remained. A pleasant garden had been made inside. I liked the place better and found that it conjured more visions of vanished glories than the palaces in Tangier and Tetuan, perfect as they were. As history went in Morocco, Chaouen was not old. The renowned soldier Abou Youma laid its foundation in 1471 as a fortress against the invaders when the Portuguese won Tangier and Arzila in the same year. It was in his war against the Portuguese that Abou Youma's famous bravery came to an end, for he was burnt alive in a mosque. His cousin and successor moved the *medina* to its present site and raised the castle's pink towers with the unwilling aid of Portuguese captives.

The ruined walls have long since lacked defenders and the attackers now were the ivy and boys with catapults after pigeons. The fortress has been scheduled as an ancient monument. The sturdy walls of stone and rubble, the machicolations and the Norman-looking round-headed windows guarded nothing more than trim hedges and flower-beds and pools. Women in white *haiks* brought their children to enjoy this last, cooler part of the day. And while the children ran in and out of the bushes or looked for fish in the pools their mothers sat on huge millstones and gossiped, presumably about the same topics as women the world over.

We could do no more than guess, for although Amor spoke English and French as well as Arabic, he could not understand the Berber language which everybody at Chaouen seemed to speak. Because of this we missed the meaning of Berber songs which drew us like magic into a café on the square. A flight of steps led up to an open courtyard. A fountain played a liquid accompaniment to the musicians and dancers in one corner. The music ran on, beguiling and gentle but insistent and apparently endless. Two tall araucaria pines shaded the court, rising above the roofs to spread fretted against the evening sky. Lemons and oranges had been piled to be kept cool in the fountain which had wooden drinking-cups also.

BERBER BERGAMASQUE

Amor and I were the only customers not from Chaouen. In rooms open to the court local men, clad in thick brown *djellabas* drank noisily from steaming bowls. The basis of the soup was the national dish, *couscous*. The pellets of semolina, steamed in saffron and spices, could be served in many ways other than soup. I ate it sometimes piled on a plate with meat and gravy, sprinkled then with raisins or dates.

Glasses empty of mint tea stood on all the tables, attracting swarms of wasps and hornets which trapped themselves in the sprigs of mint and died in vain attempts to escape. The wasps buzzed indignantly round the men with full glasses of tea. But rather than risk a sting on the lips, I asked for an orange drink. Oranges were taken from the fountain and pressed for me there and then and did not attract the wasps.

Nobody took any notice of Amor and myself, for the music and singing absorbed us all. Boys playing small, highly decorated tom-toms, sang the verse and were answered by a chorus from the older musicians with guitar-like instruments or violins held vertically on one knee. The first song lasted at least twenty minutes. Then, after an interval for mint tea, one of the boys appeared in a long blue robe under another of silver lace. A thick belt like a lifebelt was wound round his waist. He wore a red sash over one shoulder and a silk scarf round his neck and the silver chains and pendant of the *khamsa*, meaning 'five' in Arabic—which was worn as protection against the Evil Eye, even by people in Rabat's smart society.

The boy picked up a brass tray from the rush mat and carefully balanced it on his head. On the tray were glasses filled with water, four lighted candles and a silver teapot. Then he began a graceful, sinuous dance as the musicians started up again. He swayed and rocked and his body seemed to flow like liquid. He sank down on one leg, turned and rose slowly again and moved in a continuous undulation of limb and torso. He went down with both legs bent and stretched out flat on the rush mat. Then he rolled right over and slowly stood up again, all without touching the ground with his hands. And on his head the tray remained steady. None of the water spilled from the glasses, and the candle flames did not go out.

It was a fine performance and much appreciated by the audience, and the boy, who was about 18, was obviously as proud of his gracefulness as he was of his skill. Not to be outdone, a younger boy in similar garb appeared then and danced a hip-and-belly dance with extraordinary muscular contractions and jerks, also much enjoyed by the audience. These were traditional Berber forms of dancing. And so I had seen what may have been one of the most ancient kinds of entertainment in the world, for who knows how or when Berber life began?

At the *pension* Amor and I were the dining-room's sole guests. We ate not to the music of a Berber band but to a chorus of bullfrogs with no audience but the stars. Ten-o'clock bugle calls sounded from the barracks down the street as we opened a second bottle of Doumi, an excellent Moroccan wine imported even by the French. The *pension* appeared to be run entirely by two youths. So proud were they of the bathroom that they kept it locked with the key secure in one of their pockets. This may have been a precaution against the street boys who wandered in and out as they pleased. But it was embarrassing for a visitor who, having foolishly drunk water from the brass frogs at the fountain earlier in the day, was consequently afflicted in the night with a bowel condition similar to those described in the Psalms.

Getting the key to the lavatory, however, was child's play compared with the struggle to get toilet-paper. The two boys in the *pension* obviously regarded this requirement as an unwarranted, old-maidish fad on my part. Thereafter in Morocco I never went unprepared for such emergencies. The wadge of tissue-paper in my back pocket taught me a serious lesson about the country later on in my journey. Before I left Tangier a bank clerk had warned me to pin my pockets up with a safety-pin after cashing some travellers' cheques. My English guide-book said 'limber-fingered pickpockets are legion'. That is as maybe. But I was only pickpocketed once in Morocco and that was by a German hitch-hiker. Though I left my clothes on crowded beaches while I went swimming, and stayed at many hotels not on the Tourist Board's list, including some without a lock to the bedroom door, nobody ever attempted to rob me, except the German. And he got a shock on discovering that the thick roll of bank-notes in my back pocket was no more than my precautionary paper for bowel disorders.

3

Arabesques and Storks

Chaouen was the pin-up girl of Moroccan towns. Posters of its charm appeared everywhere in the country in a sufficient motley of European languages as well as Arabic to ensure the fame of its '*immuable quietude*', its '*bleibende Ruhe*' and its 'unchanging peace'. But there was no denying that the little mountain town was worth the outlay of superlatives. I felt sorry to leave, but Morocco was big and hundreds of miles lay ahead. I turned round in my bus seat to look at the trim white town sitting so neatly on a shelf of its mountain. From the flank of an opposite hill which the bus was climbing I could see clearly the huge cleft riven into the mountains, which had given the town its Berber name of Chechaouene—'two horns'.

When Chaouen was hidden by a spur of the mountains I settled down to enjoy the thrill of hairpin bends with drops of hundreds of feet. The mountain air was cool and this was encouraging, for my destination being the imperial city of Fez I knew that later in the day the heat would build up. At first I found the early-rising habits of the Moroccans alarming. A day beginning at 4 or 5 a.m. was not at all unusual. The 7 a.m. bus I took from Chaouen was regarded as the late one. But I soon discovered that, certainly in inland places, the midday heat made at least a brief rest unavoidable. Although the hottest period only lasted two or three hours, as soon as the sun came up it turned the landscape to gold.

Chaouen's last orderly olive groves dropped behind and we were abandoned to the risks of the journey out of the mountains. We were bound for the plains south of the Rif range, which stretched uninterrupted to the Atlas Mountains, and for the Sais plain on which Fez stood. Several women in the bus were sick, albeit discreetly into tin cans with which they travelled, and like them I was glad when we emerged from the slow nerve-wracking process of negotiating terrifying bends at high altitudes.

Once on to flatter ground again the driver made up for lost time and we went headlong over miles of straight road laid like a black river through the yellow fields. The landscape had a dream-like quality, as though, if approached, the whole scene would vanish like the glimmerings of non-existent water in mirage on the road ahead of us. The reaped fields were enormous in extent and the sun shone on the stubble and made it glossy like the sleek coat of summer cattle. Beyond the shining plains misty with heat were low hills clothed with green bushes as the plains themselves were dotted with herds and flocks and the lonely figures of shepherds in their *djellabas*. We sped through a forest of cork oak and past a shaggy green mountain with here and there a flash of red arbutus berries, and on through the wide harvested plains where the white stork gleaned the stubble for grasshoppers and snakes, plains that ran like a pastoral frieze of a timeless land.

Then the front tyre burst. The bus swerved off the road and in a moment of screams and shattered glass lay on its side, shrouded in a cloud of dust. Somehow, I was flung through the front window, to land on the dry mallows and dusty earth, along with others from the front seats. The dust was in my lungs and throat and eyes. When I could see again I tried to pull others out of the bus and to stop myself from trembling and bleeding from an arm. Blood was sprinkled everywhere. I searched for water in dried-up stream-beds. But there was none to give the seriously injured, and none to wash away the thick coat of ochre dust which made everyone look as if they had make-up on for some ghastly drama.

The sun beat down unmercifully in that open place. After half an hour or so a car came beetling along the road from Ouezzane, the nearest town, whence it promptly returned to raise the alarm. We waited, too concerned with our own injuries to worry about the panic-stricken squawks and bleatings of chickens and sheep still frantically struggling on the now-vertical roof of the bus. None of it seemed at all real, least of all those with serious injuries, who sat or lay moaning in strips of shade by the wrecked bus, their dark faces looking green under the masks of dust. The Red Crescent emergency box in the bus could not be found amongst the wreckage.

We heard the first ambulance coming, its siren wailing like the banshee. I went off in it with three English students who had been in the seat beside the driver. Their backs were lacerated, to add more pain to their sunburnt skin. At the new and still half-finished hospital in Ouezzane, the nurses, in caps like Victorian parlourmaids, cleaned us up. The doctor examined the damage, and then the nurses gave us an injection in the buttocks, pumping enough anti-something-or-other in to paralyse a camel. And that was that, except for a London University lecturer who brought our luggage in the second ambulance. He was quite unhurt. But just as we were leaving he leaned against the door and sank like the Berber dancer gracefully to his knees in a dead faint. 'Shock,' he explained, coming round. 'It's nothing really,' and promptly fainted again.

The journey to Fez was postponed. After interminable interviews with the police, they drove us in a jeep to an hotel on the outskirts of Ouezzane. It was quiet and within minutes of sinking into the embrace of a double bed under a mosquito net, which might have been the canopy of Holofernes, I was asleep. The hotel was only a few hundred yards from the police station. But a sense of humour made it seem the most suitable, for the hotel was called Tout Va Bien!

Everything did go well, and I had to admit that without the accident I would never have discovered the delights of Ouezzane. The town did not enjoy the poster-fame of Chaouen nor did its name appear on tourist itineraries. Perhaps its charms are not so obvious as those of the mountain-fortress town. But for the Moslem, Ouezzane was a sacred city, and pilgrims even from beyond the Nile came to visit its shrines.

When these springtime pilgrimages, the *moussems*, were not distracting the good townspeople they followed an existence based on the pastoral life of the wide countryside all around. Ouezzane was a market town for this region, on the slopes of Mount Bou Hellal. The old town had been built on the mountain's lower hills and its houses ran in layers across a series of projecting mounds and promontories. The houses were brilliantly white, cubic in form with flat roofs among the spherical forms of the olive trees. Travellers of years ago must have found this geometrical architecture more unusual than it appears today. For modern buildings with their cubes and flat roofs resemble these ancient Moroccan towns closely.

There were few tourists in Ouezzane and I was not importuned by anxious would-be guides. The people going about their business were handsome and friendly like all Moroccans, yet curious also about the odd, bandaged quintet of bus-crash victims. A constant coming and going with the countryside went on. The farmers passed by continually on their donkeys, riding side-saddle, sandalled feet dangling, heads buried in the high, pointed hoods of their *djellabas* raised against the sun. In the market-place, and everywhere they met, there were greetings of graciousness. I saw this greeting everywhere in the country, hundreds of times, and it never failed to move me by its dignity. When two people met, men and women, they shook hands and then with a deft movement kissed their own hand where the other had held it, and then touched their breast over the heart. Like the movements of a ballet, it was delicately expressive of the honour in which Moroccans held friendship. I have often thought that our English manners, regarded once as the symbol of our superiority over the world's Frogs and Wogs, are, in fact, singularly uncouth. Our greetings and partings are unmarked by demonstrative movement, and even when it is, such as the raising of a bowler hat, it is expressive of nothing. How different the quick, almost shy handshake, kiss and heart-touchings were in Ouezzane market-place. Some friends, on meeting, embraced and kissed each other on the cheeks in the French manner.

Besides the men in traditional *djellabas*, some of the younger men were riding off on their bicycles to work, wearing the shortest of shorts, riding between the high green walls of *canne de provence* as though it were the Bois de Boulogne. These and other overtones of French life merged happily with Morocco's traditions, and made me think that the country had slipped more easily into contact with the modern world than many other non-Westernized nations.

In a country town like Ouezzane, more than in cities like Tangier or Tetuan, life took on its pace from Nature's. The day began when the first hint of dawn lightened the sky above the mountain ridge. And by the time the sun was visible many people were already at work. As much as possible had to be done before the midday heat brought activity to a halt. Most foreign visitors, being on holiday, are only getting out of bed when most Moroccans, especially in country places, have already done several hours' work. Seeing so many recumbent figures already sprawled by 11 a.m. under the trees, or in the shade of doorways or walls, some tourists think Moroccans lazy.

Pace of life and physical exertion must be adjusted to suit the climate of different places. Moslem countries tend to be hot in the middle of the day, but otherwise comfortable enough. In Morocco activity tended to be crowded into the day's two extreme ends, early morning and evening. An old Moorish proverb gave good advice on how to cope with heat,

> *Never sit when you can lie,*
> *Never stand when you can sit,*
> *Never walk when you can stand,*
> *Never run when you can walk.*

'Never do in the sun what can be done in the shade' should have been added. It would be difficult to find a more industrious people, even if many of them are asleep again by the time the tourists emerge from their hotels at 10 a.m.

The Hotel Tout Va Bien was remote from the nocturnal activities of Ouezzane. I slipped gratefully under the rococo drapes of my mosquito net long before 11 p.m. The bus crash produced effects for which sleep was the only remedy. Although Morocco's mosquitoes were remarkably few, stray ones congregated, mad with frustrated blood-lust, round my net. Since even in London mosquitoes bite me, I would not suggest to any other prospective visitors to Morocco that a net was essential.

An entomologist might disagree, but I *know* that mosquitoes sleep all day in order to spend the entire night awake. The same is not true of cicadas. They never seem to sleep at all. As I lay under the net I could hear cicadas in the trees outside my window, buzzing like crossed telephone wires. The dogs of every house within miles barked at late home-goers. From the road below came the delicate clopping of donkeys' hoofs bearing their masters out into the country.

Travellers of this kind seemed to be on the move all night, so that the entire canine population of Ouezzane howled and yapped until, in the early hours, the cocks took over, calling one to another, refusing to be quiet. And in the midst of the fowls' chorus, the *mouddhins* came to their minarets, calling the faithful to prayer, though it was still not 4 a.m. The *mouddhins* were like the cocks, rivalling each other and each, it seemed, determined to have the last word. From every minaret the call went out, a reedy chant which echoed from the mountains. Some sounded like a car changing gear going uphill, others made more pious paeans as they recited the familiar lines '*Allah Akbar, Essehadou Muhamadu, Ressool-ul lah, Allah Akbar, la il lah il Allah*'—God is great, there is no God but God, and Mohammed is his Prophet.

Quite by 4 a.m. the roadsweeper's prayers would be done and his prescribed ablutions completed, and he would be on his way back to town, where a score of cafés would be serving mint tea and fried puffs under the stars. Then light seeped into the sky, the cocks began to scratch for food, and the noisy dogs slept. The dawn chorus of blackcap from out the mimosa trees was a weak performance compared with the night-long clamour, but perhaps the birds had been kept awake, too.

The kindness of the people who ran the Hotel Tout Va Bien helped our recovery from the accident and three days afterwards I was sitting in another bus, going to Fez. To avoid a morbid pre-occupation with the road's possible dangers, I made mental notes about the sunflowers, that plant of Aztec splendour, which was cultivated by the acre in many parts of the kingdom. The edible seed could be bought in every Moroccan market and I wondered if the Romans had first introduced the sunflower as food.

Eucalyptus sped past the bus window and lined the roads for miles like poplars in France. In spite of flourishing in a ubiquitous way, and looking thoroughly native, eucalyptus trees had only been introduced to Morocco in the last century. The man responsible was

Sir John Drummond Hay. The eucalyptus possessed a gracefulness rare in a landscape so often dried up by summer sun. Tall and airy, they arched over the road at one place where a most beautiful girl rode a mule and led a string of donkeys. She wore the *haik*, but her striking face was uncovered. Her serenity of bearing on the big mule reminded me of Lalla Rookh riding to meet her suitor, the young King of Bucharia, who had been with her all the time disguised as a minstrel.

Strings of men on donkeys lined the roadsides along the Fez highway. They held black umbrellas against the sun and looked like processions of courtiers. I had not seen so many asses on a road since going to Enniskillen fair as a boy. They were coming from a market, returning to the sod-roofed villages scattered along the way. These home-made houses, protected by windbreak cypresses, blended with the landscape and made a harmony of colour and shape, whose only discords were occasional sheets of galvanized iron, hideous and hot.

Native skill and materials made the finest buildings everywhere, especially in the High Atlas. An iron roof over a building of concrete blocks set up a jarring discord rarely seen in Morocco. It seemed that, as elsewhere in the world, where traditional crafts could not meet the demands of modern life all the old senses of beauty and perfection of workmanship were jettisoned.

Many of the mud-brick and mud-plastered village houses had claps of dung drying on their walls for use as fuel. Along the roadside we passed enormous concrete pipes laid out for the construction of a drain. Inside workmen stretched out fast asleep, like Egyptian kings in twentieth-century sarcophagi. Orchards and gardens bordered this road to Fez. Many of the trees seemed to be hung with white blossom like magnolia. But glimpsing some closer, I saw that the blossoms were large flocks of egrets perched in the orange and pomegranate trees. Farther on, I saw a pair of egrets crossing the road with cattle, one riding a cow's back. The cattle were a mixture of Jersey and Ayrshires, all in fine condition. They moved in large numbers which suggested communal herding. There were fine hirsels of black-faced sheep also, standing with their heads under each other's belly for shade.

We rushed on through valley after valley, each a chequerboard of green maize and golden stubble. It was a world of gold, tarnished and burnished, beaten and hammered, overlaid on the face of the earth like the golden mask of Agamemnon from Mycenae. Then the harvest fields looked as if they were made from gold thread and whole hillsides and plains were like cloth-of-gold ruffled by the wind. Rows of silver olive trees stood on the purple of freshly turned earth. Rows of saffron melons lay on their tiny green islands of leaves on the corduroy earth.

The plough was master of this ordered landscape.

When I first came to Morocco the picture on the reverse side of bank-notes made me smile at what I thought was its *naïveté*. The picture showed a peasant holding a sickle and a sheaf, but glancing longingly at a combine harvester moving across vast wheatfields. But I began to understand when I saw the arable land, stretching away from the roads, flat rich land of prairie dimensions. Though the Moroccan prairies often stopped against hills, in some places there were no hills, and the plains extended to the horizon through all points of the compass. The white heat haze blurred their edges, so that it was impossible to tell how the gold of the land merged into the blue of the sky.

I had not realized that agricultural produce was Morocco's principal product of export, or that the country sent wheat to nearly every European country, including Britain. The corn from these Moroccan prairies even crosses the Atlantic to America. I saw the work of giant combine machines in the form of straw cubes littered for miles over the stubble fields. Yet the age-old threshing-floor stood before every farmsteading. As many as six mules might be used for circling the floor of yellow corn. Men and women, boys and girls were all out at these harvest festivities, shouting at the horses and mules as they went in a dizzy circle, trampling the grain.

The colour of the background hills changed from blood red to chalk white, with black bog-like valleys between. I knew that in the manner of Icelanders and Indians the Berbers buried their butter in the earth to give it a much-relished rancid flavour. In Ireland, when I was a boy, we always hoped to find centuries-old butter in the peat bog. Finds of it were exceedingly old. Pre-Christian butter had been dug up on the Isle of Skye. Authorities dated it 2,000 years old—a notable discovery, considering that the hairs from a blonde milkmaid were found in it.

A Moroccan who sat beside me in the Fez bus spoke English and was amused by my interest in bog butter. He promised to let me taste some when we came to the next refreshment stop. But I recognized the over-ripe gorgonzola-flavoured buttermilk as *smeen*. This was something quite different. Although *smeen* might well have been buried in the earth for one year, it certainly had not been for a thousand like peat-bog butter. *Smeen* was used extensively in Moroccan cooking, imparting a pleasant, unmistakable flavour.

Now we were in the heart of Morocco. The landscape never ceased to astonish me. When I tasted the *smeen* and washed it down with an 'Atlas' orange drink I looked at the hills rising by the little roadside café which was our last stop before Fez. They were a brilliant sulphur yellow, vividly accentuated by the radiant blue sky. A dead chameleon lay on the road, squashed by a passing car. The skin was exactly the colour of the road, making the little creature look like some unevenness in the road surface.

A brown river, miraculously full, wended its way near by and giant water-wheels turned slowly, lifting the precious water and emptying it into open channels which ran among the fields. The wheels were beautifully constructed, and a music of creaking and tumbling water accompanied the endless movement. They seemed to symbolize the rotation of seasons, the planting and the harvesting, a movement which the boys swimming naked in the river knew instinctively, a movement whose rhythms they obeyed as they watched their flocks on the golden hills.

The road south from Ouezzane to Fez had given me many delights, the birds perhaps most of all. Conspicuous amongst the dry scrub and in the vineyards was the rufous warbler. He sang from telegraph wires and the opuntia and agave hedges. He was much bolder than the many other warblers. I heard his fine, disconnected phrases of song frequently and could almost believe that it was the skylark singing. Both the crested and thekla larks abounded, and the calandra and short-toed to a less degree. There were many storks and crowds of egrets.

By the streams we crossed I saw several Barbary partridges

adorned by the reddish-brown necklace patterned by white spots. At one place women and children were out in the fields frightening large coveys of partridges away from their crops. The boys were expert with slings and stones against any bird, even the tiny wheat-ear. Scarecrows defended many of the fields and cultivated patches. They looked quaint as scarecrows always do and more so, for these gentlemen of sticks and rags were the only people for miles around in Western dress.

Morocco was rich in game birds and the Tourist Board was trying to attract sportsmen. But although wild boar could still be hunted, the lion had long since gone far south of the border, and the few panthers that still roamed the mountain forests were jealously pro-tected. I was horrified to discover that Europeans going to North Africa nowadays count the bag by the hundred, much of their haul consisting of tiny birds. The Tourist Board in Fez told me about 'hunting', and gave me the Ministry of Agriculture 1964 regulation list, which included thrush, avocets, godwits, oystercatchers, red-shanks, curlews, blackbirds, sandpipers, phalaropes.

This undignified slaughter went on through the official season for waders and migratory birds from September to March. The activity of these inane tourists was not, to my mind, excused by the fact that throughout the whole year local wildfowlers and village boys shot the most splendid birds like the blue rock thrush, or that villagers often caught the birds for pets, the goldfinch being a favourite songster who could be seen in sad cages around doors in the city streets.

Eucalyptus continued to shade the road, though the landscape now was dominated by American and sisal agaves. These weird plants grew almost everywhere in Morocco, used, like the prickly pear, as efficient natural fences. The old idea that the American agave took a hundred years to flower gave it the alternative name of century plant. But this notion was a false one, for the fifteen-foot-high stalks crowned with blossom were the tallest thing in all the plains, eucalyptus alone excepted. The agaves' extraordinary blooms rose high above the roofs of farms and villages, as regal as the im-perial parasol above the Friday crowds at Rabat when the King, riding on a horse, goes to prayers. I did not like these tree-like plants, for the huge yellow-rusty blossom had something uncanny about it, like cauliflowers sprouting from palm trees on some science-fiction planet.

And so, at last, to Fez. The last miles of road stretched straight like a typewriter ribbon across the yellow paper of the fields. The final stretch of landscape was suddenly lyrical and English, a scene which Turner might have painted, except the colours were not his. A cavalcade was going to the imperial city led by a boy of 6 wearing a fez and sitting bare-back on an enormous mare followed by four horses. His eyes were black fire and he sat upright, more regal in appearance than the girl like Lalla Rookh we had passed earlier. Such strings of horses, led by similar boys wearing similar clothes, had been going to and from Fez for more than a thousand years, a city which was then, and still is, the intellectual and religious capital of the Sherifian kingdom.

Early in A.D. 808, King Idris II, aged 15, was riding across the same Sais plain when he came upon some springs. The beauty of the place struck him and he commanded his royal capital to be built there. Precisely at the place where the young King halted, the Mzara, the event has been lovingly perpetuated through the ages, and still today people leave votive offerings of wool or fragments of their coats on the iron railings surrounding it and make a wish.

Christians, Jews, Syrians, Kairouannis, Berbers, Moors and pagans were amongst the early inhabitants of the city and eight hundred families fleeing from Spain gave Fez its first Andalusian quarter. The city was lucky with chroniclers. El Bekri, the great historian, lived there before moving to Seville in 1067. Ibn Khaldun, like El Edrisi before him, left long accounts of early years in the imperial capital.

Above all other things described in El Edrisi's books, one city alone was coveted by Henry the Navigator. He dreamed of conquering Fez. By the early fifteenth century Fez was a powerful influence in North Africa, though its empire had shrunk since the twelfth and fourteenth centuries, when Algeria, Tunisia, Tripolitania and the Andalusian possessions besides Morocco looked to Fez as capital. In Prince Henry's time Fez was a formidable stronghold of the Moslem world, renowned for architecture and for the university—the oldest in the world.

The Infante did not dream on his own about conquering Fez. Every Christian monarch in Europe and every succeeding Pope concerned themselves with Fez. It represented the power of the Crescent, which, at all costs, must be subjected to the Cross. In addition to this worthy cause the Portuguese had personal suffering to avenge, for immured within Fez's mighty walls in a foul prison lay Prince Fernando, another son of Philippa of Lancaster. Fez had many famous prisoners from its early days until as recently as 1912. But few could have caused as much bloodshed as Prince Fernando, for various nations were involved in rescue attempts. But the Prince was neither rescued by his friends nor freed by his captors. At his death in the Fez prison the Church canonized him. Henry the Navigator never forgot his favourite brother. But Fernando's misfortunes hardly justified the consequent action of Henry and other Christian princes in subjecting thousands of 'Saracens, Pagans and other enemies of Christ' to slavery, even though such action bore the papal blessing.

To go through one of the great gateways of Fez was to pass from the twentieth century to the days of Fernando's imprisonment, and then beyond to further recesses of history back to the line of Merinide kings secured on their throne by Syrian archers. It was the sight of old Jews in black levite and skullcap going through Fez's ancient streets to the Great Synagogue which carried my thoughts away to the days when Ezekiel was a priest in the land of the Chaldeans.

I imagined that almost nothing had changed, except for the massive tawny walls which had crumbled here and there. As soon as the three English students and I got out of the bus a young boy came up with a tray of fine-combs. His head was shaven, his smile ingenuous. In his ragged brown *djellaba* he might have been a boy of Fez from any age. Ezekiel himself probably looked at faces exactly like that boy's. Fortunately, I never had need of the particular combs he was selling, though I slept in a few dubious beds.

The walls of Fez still retained barbaric splendour. Remembering super-epics in the cinema, I could people the walls with fierce

Saracens—the crowd-scene extras in long robes were already there for me to see in reality. What a scene that must have been on the day when horses' hoofs sent dust into the air and when banners flew and armour glinted and Prince Fernando was led captive into the city.

I walked into the labyrinth of the *medina*. No motor-vehicles could go in, because the streets were too narrow. Only mules and asses struggled up and down the wider alleyways, though even they could not enter the smallest, some of which were no more than two feet wide. Pack-animals went to and fro continuously, for they were the only means of transporting goods within the extensive network of the *medina*. Every booth and stall and restaurant and every workshop received and dispatched its goods by the animals. The drivers' cries mingled with the hubbub of clatter and chatter. Several times I had to leap nimbly to avoid being crushed against the wall by a passing ass, its panniers perhaps built of wooden crates, loaded with Stork beer, or hundreds of Coca-Cola bottles—two products which were certainly new since the unhappy Fernando's day. Yet though the tiny shop-booths, open directly to the constricted streets, had many other things to sell made in the industrial world, from transistor radios to plastic brooms, most of their commerce was quite unchanged. It was possible to stand and watch skilled craftsmen making intricate things by hand exactly as they had done for centuries.

Fez stood on the plains, but the plains were not without hills and the city's streets were steep in places, adding to the architectural excitement of the intricately linked, confined ways. The pack-animals trod the steep streets carefully, sometimes slipping on the cobbles or stone setts, threatening to send a load of fruit tumbling. When the alleys were wide enough to allow hot fingers of sun to penetrate, bamboo screens stretched overhead, creating a pleasant filter of light and keeping the alleys cool. In some places big reed mats served the same purpose and shady vines hung on wires.

'This tree three hundred years old. Come and see,' said a voice behind me when I stopped to admire one fantastic vine.

But I went on, not wishing to get embroiled in one of the tourist bazaars, which looked surprisingly spacious through the small entry from the street. A venerable man sat beneath the vine selling a strange collection of spectacles, ranging from gold-rimmed to horn-rimmed, and old-fashioned box-irons. He looked as if he had been sitting there selling his oddly unrelated pairs of glasses and box-irons since the vine's planting three centuries before.

Contrary to what I had been told, the tourist bazaars were not selling rubbish. All the jewellery and the beautifully worked leather goods had been home-made in some tiny workshop no doubt near by. None of the metalwork teapots or trays came from Birmingham. But I preferred to make my purchases from the craftsmen themselves rather than from the salesmen in the tourist bazaars. The main reason for this was that the craftsmen, proud of their skill, would show me how they worked and how the things were made. With a few deft movements of deceptive ease, a youth made me a small collapsible box, cut and folded from a square of leather. He passed it to his grandfather, who stamped and gilded it with a pattern of star-shapes. It was a beautiful thing and cost only two dirhams, about three shillings. At another craftsman's booth I bought a pair of *babouche* of yellow goat leather, those Moroccan slippers, open at the heel, which were worn with the *djellaba*.

All the trades were grouped together in the streets and alleys traditionally associated with them. And all were members of the city's many guilds, which not only protected the tradesmen but ensured that their high standards of skill were maintained. Each corporation was supervised by an *amine* and the united guilds controlled by the *mohtasseb*. Thus, in Fez, a system of guilds still thrives similar in structure, function and rights to the guilds of medieval Europe, now long since vanished.

Herbalists sat beside festoons of tree bark, mountains of dried henna leaves and baskets of mint whose combined scents were even more powerful than the drifting blue trails of smoke from the incense market. The Arab people as a whole love incense and the air was laden with the fragrance of amber and storax, musk and witch-hazel, aloes and cascarilla. This tinting of the air occurred even away from the incense-sellers' booths, for many houses seemed to have incense burning inside.

Jewellery was as popular an enrichment of life as incense. No

71

matter how poor a woman might be she would be adorned with jewellery, and not only on special occasions but during the ordinary working days, even, in Berber regions, when working in the fields. The large, pear-shaped emeralds of the city's rich women were substituted by the even larger, tomato-sized amber-ball necklaces of the poor. Garnets and pearls and the 'rubies of Fez' set in gold made up the wardrobe of the well-to-do Arab bride. Berber women preferred stones set in silver—the symbol of freedom and purity.

I passed from watching a young cripple making a necklace of pierced rosettes to the short street of silk-tassel makers. The craftsmen sat crosslegged on the raised platforms of their tiny booths, twisting the silk strands of violent purples and reds, yellows and greens, into elaborate ropes and tassels. The strands were hung over two-foot-high stands while the skilful fingers wound and bound and threaded sequins into these brilliant baubles. The tassel-makers' alley was a cul-de-sac ending in the forecourt of a mosque whose painted decoration and coloured tiles were as colourful as the silken ropes.

No other *medina* in Morocco had the fascination of those myriad, busy alleys of Fez. The old city was not only more extensive than others but had more mystery and surprises, as though the still-living centuries of tradition radiated from the walls, as though the centuries of religious activity had imbued the air with an intensity like the incense which gave it fragrance. The Gillette razor blades and Singer sewing machines, the Coca-Cola signs, the sweets moulded in miniature as the Manikin Pis, none of these Western things could damage the subtle atmosphere of Fez.

A pin-prick in an elephant's hide would produce more reaction than the American Cultural Centre would make in this venerable city of learning and skill. The French Library was a lingering memorial of an occupying nation that had come and gone within a few decades. Even the cinemas with their thrills and unreality could do no more than add incident to this city of incident. It would be impossible to discover what, if anything, the people of Fez made of American culture. But how, I wondered, did they regard the films, one of which, shown on posters everywhere, was labelled simply SEXY? Whether this was a critic's comment or the film's title did not seem clear. What did the modestly veiled women think of the poster's near-nude girl whom they studied seriously?

The *medina*'s buildings, crowding in the restricted alleys, were old. From the streets the only features visible were the doorways. Many of these boasted elaborate wood carvings, the skill of forgotten craftsmen still beautiful after hundreds of years. Bracketed canopies projected above the heavily studded doors, and since the doorways were round-headed, the tympanum was filled with wood carving. Some doors boasted hinges and handles of splendid wrought iron. At frequent intervals along the alleys wall-fountains were placed, gushing perpetually for the buckets and pitchers of the children and housewives. Most of the houses projected eighteen inches at the first floor, to gain more space for the upper rooms.

In Fez the golden age of architecture seems to have been the fourteenth century. Most of the great buildings of that time are still in use, and more often than not for the same purposes. Renowned among that century's works were the Bab Segma gateway, the Merinide tombs and the magnificently carved ceilings of the Tetuan Fondouk, used as a caravanserai by merchants from the Rif region who came on business to Fez, and, surpassing all these, the *medersas*, or colleges.

Unlike most of the mosques, the *medersas* were open to visitors. These buildings, arranged around courts paved with onyx and marble, expressed at once their detachment from the life of everyday buying and selling. Their high walls shut out the streets' commotion and in the shade of the colonnades there was an atmosphere conducive to thought. But perhaps these islands of quiet in the city's sea of activity were deceptive. The vacations kept them empty and cloistered. Perhaps when the students returned at the end of the summer the colleges rang with the noise of youth which is the same all the world over.

For the moment only a few visitors and the custodians were there to admire the carved cedarwood friezes and the walls of mosaic. The loudest sound came from invisible typewriters and from the birds. Swifts made the most din. Besides the common swift swooping over the courtyards getting insects on the wing, there were pallid and alpine swifts also, all screaming dementedly on their foraging flight. The three species appeared to live happily in mixed colonies, making homes not only in the colleges' and mosques' eaves but in the city walls, whose holes were perfect for their nests.

Of all the colleges the Bou Anania, built in 1335, was considered the most important. This *medersa's* mosaics and polished enamels and sculptured plasterwork were classics of their kind. Because they were undeniably beautiful, I allowed myself the luxury of quibbling as to whether I *really* liked the way that this Andalusian, or Western Arabic, architecture was covered intensely over every available square inch of surface with intricate designs. The effect was undoubtedly rich. But I longed sometimes for some respite, some pause in the cascade of filigree and mathematical patterns, some breathing-space among the handsome designs wrought from the Arabic letters of Koranic quotations.

The basic form of the architecture was noble enough, the proportions of high rounded or pointed arches, the spaciousness of courtyards satisfying enough without the unrelieved excess of the carver's skill. Because the gateways through the city walls only occurred occasionally, and their elaborateness was offset by the walls' massive plainness, the effect of their richness was all the more powerful. Even in the non-stop decoration of baroque or rococo churches the voluptuous invention is gathered into areas of greater or lesser concentration. In this Hispano-Moroccan architecture the proliferation tended to defeat its own purpose and to result in monotony.

Nobody could tell me the origin or purpose of thirteen bronze gongs fixed on brackets at first-floor level in the wall opposite the college entrance. The gongs were like giant soup plates. Some people believed they were intended as chimes. But nobody actually *knew*, not even the tall man wearing a *djellaba*, who had a pock-marked de Gaulle type nose and a large pirate gold earring in one ear. Consumed with curiosity, he came over to watch me writing notes. Tourists equipped with the last possible of all words in cine cameras aroused not a whit of excitement. But a writing tourist did. The man watched fascinated as I scribbled across the notebook from left to right. He was not used to people writing backwards, he explained in mime. I knew how he felt, for I never failed to be fascinated by Arab script and the way *they* wrote backwards. Then, perhaps as thanks for the entertainment, he brought me four delicious, still sizzling doughnut puffs on a grass string.

Hardly anything has changed since a sixteenth-century author was writing about a street called 'the Place of Smoke' where fritters and fried puffs were sold. The same large ovens he described are still fed by the charcoal-vendors bumping down the streets with overloaded donkeys, even though the shop next door might well be selling the latest American refrigerators. The shops with such modern things to sell did not destroy the age-old character of *medina* shops by a plethora of plate-glass windows. Nearly all the shops had extremely narrow fronts, so that the shopkeeper was obliged to barricade himself in behind piles of fruit or shoes or nuts or whatever happened to be his speciality. In order to get in and out he swung himself, like Tarzan, on a rope which hung over the counter for this purpose.

The tailors worked cross-legged on the floors of similar shops, though often they sat on the pavement outside, especially when making the beautiful edging to *djellabas*. A deceptively simple operation, this edging process was fascinating to watch, for it was done by hand. Children, from the age of 4 upwards, helped the tailors by holding the long strands on the fingers of each hand. While the tailor neatly sewed all the strands together into the seam, making a kind of thinnish cord, the boys cleverly twisted the strands, crossing and recrossing them by passing the threads from one hand to the other.

Children began work while very young indeed. The tailors' children were lucky compared to boys sweating over the bellows in blacksmiths' workshops, though they all seemed to be happy enough and would become highly skilled craftsmen themselves while still only young men. Less fortunate were the children whose apprenticeship was in the ancient craft of begging. With a professional expression of pathos fixed on their handsome faces, some of them led blind parents about the streets. On the whole, however, the Moroccans were of an independent spirit, and though beggars begged everywhere, there were not swarms of them, and most were undoubtedly genuine hard cases.

The best beggars were the mischievous boys who went up to the modern, French part of the city to cadge pocket-money from the tourists. 'Me no mamma, no papa,' they would whine sadly with head lolling appealingly on one side. I knew perfectly well they usually had both mammas and papas who might even be angry to know their children were on that game. Moroccan parents were strict with their children and this balanced an intense affection.

Islam enjoins alms-giving, or *zakat*, upon believers and it is regarded as equally important as prayer and fasting. God himself instituted *zakat*, by which every man must give a portion of his goods to the poor and needy. It may, of course, be argued that poverty and need of the direst kind have largely gone from countries with an enlightened programme of social services. This is true, but meanwhile, until countries like Morocco can reorientate themselves in this direction, the poor go on being poor and *zakat* remains as some source of comfort.

Blindness drove many on to the streets, and their cry of '*Allah Akbar, Allah Akbar,*' droned on continuously as they drifted about like rudderless boats, with hands or money-bowls extended. People gave steadily to such beggars, even people who looked desperately poor themselves, but who were, presumably, thankful for their sight.

Much of the blindness in Morocco was caused not by obscure diseases or hereditary defects, but simply by trachoma. And this annoyed me, for trachoma is carried on the feet of flies, and Moroccans allowed flies to walk about on their eyelids. Though the country was extraordinarily free of flies, those that did exist were persistent. Moroccans presumably grew up accustomed to flies and did not notice them. Many young people were afflicted by trachoma and I was not surprised. Women, with their arms wrapped inside the *haik*, with only their eyes exposed, could do little to keep away the disease-carrying flies. Babies bound to their mothers' backs could not brush away the flies that came to walk about on their bright black eyes.

Allah Akbar sang out the voices of the blind. God is Great! they chorused as groups of two or three, blind leading blind, tapped their way through the jostling alleyways. Centuries earlier Allah's greatness had caused the Attarine Medersa to be built for study. I tried to find this famous college, threading my way among the mothball pedlars and skin traders, wool merchants and garlic hawkers, past stone-masons chiselling sinuous inscriptions from the Koran on gravestones, past false-teeth repairers and wooden-plough makers.

I went up and down steep alleys where blacksmiths worked at wrought-iron grilles, the fire glowing and fading as the small boys stood over the bellows, the anvil ringing as youths wielded the heavy hammers. I passed courtyards where camels and horses were stabled and where obstinate asses and mules stood rooted to the ground oblivious to the angry curses of their drivers, and where scores of pigeons flocked about the rich droppings.

I paused to watch the makers of small-toothed combs, sitting in the foul stench of cow horn held against the sides of their feet as they sawed each tooth carefully by hand. In other places the smell of hay-lofts brought the presence of summer meadows into the dappled light and shade of the *medina*'s warren of booths and shops. And there were butchers who only sold camels' humps and others only sheeps' heads, complete with skins and horns, reminding me of the grisly 10,000 heads of Shavoian men, women and children which Moulay Ismail put on the walls of Fez and Marrakesh.

At last I found the Attarine College and, stopped by nobody, went by the great bronze doors into the courtyard. Though smaller than the Bou Anania Medersa I had seen earlier, it was a finer example of the splendour which the Merinide kings lavished on their buildings. Instead of the more usual decoration of geometrical arabesques, the mosaics by the prayer room had conventionalized floral designs and flowing curves in abstract patterns. The college was built in 1323, yet still serves exactly the same purpose today.

Although the Merinide kings built this masterpiece of Hispano-Moroccan art, it was only one of the splendid architectural works which these great builders gave to Fez during their two hundred years of power between 1248 and 1465. But before their time a prince of the royal house of the Almohades was the most renowned patron of the arts, not only in Morocco but in Spain also. The Almo-hades were Berbers from the Atlas Mountains and made Fez the most modern city in their huge empire. At a time when Europe festered in squalor, relieved only by the presence of the monasteries, Fez was already a great city equipped with a network of water supplies and sewer systems.

Yacoub el Mansour governed the Moroccan Empire from 1184 to 1199. But though he rebuilt the walls of Fez he did not give the city any building which could compare with the Giralda he built in Seville or the extraordinary Hassan tower at Rabat. El Mansour may have felt, not unjustifiably, that Fez already had enough public buildings, though he did rebuild the Andalusian Mosque and its fantastic gateway. But this building, like every other in Fez, was secondary to the wonders of the Karaouine Mosque.

On 30 November A.D. 859 Fatima el Fihria paid sixty ounces of silver for the site of a mosque which was to be a memorial to her father, a refugee from Kairouani in Tunisia who had settled in Fez. Within a century the place proved to be too small and a larger mosque was built. The Karaouine soon became a famous school for Koranic theology and Moslem law. Students assembled from all over the Islamic world, and continued through hundreds of years to hear the Karaouine's celebrated dons lecturing on philosophy and music, mathematics and astrology. The school's fame spread to Europe, and during the Middle Ages students from many European countries enrolled there. One of the last Europeans to attend the university, before the anti-Christian movement sprang up in the sixteenth century as a counter-move against a militant Church, was a Professor Clenard from Belgium. 'Seek knowledge,' the Prophet was reputed to have said, 'as far as China.'

The Karaouine Mosque occupied a considerable site in the mesh of the *medina*'s streets. Unbelievers like myself were not allowed in. But from the alleys outside the great building's walls I caught tantalizing glimpses through high arched doorways. Here, as in all those magnificent buildings, there was richness and spaciousness, and an embellishment beyond the normal, everyday life. These were achieved by the immaculate, tiled courtyard and the gorgeous coloured woodcarvings picked out in myriad touches of white and blue, red and yellow, and by the cool, shadowed, arcaded aisles between row upon row of columns, where old men curled up on the reed mats and slept serenely.

These sleeping figures were a silent yet eloquent expression of the Islamic faith's simplicity. The Karaouine was the most important mosque in Morocco, and a building of architectural and historical significance. But it was not a showplace like St. Peter's in Rome or St. Paul's in London, or even the Badshahi Mosque in Lahore, which was built over a single hair from the Prophet's head. No deans or canons came rushing through the columned halls to wake the sleeping men, no ordained priests or pompous vergers to tell the young boys to make less noise, for the mosque was also a meeting-place.

The only people attached to the mosque because of religious office were those who led the prayers and recited the Koran and the *mouddhins* who called from the minarets. Even these men were not ordained, nor was there any complicated liturgical observance. The five pillars of the religion were profession of faith, prayer, almsgiving, fasting, and the pilgrimage to Mecca. The profession or creed, the *chahada*, consisted simply of the bald statement 'I affirm that there is no God but God and that Mohammed is His Prophet.'

Beyond the street of second-hand booksellers which swarmed with students and Koranic scholars, I discovered another, smaller mosque, and here the *mouddhin* invited me in, though his own people were coming and going, kneeling to kiss the ground before saying their prayers. The mosque's gateway had a pair of beautiful doors of wood plated with thin, delicately worked sheets of bronze. A flight of steps led up to the courtyard. Once inside, I was again powerfully conscious of the Islamic belief's intellectual quality.

In spite of the decorative elaboration I had by now learnt to expect in the form of marble panels and blind arcading, columned cloisters, low reliefs of plaster and wood, bracketed superstructures and eaves, the mosque had nevertheless an emptiness, an absence of distraction from the central concept of God's oneness. Idolatry and therefore figurative representation was absent. There was no physical object which could be selected as a focus for worship by a superstitious mind. No part of the building dominated. And though the faithful turned towards Mecca when praying, only an empty niche, the *mihrab*, on the eastern wall indicated the direction of Mecca.

Murky water was flowing through a marble-lined channel to one side of the mosque's courtyard. This was the River Fez. It emerged from one culvert and vanished into another, pursuing its underground course through the *medina*. In some places the river flowed through cellars and was harnessed to water- and cornmills. Two serious, bare-foot boys with palm brooms were washing the marble courtyard of pigeon droppings, and this, too, was swilled into the waters of Rio Fez, as I suspect was some at least of the city's sewage.

From the courtyard I could see storks' nests on convenient projections, though the birds were not breeding. Islam proscribed idolatry. Artists could not portray human or animal forms in religious art, yet in Morocco the stork was a sacred bird. To have a stork's nest on the rooftop was considered a sign of favour and honour. If a stork did not return to its nest, this was a sure sign of the Evil Eye being around.

Fez and storks had been associated in my mind since boyhood, when I first heard about the stork hospital. A long time ago, at some period unspecified, a stork dropped a rope of pearls inside the office of the Kadi of Fez. He tried to find the owner of the valuable necklace, but without success. The stork, however, was recognized as one whose nest had recently been cleared away by a man who could not bear the untidy mess. Since the man clearly disapproved of the bird, the Kadi asked him if he would sell his house, for normally a house favoured by storks was a prized possession. The man readily agreed to the good price offered, which came from the sale of the ownerless pearls. And the house was turned into a hospital for sick storks and the street renamed Zunkat Bilarj, in compensation for the offence given to the sacred birds. Enough money remained from the sale of pearls to buy other houses whose rents supported the stork hospital for many years.

I wanted to see this renowned place and inquired about it at the Tourist Office up in the modern part of Fez. The Director was attentive and kind and gave no indication that he thought *me* a weird bird for asking such odd ornithological questions. The Director and his assistants most patiently tracked down some bird photographs for me. I felt guilty in refusing them, for they only showed French women laden with hundreds of tiny waders shot in a day's 'hunting'. The Tourist Office had many inquiries from visitors about birds, but usually from sportsmen with guns.

Laughing matter—
she has many charms,
her own and the
soothsayers'

Serious affair—
only charm, an amulet,
is round his neck

Raiser—woman with dough at local bakery

Razor—boy with tonsure from local saint

Nevertheless, the Director was able to help me about the stork hospital. One of his staff, an elderly man in a silky cream-coloured *djellaba* and a red fez, who spoke some English, took me outside into the wide, palm-lined Avenue Hassan II and told a taxi-driver to take me to the stork hospital. He did, but not to the ancient institution supported by the pearl necklace as I had anticipated, but to a brand-new animal hospital. Among its other functions this modern foundation, the American Fondouk (an inn or stable in Arabic), had taken over the responsibilities of the ancient stork hospital. On entering the large central courtyard I saw some storks hopping around. But the Fondouk's main service was to horses and mules and donkeys badly treated by their owners.

Dr. André Rousseau, a young French-Canadian veterinary surgeon who ran the Fondouk, showed me the beautifully kept pens and stables. Many of the animals were brought in, he said, in a terrible condition. We looked at rows of recuperating donkeys contentedly foraging in the hay-racks. Nearly half the patients were brought in voluntarily by their owners, but in spite of all treatment being free of charge, most of the people regarded the Fondouk as a prison. Mistreatment of animals was, officially, illegal, and inspectors had the right to detain any animal in bad condition. The owners, insensitive to the sufferings they inflicted, did not like to be deprived of their donkeys. Although these beasts were their means of livelihood, they had no qualms about damaging their animals by neglect, overloading, starving and beating—the age-old fate of the beast of burden.

If blindness, lameness or tumours developed, the owners regarded this as the work of the Evil Eye, and to drive the evil spirits away branded their animals on the affected part. So a beast already suffering would have terrible burns as an additional cruelty to bear. Many of the horses and asses we looked at were suffering from the awful sores that followed such branding. There was also a wretched little stallion with a fearful wound in the neck where the owner had started to saw its head off when the stallion had been obstinate. Three months of treatment in the Fondouk's airy stables had been necessary to heal the gash.

In contrast to this kind of brutality, there were those who brought their pet doves and monkeys for treatment to the Fondouk, as did snake-charmers, and even cameleers whose herds had to be in top condition when slaughtered for human consumption. And, of course, storks were brought, perhaps with broken wings or legs. Dr. Rousseau was pleased when the storks decided to stay on at the hospital, for they were expert at catching rats as well as snakes.

Leaving the attention lavished on me by three wonderful gazelles, I went into Dr. Rousseau's office. He showed me his operating theatre and equipment, and a display of fearful implements which brutal drivers had used on their animals, things like thick sacking needles on the end of sticks. Apart from any question of sensibility, it would not seem to make sense for the owners of pack-animals to damage their only source of income. The Koran mentioned kindness to animals. But perhaps Islam was still too new to have overlaid more ancient and more barbarous ways.

Fez had seen much slaughter in its long history—even in the twentieth century—when fifty years ago a contestant for the throne of Morocco was brought prisoner in a cage fixed to a camel's back on his way to be thrown to hungry leopards. But Moulay Hafid, who had given his would-be rival this treatment, was practically a prisoner himself in Fez by 1912. Tribes from all around revolted against him. In desperation Moulay Hafid asked the French to save Fez, his capital. The French duly obliged, but demanded a protectorate of the country. The protectorate only ended in 1956.

By any standards Moulay Hafid was a cruel man. His feeding of opponents to the leopards was kindness compared with the salt tortures he gave to captive tribesmen. Their hands were cut with daggers and salt sprinkled on the cuts. A stone was placed in each palm and tight leather gauntlets drawn over the clenched fists. Death came as a relief after months of madness which resulted from the torture.

Perhaps the Sultan Moulay Hafid was mentally unbalanced. He lived in a world of suspicion. Having signed the Protectorate Treaty between Morocco and France in 1912, he at once began to suspect the French, particularly as rumours circulated at Court that he was himself about to be imprisoned. The outcome of this was that practically the whole European population of Fez was murdered one night. Marshal Lyautey hastened back to the royal capital to find 20,000 Berbers come down from the Atlas to finish Moulay Hafid. The Sultan's excesses were even too much for the French and he had to abdicate.

Rivalry exists between Moroccan cities. The darker-skinned, carefree people of Marrakesh, for instance, distrust what they regard as the intellectual snobbery of Fez. The tribes of the south detect some sinister character about Fez's long-faced scholars and city fathers. The people and ways of the south really belong to Africa and they have led the tribes for many centuries against Fez, which belongs to the East. People I spoke to in Tangier, besides many tourists preferred Marrakesh to Fez. The southern city, they insisted, was more jolly and friendly. But in any case, they said, I would not be able to go near Fez in July because of the heat. The temperature at that time of year went up to 120° F. and more, my informants went on, and the Fez people themselves left the city for hill stations or went to Tangier and the sea.

But I liked Fez and I decided that nothing was to be gained by trying to compare it with Marrakesh or any other Moroccan city. Fez was Fez. Its history, its setting, its people were unique. And even if the thermometer did record 120° F. while I stayed there, this outrageous-sounding heat was bearable because the air was exceedingly dry. The low humidity made nonsense of temperature readings and even in the hottest hours after midday I did not experience the heat discomfort I knew well from South America. I was surprised to find the people of Fez had not all gone to the hills or the sea, and that like myself they walked about the *medina* in the 100°+ quite unperturbed.

I established a kind of headquarters at a little roadside restaurant. Though small, it was a landmark, for a great mimosa tree filled it with green filtered light. Whitebait sizzled over the pavement fire, and while I waited for it I drank orangeade and watched the owner's cats letting their instincts loose by chasing grasshoppers through the dry dust. The cats had long ago given up hope of catching any of the big alpine swifts that dived almost to the ground in their hunt for evening insects and darted upwards and back again over the tawny, pock-marked battlemented walls.

Messenger-boys came along talking and gesticulating in an animated way together without upsetting the precariously balanced towers of shoe-boxes they carried on their shaven heads. Then the sun went behind the dry hills seen over the city walls, seducing the sky from its day-long blue. But herds of donkeys still clattered through the Moorish gateways, many of them bearing fresh loads of mint for the long night sessions of green tea.

Solemn and stately, unperturbed by the dust and noise of buses and cars, the camels sailed through the gates, their aristocratic heads held disdainfully high, unaware that they would not see tomorrow's sunset. People in Tangier had asked me if I knew why the camel held his head so high. Undoubtedly the camel had some kind of *noblesse oblige* to fulfil. I was told what it was. Although the faithful recite the ninety-nine names of God, only the camel knew the hundredth. But this knowledge could not save him from the slaughter-house.

The mimosa outside the city gate provided a meeting-place for old men, and several of them sat under it to have their heads and armpits shaved. Then a Land-Rover passed the café. On its side was a sign *5th Potters Bar Rover Crew 1964 Summer Overland Expedition London–Morocco–London*. Fez may have seen such expeditions before. But the London suburb had certainly never seen the twilight spectacle of donkeys and camels and their long-robed riders entering the horseshoe gateways. And the people of Potters Bar, I felt sure, did not greet each other with *Salaam-o-alikum*—Peace be unto you.

4

Eclipse of a Sun King

The people who had advised me to keep away from Fez because of the heat were equally insistent that I should go to Ifrane. It was, they said, the queen of the hill stations in the Middle Atlas. Surely enough, for every poster of Chaouen's *immuable quietude* there was another showing Ifrane in winter with ski-laden tourists and snow-drifts among the cedar forests.

I had postponed my departure from Fez several times, but at last I boarded a bus going across the Sais plain, through the wheatfields and up into the mountains, stopping on the way at a charming town, Imouzzer du Kandar. Up there the air blew coolly, and came sumptuously laden with the scent of mountain trees. Fast-flowing waters rushed through Imouzzer, coming down from trout streams and irrigation channels that coursed through cherry orchards and alpine meadows, mushroom farms and strawberry fields. Underground reservoirs and springs fed the surrounding lakes and streams of Imouzzer. Dr. André Rousseau at the American Fondouk had told me how these deep, powerful waters were a menace to families who still lived in underground caves.

The town perched on a fertile plateau was founded by the Berbers long before the French built the modern town when Morocco became their protectorate. I saw some very French-looking villas among the quince and mulberry trees. But the cave-dwellers had no such love of gardens. They only loved the natural grottoes, even when some of their people had been drowned recently in floods from hidden subterranean rivers. Safe houses were built above ground by alarmed authorities. But the troglodytes drifted back to their dangerous burrows.

Imouzzer's streets were themselves cave-like with weeping willows and plane trees meeting low overhead. Fruit trees and bushes crowded the mountain ledges and I could see a motley of peaches and pears, loganberries and apples, plums and figs. Flowers and fruit rejoiced in their rich situation. But the houses whose yellow walls and shuttered windows peeped above the orchards looked forlorn. Many were for sale and they told their own story of the French owners who had gone away since Morocco's independence in 1956. Their architecture was unremarkable. Their care had been lavished on the gardens and these went on flourishing despite the fortunes of politics.

Ifrane lay much higher up in the mountains, 5,143 feet above the sea, a place of brilliant sunshine and rarefied air. At first sight Ifrane offended me with its pretentious would-be European buildings. The first thing I did on arrival was to inquire how quickly I might get out again. No bus, however, left for Meknes until the following day. I was trapped in a suburb of steep-roofed and gabled houses which were waiting for the first snowfall to complete the picture-postcard scene. Ifrane was deliberately and perversely quaint. American producers would find it ideal for a film about Hans Andersen. The royal palace at Ifrane was built like a *schloss* on the Rhine. I found it difficult to believe that this extraordinary French colonial hill station was not a German suburb.

My stay among the architectural splendour of Fez and the taste I had there of Morocco's time-honoured way of life made Ifrane's superficiality unacceptable to me. By sundown, however, my hostility had subsided. After all, Ifrane *was* deliciously cool and it was refreshing to look at tall green pines and cedars covering the hills. And to be fair, Ifrane only came into existence in 1929, which was a bad year for architecture generally.

My translation from Fez to Ifrane had a dream-like quality. It looked most odd to see men in *djellabas* and women in *haiks* coming out of the steep-roofed Grimm fairy-tale houses and going into Austrian-looking hotels complete with Gothic lettering and Swiss balconies. But when I realized Ifrane swarmed with children of all ages and that the Moroccans had turned the odd French hill station into a summer paradise for children I forgave all. I could not quite imagine what the place would be like in autumn and winter, when the wild-boar hunters and beaters flocked in, followed by skiers from all over the world, but I could see how the summer children transformed Ifrane, because Moroccan children had an especial beauty. Long crocodiles of orphans from holiday homes went about the tiny town and through the trees. They made a splash of colour with their neat, French dress of white or khaki skirts with blue shorts and red or yellow hats or baseball caps. These children were handsome, healthy and happy, as could be heard from their bouts of community singing as they went home through the oak woods, their slender, perfectly formed brown legs moving like gazelles through the trees. Their leaders were young themselves, some still in their teens. I watched one long file of girls. Not one among fifty was ugly or even plain. Their raven hair was lustrous and without henna. It was the first time I had seen what beauty Moroccan women must have under their veiling *negabs*.

All the children, both from the holiday homes and those with parents, eventually found their way down to the water-meadows which lay between the village and the palace on the hill. The road to the palace ran by the meadows, and it was from there that I saw the King arrive with his entourage to take up summer residence in the German castle palace.

Being itself only small, Ifrane could offer the King only a small crowd of welcome. These loyal citizens lined the road and clapped and cheered politely when, after a succession of motor-bike outriders and police radio cars with huge aerials looped like giant fishing rods on the roof, the royal limousine itself swept by in a long, low, black and shiny symbol of kingly elegance. Three Ministers in red fezzes sat in the back, while King Hassan II himself was in front beside the chauffeur, wearing shirt-sleeves. He leaned out of the window and waved in a friendly way like a young man going on a holiday, which, I suppose, he was. The entourage concluded like the other half of a pair of book-ends, as it had begun but in reverse order, motor-bike outriders coming last of all.

Meanwhile there had been some extraordinary limousines like

small buses, each with eight doors, and filled with ladies of the royal household in dark *djellabas*, the last of these cars carrying a bird cage. Since each of the ladies in black exactly resembled every other one of the ladies in black, it was impossible for a stranger like myself to form any notion as to rank, station, function or relationship, if any, to the King, though presumably those in the first eight-doored car were more important than those in the last one.

The whole procession was gone in a moment, swallowed up by the woods below the palace. If it had been like former processions which some of the old men at the roadside might have seen, I would have had more time to take in details, for the Sultan's predecessors went from palace to palace on horseback, with the seals of state hidden under their saddle-cloths.

The meadows, streams and pools which made up Ifrane's public park occupied a flat valley between the high ground on which the village stood and that on which the palace had been built. The mountain streams came down pure as crystal, winding and twisting through the low banks, crossed here and there by wooden bridges like those in miniature Japanese gardens in ceramic bowls. Noble boles rose out of the gurgling streams and dragonflies darted close to the surface with iridescent flashes green as a plover's back, yellow as ragwort, more blue than sky, red as the rubies of Fez. Children lay flat and drank the water, alarming nobody but my microbe-conscious self. Perhaps they were born with immunity against infection, though I looked at the thousands of tiny black snails clinging to the stream-bed rocks and stones and wondered if these were the sort that caused bilharziasis. To heighten my hypochondriacal thrills an olive-green snake, three feet long, slithered away through the grass when I sat down to watch the *fête champêtre*.

Families crowded the meadows and the children darted about like dragonflies and nearly as colourful. The men, however, sat together in groups under the trees, playing cards for hours on end. They sat on rugs or cushions and drowned the children's shouts by transistor radios on which rival stations competed with jazz and Arab music. Their womenfolk, at some discreet remove, also sat cross-legged in groups, some removing their handkerchief-veils perhaps to reveal a face totally covered by tattoos. The ladies' occupation was to gossip and keep an eye on the children.

Somehow the whole scene recalled the French Impressionists' idea of Sunday. There was the same golden atmosphere, the same sense of relaxation, the same composition of groups and the same, indefinable air of warm sensuality. French Impressionist women, whether Seurat's serene and monumental Venuses with bustles or Renoir's Parisiennes with *parapluies*, were not unlike the women at Ifrane sitting or walking in the meadows, for the dark, full-length *djellaba* glimpsed in the willow shade was not dissimilar to the Parisian dress of the 1890s.

To link the groups sitting on the grass by the stream with Degas's and Tissot's picnic scenes was a fancy of mine. But I was awakened from it not, as would have been right, by a French voice but by one in English with an American accent. My hand was shaken by another twice its size which belonged to a huge negro in a blue boiler-suit and baseball boots.

'Pretty nice, isn't it?' he asked, indicating the holiday crowds. I agreed that it was.

'I've got an hour or so off,' he went on, dropping down on the grass beside me.

'Off from what?' I asked.

'Duty.' He pulled a red beret from a pocket in the boiler-suit. 'I'm a King's guard,' he said proudly. He went on to say how displeased he was with the way things were turning out. Traditionally, the Imperial Black Guard *was* black.

'But now,' the soldier explained, 'they're bringing in lighter-skinned men.'

Originally, the King's guardsmen had come across the Sahara to form Moulay Ismail's bodyguard in the seventeenth century. Now it seemed that the negroes' traditional place was threatened. My new friend talked as fast and as flowingly as the stream we crossed when he insisted on taking me through the woods to see the chalet-like barracks which had been built as a holiday centre for the now-departed French Navy. He was, he said, one of the royal chauffeurs.

'You been to Marrakesh?'

'Not yet,' I said. Then he told me all about Marrakesh, where he was born, though he thought Tangier better.

'Why don't you come fishin' tomorrow?'

Quite a number of the soldiers were city boys who liked the King to come up to Ifrane, because this gave them an opportunity for fishing. My friend and some others were off duty again the next morning and would be going up to one of the lakes. Alas, it was as difficult to drag me from bed next day as it was to heave a black bass from the lake. An evening's celebration on fiery fig brandy left me in no mood in the morning for rainbow trout. My hand which the King's guard had nearly crushed in his grip was much too shaky to tackle a fighting pike from a run of reeds. And this put me in a bad mood, because angling friends in Britain had talked to me of splendid trout and coarse fishing in the many lakes and multitude of streams coursing the extensive woods around Ifrane.

I had a room under one of the village's steep roofs. The sleep induced by fig brandy lasted until eleven o'clock. I got up and sluiced a haggard face, annoyed at missing the fishing trip. The soldiers would have started at dawn and already be on their way back. A strange noise came from outside my window. It was not a plague of locusts as the sound suggested, but rain pattering on the poplar leaves, the first and only rain of my whole stay in Morocco. The short shower was refreshing, as much for its novelty as its freshness, though the sun was not long in coming out again. I thought about the sisters of the rash Phaethon who stole the chariot of the sun-god and fell from the sky to be turned into poplars forever to shed amber tears into the Eridanos River.

The tears of Ifrane's poplars dried up before I had breakfasted on tomatoes and Finnish cheese. I swallowed this frugal meal as an act of will rather than from appetite, because the journey to Meknes, though only forty-six miles, needed firm foundations. My women fellow passengers in the bus were losing their foundations into tins held discreetly under their veils. But their bus-sickness, I decided with firm, confident callousness, was psychosomatic. If only last night's fig brandy could be finally dealt with by the cheese and tomatoes, I considered my journey would be fine. I ate six prickly pears also by the time we reached the first stop at El Hajeb. Without a qualm of stomach or conscience, I thoroughly enjoyed the journey down through the Vale of Ifrane, where trees bordered rivers and waterfalls, making beautiful places for the families already picnicking on the banks.

It was difficult to believe that the drive through the green-oak forest of Djaba was in the middle of Morocco. The bus went too fast for my comfort, since the bus crash outside Ouezzane had left me nervous. But my bandaged arm, full, I suspected, of glass chips, was not the main concern. Because of the driver's speeding I could not see as much of the countryside as I would have liked.

After the forests we sped like an intercontinental missile through landscapes whose only buildings were herdsmen's tents, the big brown tents of the Beni Mtir tribe, Berbers who have been recorded as camping there as far back as the fourteenth century. The open country was arid after Ifrane's verdant valleys. A buzzard circled overhead on taut, motionless wings, waiting to pounce on young hares or partridges amongst the dwarf palmetto. At El Hajeb the world was green again.

I bought more prickly pears from a small boy wheeling them in a pram, and walked over to the fir woods, where there were caves and grottoes with connecting passages which people had lived in for centuries. The stork's nest on the police-station roof was clearly of a much later date, and undoubtedly shortlived would be the fat rams being tied on the bus roof for the remaining miles to Meknes.

The last lap proved to be rolling farmland. Mile succeeded golden mile, broken only occasionally by olive trees blown by the wind so that they resembled the soft texture of satin in eighteenth-century portraits. The shimmering distance half revealed lines of hills, including one with a profile like Firle Beacon in Sussex. Much of the land had already been ploughed and the freshly furrowed earth resembled the brown velvet of autumn reed-mace. Not even in Canada had I seen such acreages ploughed by the first day of August. Some of the plains were given over to maize and vineyards and all of these had little straw pulpits built on high agave poles where watchmen sat guarding the crops.

Throughout history these wide-open spaces must have fed the lust of many ambitious men. I could sense the effect the land must have had on the fabulous Moulay Ismail, how his imagination and desire must have burned for possession and power over the wide sweeps of earth and sky, and how the emptiness of the plains must have filled him with the obsession for building monuments that would stand for ever as witness of his greatness.

Moulay Ismail's ambassadors had failed to bring the Princess de Conti back from France for their imperial master. But they did bring him accounts of Louis XIV's doings at Versailles. In those days Meknes was an undistinguished, modest-sized town. But its site, with the limitless plains around, offered Moulay Ismail a bare canvas on which could be painted wonders to exceed those of the French Sun King.

Architecture on the grand scale has always been an accessory to the megalomaniac dreams of tyrants from the Pharaohs of Egypt, the Roman emperors, the Popes of the Renaissance and the Czars of Russia down to modern dictators. In 1672 Moulay Ismail settled in Meknes to supervise his grandiose schemes. To him, as to others of his kind, life and limb meant nothing. Some 25,000 Christian slaves and 30,000 native convicts were among the huge army of workmen employed.

According to one of these, Thomas Pellow of Penryn, the slaves were often stamped alive into the mortar of a wall. Pellow escaped such a fate and rose to be an official in the royal service. He later wrote in his interesting book, *Captivity and Adventures*, about the King, 'Voluptuous, covetous, passionate, treacherous, more than a tyrant, he tamed the natural savageness of his subjects by showing himself still more savage than they.'

The Sun King of Morocco concerned himself personally with the works. Every morning the Sultan toured the new projects, accompanied by a negro slave who carried his pipe, another who carried the tobacco, and a third who bore a jug of hot water for the King to wash his hands. Other negroes followed with clubs for the Sultan to throw at slaves who were not working to the royal satisfaction. Another array of black eunuchs held handkerchiefs at the ready to catch the royal spittle and excrement. This was not allowed to fall to the ground and was kept in jewelled boxes by women who believed that anything from out of the little black body was a cure for distemper.

One palace alone, with walls twenty-five feet thick, was four miles in circumference. In fact, he often did the rounds on horseback. He was very agile. Even when over 60 years old he could, in one move, mount his horse, draw his sword, and sever the head of the black eunuch who held his stirrup. On the other hand, the Sultan was not without feelings. He cared well for his horses, and those animals which had been to Mecca were never allowed to be ridden again. His personal dromedaries were shampooed three times a week, and the palaces were full of cats. He fed his favourite dog on nothing but the best, and the best was pieces of buttock cut from a living woman.

Not unreasonably, it might be supposed that this sort of thing could not possibly go on for long. But it did, for fifty-five years. Moulay Ismail was only 26 when he came to the throne in 1672 and he stayed there until 1727. Among the many accounts of the Sultan was one by Simon Ockley, Professor of Arabic at Cambridge. He described the Moroccan King as 'A mulatto of a dark complexion and of a very lean and thin body, exceeding amorous and as eminent for the Sports of Venus as for his Martial Exploits. Next to Women, his Recreation consists chiefly on contriving and building houses, and walls, in levelling mountains and filling up vales.'

Moulay Ismail has long gone and the horrors of his reign are forgotten. But the works remain, or at least sufficient of them to show the barbaric splendour that once possessed the city of Meknes. Even today the gates and walls and towers have about them an air of intimidation as well as grandeur. Much has fallen into ruin in the three centuries since their erection.

The Bab Mansour gateway survived decay and it still makes passage through the invincible tawny walls a ceremonial experience. The gate is wide and high and flanked by enormous marble monoliths brought from Volubilis, a Roman city twenty miles from Meknes. The central horseshoe arch of the gateway and those of its projecting pavilions only filled half the height. Panels of geometric, three-dimensional tracery covered the solid upper half and long strips of Koranic inscriptions carved in low relief ran across the top. These panels and the tympanum above the arches glittered in the sun with green and gold mosaics.

Moulay Ismail seems to have had an eye for talent, because this gate, finest of the surviving works, was designed towards the end of the Sultan's reign by a Portuguese slave on his conversion to Islam. One of the King's 800 sons completed the gate in 1732. He was one of the lucky sons, because, with so many offspring, Moulay Ismail was not perturbed at the loss of a few here and there. He killed several of them himself, one having his right hand and left foot cut off. However, the Sultan was a good father at heart—he always made certain that they had fine mausoleums, some of which still remain.

Inside, the Bab Mansour consisted of a high tunnel which turned left and then right, a device no doubt used for defensive purposes. Carts and carriages and cars have necessarily to slow down to manoeuvre past the tall arched niches on whose platforms beggars were sleeping when I walked through. Beyond, the outer wall was echoed by an inner wall, crenellated and with square bastions at frequent intervals. There was an open square, dominated by the green-tiled minaret and golden spheres of the Dar Kebira Mosque. An old blind man sat there with a little guide-boy beside him. He played on the *thilats*, small kettledrums made of pottery, one smaller than the other and producing a sound not unlike the bongo drums of the modern dance band.

Inside the inner ring of ramparts the extent of Moulay Ismail's building operations could be appreciated. Immense walls spread in all directions, though much fallen in places. Unlike the walls of castles and forts in Europe, Moulay Ismail's were not constructed of ashlar masonry, but in a mixture of roughly coursed stones and coarse mortar infill. Though adequate for immediate purposes of defence, such construction was not proof against time. Nor indeed was it proof against the picks and shovels belonging to a later generation of car mechanics and blacksmiths who had dug workshops for themselves into the walls' thickness.

Farther into the network of this city of walls, past Moulay Ismail's own tomb and the prison of his Christian slaves, I found the Bab er Rih gate. This was an unusual affair, as large as a Norman parish church in England, complete with a long aisled hall which the road passed through between side aisles separated by squat monolithic columns supporting a Moorish arcade. Large open carriages lumbered along the main aisle's hundred-foot length. These carriages were too dilapidated even for use as tourist traps. Former glory gone, like the Ambassadors' Pavilion just beyond the aisled gateway nobody but the poorest people used them. The economics were simple—the more people per journey the less each passenger must pay. So the disintegrating vehicles were hopelessly overloaded. The owners had fixed barbed wire at the back to prevent stowaways cadging rides on the springs and axles. Thus weighed down with humanity, a humanity usually itself loaded with sacks and bags and boxes from the markets, the carriages creaked and groaned, drawn by starved, straining horses, through the ghost town of the Sun King's crumbling palaces.

Fifty of these palaces, each with its own mosque and baths, had once adorned Meknes. There had been a stable three miles long, with thousands of magnificent Arab horses, and vast barracks to house the imperial cavalry and harem guard of black eunuchs. Now they had all come to silence and ruin. Only a few egrets flocked in old mimosa trees where white peacocks once strutted over clover lawns.

European governments kept anxious, watchful eyes on Meknes during Moulay Ismail's reign, and the British Government was no exception. They knew all about the royal menageries of lions and tigers, leopards and wolves, which were fought by as many as sixty slaves a day who preferred to take that sporting chance rather than be thrown alive into lime kilns. And worse, for apart from strong young men being forced into building operations and strong young women into harems, aged clergy and nobles were sent in chains by their owners into the streets of Moroccan towns to sell water and sweetmeats.

Prompted either by conscience or expediency, a mission was dispatched from London. It included John Windus, who wrote *A iourney to Mequinez, the residence of the present Emperor of Fez and Morocco, on the occasion of Commodore Stewart's Embassy thither for the Redemption of British Captives in the Year 1721.* The British mission arrived during the last years of the Sultan's life. Moulay Ismail was 75 by this time, but according to Windus 'very active for such an Age'.

The Redemptionist Fathers also undertook many dangerous journeys to Morocco to redeem Christian slaves. Their accounts resembled John Windus's, though they had much more to say about the way Moulay Ismail pulled down palaces to build even larger ones. This high-mindedness was, of course, commendable, and no doubt many of the Meknes slaves hoped for some such release from captivity. But why did these Christian rescuers make such a fuss about Morocco when equally outrageous things were going on in their own countries? Why did they say nothing about the cartloads of dead labourers who were carried away from Versailles? Why did the estimable John Windus and Commodore Stewart say nothing about the fact that Charles II of England and his Queen were large shareholders in the 'Company of Royal Adventurers of England into Africa' that claimed 'the sole and entire trade in Negroes on the African Coast'.?

Commodore Stewart and his mission returned to London with 296 rescued slaves. There were, however, curiously enough, many others who did not want to return home, possibly because their individual lot was not too hard, perhaps less hard than they had suffered in Restoration England. It would be interesting to know how many of the 15,585 negro slaves sold by the Royal Adventurers of England in 1673 for 3,500 tons of sugar would have preferred the chain gangs of the plantations to their freedom.

During the same year in which John Windus wrote of Moulay Ismail's excesses the British headed the list of slave transporters, with the French second and the Portuguese third. Bristol and Liverpool were growing richer on the profits from the slave trade than Meknes ever became. Powerful voices, like those of Dr. Johnson and Adam Smith, Montesquieu and Rousseau, were constantly raised against the evils of slaving. Cowper summed the situation up;

I pity them greatly, but I must be mum,
For how could we do without sugar and rum?

John Windus commented on the Sultan's way of dealing with colour questions, 'He always yokes his best-complexioned subjects to a black help-mate, and the fair lady must take up with a Negro. Pointing to a man and woman married them with *Hadi yi houd hadi*— That take that.

Compared with modern methods of extermination Moulay Ismail's

Mud—around Ouarzazate the Berber's home is his castle

Mouloud—at Sale the Prophet's birthday presents are wax lanterns

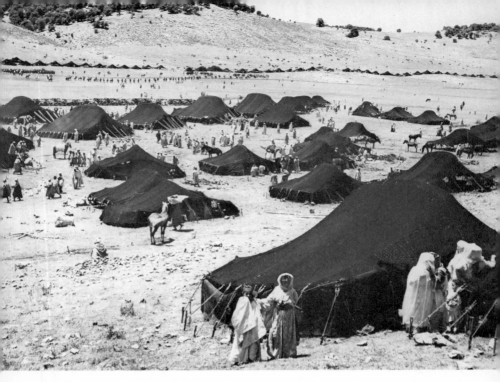

Festival of tents

Fantasia on horseback

excesses were, of course, child's play. He could never have emulated the extinction of six million Jews in the Second World War, or the sudden disappearance of Hiroshima. And in his own century the Sultan appears no worse in terms of cruelty than European royalty like Alfonso VI of Portugal, whose hunger for cruelty and debauchery was so outrageous that he shook the structure of belief in Divine Right to its foundation.

Moulay Ismail's cruelties are not excused on the grounds that he was only doing, to greater or lesser degree, what many other crowned heads were doing. Yet seen in this way, the praise he received from contemporaries can be better understood. If many of his acts were those of a madman or monster, other deeds showed him to be a genius who had succeeded in uniting Morocco as far as the borders of the Sudan. This was an enormous empire in which his power was completely respected and 'public life and property never more secure.'

At his death the royal princes swooped on Meknes and seized everything that was valuable. The palaces and courtyards fell into ruin. But the Sun King bequeathed his country something infinitely more precious than stone monuments. By his actions of forcing miscegenation Morocco could never be torn asunder by racial strife. In the Morocco I saw the people had a rich mixture of Arab blood which long ago mingled with the mysterious Berber, the negro, the Jew and Christian slaves from a score of nations. There was no Moroccan 'type' except for an extreme handsomeness of features and a skin colour the like of which sun-tan manufacturers would give fortunes to reproduce.

Such was the beautiful colouring of Hassan Lamrani and Ahmed Fellah, two schoolboys who came up to me outside Moulay Ismail's tomb. They approached me shyly and then began to speak a flood of English, offering to show me Meknes and to tell me anything I wanted to know about their city. Their special delight was in being able to speak English with a 'real Englishman'. It seemed too complicated to explain I was Irish. The boys talked fluently and with good accents. They not only read Edgar Wallace and Agatha Christie avidly but never missed a film by these two authors. When I met them the boys were carrying swimming-towels. During their long summer vacation they studied, went to the swimming-pool and the pictures. We met again several times and I was immensely impressed not only with their command of English but their range of knowledge and interests generally. They talked about religion and French philosophers and English writers other than Wallace and Christie. I found it difficult to believe that the boys were only 16. Hassan wanted to go to England and see London's *purée de pois* and his girl pen-friend in Newcastle. Ahmed wanted to go to Tahiti, following Gauguin's footsteps—talking of feet, he said, his own were so big and broad through playing football barefoot.

I was on my way back to the hotel up in Meknes's modern town and so, talking and laughing and explaining many things to me, the boys walked up the hill. By looking back we could see Moulay Ismail's city spread out, white and tawny, punctuated by minarets, low behind the encircling walls. Meknes had a population of 200,000. But this figure was meaningless, because it was impossible to tell how many people there were, for the *medina*, as in other cities, could not be comprehended as a whole, and with the French new town tacked on any sense of size was impossible. Perhaps the best way to judge the size of a town was by the number of cinemas. Meknes was well blessed with cinemas, whose films seemed to be either of the sex or swashbuckling type, or both. Certainly more customers were going into the Regent cinema than into the Assembly of God mission hall next door. A Victorian traveller called Budgett Meakin knew Morocco well. In one of his books on the country he claimed that 'Mequinez has earned the worst possible reputation for morals, rivalling Sodom and Gomorrah in the tale of its wickedness'. Alas, such excitements can now be found by the locals only in spectacles shown at the cinemas.

Hassan and Ahmed were excellent guides. Under the canopy of orange trees on the main shopping street, naturally the Avenue Mohammed V, we found a Monoprix, Morocco's Woolworths, where I bought a bottle of good Martinique rum for 17s. 6d. The store manager asked if I would like the cork removed, rightly guessing I was going to drink it in my hotel, where cooking in the room was the only thing expressly forbidden by the notice on the back of the door.

The room evoked a whole epoch. Its rain-forest green walls, with

curtains and bedspreads to match, the chromium-plated wall telephone shaped like an ear-trumpet, recalled the 1920s, thé dansant
and potted palms and wicker furniture and long beads and tasselled
flat-bosomed women and wind-up gramophones—all of which this
hotel had probably seen in its heyday when Meknes was Morocco's
second most important military centre.

Since most hotel rooms in England remind one of the post-
Franco-Prussian war rather than post-Great War, and speak of
Dickens rather than Hemingway, I had no complaints. Where in
England could 9 shillings buy a night in a large room with a large,
perfectly clean bed, plus a private bathroom with hot running water
and a bidet? The bidet was standard equipment for nearly all
Moroccan hotels. The rooms which had a basin naturally had a bidet,
too. I came to expect this sanitary duet as a matter of course, though
I never met a duet like the bath-room which a rich pasha installed
with two baths, one for the hot tap and one for the cold.

I took shower-baths more frequently in Meknes than anywhere
else in Morocco. The city seemed much hotter and more humid than
Fez, and it seemed noisier at night. In the room next door the
Moroccan swimming champion was celebrating his victory won that
day at the city's pool. And when his late-night session subsided the
dogs began to bark, eventually leading, at 4.30 a.m., to a blood-
chilling yelping and screaming which I thought meant that one of
the sleepless dogs had been run over. But from my window I saw
that a man in a café across the road was having a fit and the terrible
cries only ceased when an ambulance arrived.

Since the hotel was near the Avenue Mohammed V, I ate at the
Central Restaurant, a small and pleasant place with tables in a patio
behind the Avenue. The noise of traffic was excluded and cool
breezes blew through the courtyard, ruffling the tiny garden. Lizards
stalked over the whitewashed walls after mosquitoes and large moths
fluttered into the patio's orange trees and rose bushes. I was happy
eating at the Central Restaurant, but Omar had other ideas. We had
met the moment I arrived from Ifrane at the bus station. A begging
woman, with a child on her back swathed in the usual manner over
her *djellaba*, had come up and spoken in perfect American English.

'Hi, boy! What you looking for?' Her veil revealed enough for me to see her beautiful face. While I was getting her sad story of an American airman Omar came to the rescue, thinking the girl had molested me. 'I get you a good clean girl,' he had said in disgust.

Omar did not really understand when I explained that the young woman's story interested me. It was Omar who took me to the hotel which lay just across the street from the apartment block where he lived with his wife. Omar was 19 and Chedlya 18. Apart from the tents at Tetuan and the barracks at Ifrane, theirs was the first Moroccan home I had been into. The young couple lived with Omar's parents. His father was a well-established Civil Servant. But I never saw the older people, because Omar and Chedlya entertained me in their big bed-sitting-room, whose chief piece of furniture was the hi-fi radiogram. Jazz obsessed them. They spent most of their time together dancing to the strains of the hi-fi. Late at night I would see them out on their balcony doing the Twist or the Shake or the Blue Beat or some such American craze. In the street Chedlya wore a *djellaba* and was a model of Moroccan propriety. At home she wore ballet tights ('She's real sexy,' Omar kept saying), while Omar himself wore a singlet and blue shorts. They were like a French film about teenagers.

But in spite of their wild sort of happiness together, something had gone wrong in their young marriage, which neither of them was the least shy of talking about. And through it I discovered that even behind the façade of the most up-to-date apartment blocks age-old Arab traditions persisted. Although Omar and Chedlya had already been married nearly two years, she being 16 at the time, she had not conceived. They were deeply and romantically in love. Yet both of them recognized that, fundamentally, Chedlya's role was to produce sons.

Although I could not discover with what degree of effectiveness, aphrodisiacs were much used in Morocco, not only as stimulants but as preventatives against sterility. Every *medina* had shops specializing in love potions. These were easily known by the odd collection hanging from the doorposts or heaped on the counters, old skins of foxes, hedgehogs, snakes, weasels, colocynths and roots and dozens of herbal mixtures. The bones of animals were ground up with insects and bats' blood and tree bark.

Another powerful dish against sterility used in many houses was a black sausage smelling even stronger than the strong buried *smeen*, and which was made from the testicles of a sacrificial ram. Aid El Kebir—The Great Feast—was a major festival held fifty days after Ramadan and every family killed a head of livestock at this time. This consisted normally of a sheep and for weeks beforehand the children paraded their family's sacrifice-to-be through the streets seeing who had the biggest and best. On the morning of Aid El Kebir, the head of each family turned the animal towards Mecca and slaughtered it.

Though Chedlya served it to me, I did not enthuse about the pieces of black sausage, kept for months after the day of sacrifice, which were in a stew she made. It was full of *baraka*—blessing—according to Omar. Apart from this, however, I ate voraciously in their house, because Chedlya was an excellent cook, though many of the herbs were, I knew, put in not only for flavouring but also in the hope of exciting Omar's love. Many of the herbs and powders in the markets had additional uses as charms besides their aphrodisiacal and flavouring properties.

But at 18 Chedlya took her cooking most seriously. The black sausages had not performed as they ought to have done in respect of sterility and neither had the menstrual blood she sprinkled on a score of holy men's tombs, and on the mules, who by nature, of course, were sterile, and into the water of the local river Bou-Fakran, Father of Tortoises. She endeavoured now to put the matter right by cooking with the most extraordinary, but always delicious, ingredients. My tendency to be sceptical about these ancient practices was corrected when I considered the mumbo-jumbo which goes into Western processed food. Chemists and advertisers between them have concocted a modern set of myths and superstitions about food, a jargon compounded of words like goodness, strength, fresh, pure—all eked out with popular pseudo-science about vitamins and proteins and calories. None of this nonsense which surrounds our debilitated food is true. 'Fresh' and 'pure' mean nothing after weeks and months of storage, processing, and oddities like colouring have all played their part. And, moreover, none of this pre-packed, vacuum-packed, sealed-in-flavour food tasted half as good as the dishes which Chedlya gave me in Meknes, for all their superstitious association.

My favourite dish of Chedlya's, though even this did not make me unusually amorous, was mutton cooked slowly in honey with raisins and almonds, nutmeg and thyme, myrtle and lavender, ash tree-seeds and garlic, mint and stavesacre seed, roots of strapwort and locust beans, all generously sprinkled with common as well as red and black pepper.

What I found particularly pleasant as I picked up my spoon carved out of lemon wood was Omar solemnly pronouncing, against a background of the Beatles' ya-ya-ing, the gracious *Bismillah*— In the name of God.

'*Bismillah*,' he said, and in the same breath, '*Bon apetit*.'

Chedlya was as eager to learn new recipes as she was to prepare familiar ones. I told her about a recipe the Queen of Sheba used with desired effect upon Solomon. Chedlya had never heard of it, and I was surprised that it was not known in Morocco, for many Moslem countries served milk pudding coated with the thinnest diaphragm of beaten silver. In the streets of Lahore housewives could be heard beating the silver to a spider's web frailty in order to give nourishment to the heart. I was first given this silver-coated pudding in 1957 at a welcome-home dinner to the Pakistan cricket team from England. Chedlya's eyes sparkled at the prospect.

Talk of Solomon and the Queen of Sheba brought Omar back to his favourite character in history—their own Moulay Ismail. On the pink-tiled bathroom wall they had put up some travel posters. Between a Spanish bull-fight and a view of the Parthenon was a poster from the big 1962 tercentenary for Moulay Ismail. The reproduced contemporary engraving showed the Sultan with his sceptre and long pear earrings. Omar was proud of Moulay Ismail, as were all Moroccans with whom I spoke about him.

'Imagine,' Omar mused in a far-away voice. 'Think of it, eight hundred sons! Think of being able to have a palace full of a thousand beautiful women.'

Chedlya disliked this sort of talk. It reminded her too much of her own misery.

I let the subject drop. After all, nothing was to be gained by telling Omar that, according to the British Embassy led by Commodore Stewart in 1721, the royal harem at Meknes contained over two thousand women, and the Sun King at the age of 75 managed to keep most of them in happy motherhood—a fact which makes the Kinsey Report dull reading.

5

Roman Footprints

When Carthage was destroyed in 146 B.C. Carthaginian trading-posts along the Moroccan coast became Roman, and they built a city to serve as a capital of the interior. This was Volubilis. In later centuries, twenty miles away, Meknes sprang up.

Moulay Idris I came to Volubilis in A.D. 788, when he fled the Middle East. Arabs had already settled there among the Berbers, Jews, Christians and Roman soldiers. Because Moulay Idris was a great-grandson of the Prophet he was soon elected King. He moved his capital to a town three miles away from Volubilis on two prominent spurs of the surrounding Zerhoun mountains.

He preached the new religion of Islam, founded by his great-grandfather and recorded in the Koran. The Holy Book, of course, had been revealed to Mohammed by one of the four archangels, Jabrail (Gabriel)—the Divine Messenger. Depiction of anthropomorphic form was forbidden in North Africa, though I saw that the German engraving of Moulay Ismail was popular in Morocco, along with portraits of more recent sultans. The ban on figurative art meant, however, that no early art in Morocco shows the archangel bringing the Koran to the Prophet. To see pictures of this, it would be necessary to visit Persia, where there are archangels complete with wings and moustaches.

Moulay Idris died from poisoning in A.D. 793. By this time he had established the first Arab dynasty in Morocco—the Idrissides. His son, Idris II, founded Fez. Although Moulay Idris had only been in Morocco five years he became the patron saint of the country. The capital he built took his own name. Perched on its two mountain spurs, the little white town of Moulay Idris became the most vener-ated place in Morocco and one of the sacred cities of Islam. Even today, when little is left in the world for tourists to violate, infidels are not allowed to live in Moulay Idris or buy property there and may only visit the city between sunrise and sunset.

Until recently entry to the city, even in Arab disguise, was as difficult as getting into Mecca. Travel books about Morocco used to be enlivened by stories of the authors' attempts to go inside the gates of Moulay Idris. Colonel Trotter had to flee before an angry crowd chasing him from the Holy City. The American missionary Rocke-feller was badly stoned while trying to pass through dressed in a *djellaba*. Today, Rockefeller dollars work missionary miracles in various kinds of aid to Africa and old barriers have come tumbling down.

Omar, my friend in Meknes, said it was unthinkable for me not to go there and told the driver of a petite taxi to take us into the *medina*, where we could catch a Moulay Idris bus. Most Moroccan cities had a fleet of petite taxis which scudded about like water-beetles, and were extremely cheap. The bus ticket was not issued from the office, as it would have been for a longer journey, and the bus had no scheduled departure, leaving when all the seats were full, and, even more importantly, when no more livestock, furniture, sacks of cereal, bundles of personal possessions and household paraphernalia could be packed on top.

Bus services in Morocco were extremely good, and long-distance ones operated exactly to time. I travelled hundreds of miles, but never once encountered confusion about tickets or seat numbers. Although the engine of the Moulay Idris bus was running when Omar and I arrived, as though about to depart at any moment, I knew by now that all drivers ran their engines perhaps for twenty minutes before leaving, no doubt with the intention of making stragglers hurry.

At last we pulled into a street near the great Bab Mansour, leaving the crowd of sweet- and cake-sellers and mint-vendors with enormous bunches cleverly tied in balloon shapes by palm leaves that could be opened and closed like a green cage. The conductor entertained the passengers to distract the women from being sick. He made faces, held a cigarette in his chin and made play with a long dagger. He stopped the bus when we passed a bridal procession outside Meknes, so that we could enjoy the gaiety of the village crowd and hear the reed pipes and drums and watch the bride riding on the horse with her husband, shaded from the sun by a pink parasol. Women waved long scarves, bright yellow and green, at the happy pair, though whether to keep the flies away or in some ceremonial act, I did not know. Scores of children milled round the procession and from what little I could see of her the bride herself looked hardly more than a child.

We were out in the rolling, golden, open land which surrounded Meknes, passing through olive groves and orchards and fields where prickly pear was planted in rows as a crop and not as hedges. Shortly, the slow climb into the Zerhoun hills began. Away to the left, on a long low swell in the landscape I saw the indistinct forms of fallen buildings.

'Volubilis,' Omar said.

And almost at once, round a bend in the road, we saw Moulay Idris also, clustered white on the mountainside. The climb was suddenly steep and the road snaked back on itself, giving a fine dramatic approach to the Holy City. Unlike other Moroccan cities, little had spread beyond its wall. The small mountain town was hunched on the mountain shoulders, at once complete, protected and rejecting infringement of its isolation. In spite of the sparkling, mountain sunshine and the bright scatter of light on the white cubic houses, Moulay Idris looked mysterious.

The approach and the sense of growing climax forcefully recalled Mycenae, set similarly in the Greek hills. But whereas Mycenae was a forbidding place of chill ghosts, Moulay Idris, though sacrosanct, was bustling and alive. On the slopes below the walls whole families were out working in the steep fields, the air filled with golden dust as mules and donkeys trod the threshing-floors.

After much grinding and winding and hard pulling on the steering-wheel, our bus entered the outer walls, and though Moulay Idris had nothing to compare in size or grandeur with the gates of Meknes, I had a greater feeling of enclosure, of separation from the outside world than in any other Moroccan city. Omar knew the town well and had been to many of its festivals. He led me down a narrow street beyond the inner gate, whose activities must have been almost unchanged since Moulay Idris was first built. Blacksmiths worked in their booths lining the street and kebabs were being grilled at the pavement cafés and fresh puffs sizzled in pans of oil. We came to a small square, surrounded by a low stone arcade, a miniature place of immense charm. Tailors' shops opened into the arcade, and the men sat cross-legged working at tiny stitches. Some of them wore fine, gold-rimmed spectacles and had a thin line of white beard round the chin and jaw, altogether like tailors in a fairy story.

Omar was anxious to show me the mosque where Moulay Idris himself was buried. Although I could not go inside, he wanted me to see the long forecourt and archway approach. Though again small in scale, the buildings' architectonic effect astonished me. Omar went into the mosque while I stayed on the unbelievers' side of a wooden boom barring the courtyard entrance. Beyond this bar criminals could seek sanctuary in the mosque's outer courts. Most of the mosaics and the actual mausoleum itself dated only from Moulay Ismail's time. The Sun King had been a great devotee of the national saint enshrined there in the eighth century. While Omar said his prayers I looked around the small shops under the arched approach. Candle-sellers occupied most of them. These devotional candles, some three feet long or more, had gaudy decoration over the brown wax.

Not only infidels were kept at bay from the Holy City, but infidel architecture, also. Since modern builders have largely lost the art of making towns, Moulay Idris could consider itself fortunate in not possessing modern additions. It was completely Moroccan, an example of what most *medinas* must have been before the chances of time and politics and economics surrounded them with twentieth-century avenues and squares and concrete buildings.

The tall houses of Moulay Idris crowded across the two spurs of mountain, leaving only the slimmest of alleys between, going like switchbacks over the steep ground, twisting and turning, surprising by views of higher or lower parts of the town. All the streets were paved with stones or cobbles and many consisted entirely of shallow steps. Vehicles could not get in. Only donkeys with panniers could squeeze through streets hardly wider than five feet between crumbling, high walls whose cracks sprouted fig saplings. The donkeys not only carried market produce and other goods but also took away household refuse which was dumped outside the front doors, not always with salubrious results.

As in all *medinas*, the houses and their courtyards turned a blind eye to the alleys. Few windows overlooked the streets, except for tiny, iron-grilled openings and a few shuttered windows higher up. This gave privacy and security. Street doors were solid, heavy affairs, studded by iron nails and fastened with wrought-iron hinges and handles. Some of the doors also had a tiny grille like the spy-hole on a monastery door.

Moulay Idris, compact, dense, was a perfect Moroccan town whose streets made a perfect chiaroscuro of dazzling light and deep shadow. It captivated me completely. I would have liked to spend some days there. But since I would not be allowed to stay overnight, I waited until Omar had come out from the mosque and put his shoes on, and then suggested that we went straight away across to Volubilis. He agreed on condition we had a drink first. Walking down from the mosque we met a weird-looking friend. Omar, a suave cosmopolitan in the smartest of clothes from Paris which put my own jeans and shirt to shame, caught the scruffy old Berber by the hand and kissed him on both cheeks and walked hand in hand with him to a café. Omar's friend was amused that I could speak neither Arabic nor Berber. The old man showed me the baskets he was going to take on his donkey into Meknes, a journey which would occupy the rest of the day. I had never seen such enormous baskets, eight feet long and three in diameter, like straw sewers. Our drink together was a celebration of the chance meeting and had, of course, to be mint tea and at least the traditional three glasses to ensure good luck. Omar talked about Moulay Idris in the festival season. At the annual pilgrimage the town became a large city of canvas tents, put up by thousands of both rich and poor who flocked to the Holy City in the mountain to pray and enjoy the celebrations. The horsemen I had stayed with by the Rio Martin outside Tetuan came every year to compete in the big *fantasia* at Moulay Idris.

Nobody ever took mint tea with milk, and always drank it scalding hot. I could not gulp it as the others did by sucking air and tea together, with the inevitable musical noises as part of the occasion. Although I wanted to find transport to Volubilis, the mint tea turned into a midday meal. The old trader had to eat, Omar explained, because he had just acquired a third wife. I was wrong in judging the Berber from his looks. He was not in his mid-seventies as his thin cavernous face suggested, but had only recently passed his fiftieth birthday. Stewed steak with black olives and capsicums came from a pot on the pavement fire. The wicker-work trader was not hungry so much as concerned to keep up his virility for his newest wife, a concern which occupied many Moroccan men and determined their personal habits.

Omar translated excellently, though conversation became inaudible at times, because the trader's jack-ass stood patiently beside us and brayed with unusual loudness at passing asses burdened as heavily as himself. In spite of these love calls I gleaned the fact that the trader belonged to the Aissaouas. This roused my curiosity, for I knew that this religious confraternity had its extreme rituals banned by the authorities. Years previously I had seen some of the sect's mosques in Tunisia and heard a lot about their frenzies and extraordinary dances and rites. Blood was the central object of the confraternity's performances. Participants worked themselves into wild trances and cut themselves with daggers and hatchets, banged their heads on the marble floors as they prayed, ate broken glass and live snakes and sat on beds of nails. When sheep were sacrificed they flung themselves savagely on the beast and while it was still alive sliced portions from it to devour.

Aissaouas existed throughout North Africa, and only now I learnt that Meknes was their spiritual home, because their patron saint, Sidi ben Aissa, had his mausoleum there. This tomb was the scene of pilgrimage when Aissaouas came from far and wide and paid homage to their leader's remains. Omar said that the bloody excesses were strictly forbidden and if performed nowadays only done in secret.

Omar explained that their sacred blood dance was powerful in driving djinns away. These evil spirits manifested themselves in any form, as a stone or a river, as a storm or an animal. Djinns were powerful in women and caused many female diseases.

The survival of the Berbers' ancient pagan beliefs and rituals was a tribute to Moulay Idris's tolerance and benevolence. The patron saint of Morocco left another memorial. In most Moslem countries preachers in the mosques carry a sword at their side as a symbol of conquest by force. But in Morocco, the sword is replaced by a stick in memory of Moulay Idris.

The cult of saints and their organized confraternities had a stronger influence with the Berbers than among other Moroccans, and this cult was again a survival of pagan beliefs which existed before the Arab conquest. Tombs of these holy men, *marabouts*, stood in the Moroccan landscape, their whitewashed walls and low *koubba* domes sometimes being the only building visible for miles in a plain's endless reaches.

These small oratories also existed in the towns. Square, squat and simple, they recalled small Orthodox churches in Greece, and marked places where saints prayed or died. Women frequented such tombs, for a saint's *baraka* was powerful in fighting the Evil Eye. Young country girls went to learn weaving or knitting by the shrines while their fathers invoked the good spirits to protect their crops from locusts or partridges, or asked the spirits to find a lost heifer. Every hamlet had its saints and nearly every street, and they revealed to the women which kind of extraordinary coiffeur they wished the babies to have as a protection against the Evil Eye.

The grounds around these tombs were favourite burial-places. People wanted to be near their own saint when the Archangel Izrafil (Raphael) sounded his trumpet on the Great Day of Judgement. The whitewashed shrines differed from mosques in that the faithful could ask favours instead of merely reciting the names of Allah. Votive gifts could be brought to the little oratories, anything from ostrich eggs to large clocks, which would please the saint as the believer prayed with his hands touching the tomb.

Although veneration of this kind was, strictly speaking, on the outer fringes of orthodox Islam, the domed shrines featured as immensely popular places of religion. Some of them developed into proper mosques, and others became part of the mosque wall like that at the Koutoubia mosque in Marrakesh which I had yet to see. And even the most devout and strict observer of orthodoxy went to Moulay Idris, visiting the mosque-tomb of the national saint.

At last the Aissaoua left us to go on his long, dusty trail to Meknes, while we looked for transport to Volubilis, since no bus went there. A tall Dutchman and his short wife joined us and agreed to share the expense of a car to the Roman city and afterwards all the way back to Meknes. Following a great deal of bargaining, in which a score of bystanders took part, a man agreed to drive us, finally reducing his price from 50 to 20 dirhams. The vehicle was a small van, though luckily a new one, and we had to sit in the back, bumping over a rough road and churning up a dense cloud of dust.

'We are like the army of Rommel,' the Dutchman said, lowering his head to look out of the back window.

'That was one army which never marched here,' Omar added, 'though plenty of others marched in the dust.'

Roman soldiers filed through the gates of Volubilis during hundreds of years. The wild Zerhoun hills and the plains beyond, eaten up in the midday haze, had been there then, no different from those we saw when the van crunched over the gravel and stopped by the entrance to the ruined city—Kasar Faraon—Pharaoh's Castle, as it was locally called for a long time.

Volubilis dominated a shallow valley where the Khoumane River flowed, almost lapping the city's ramparts. These walls were built of stone, flanked by projecting semicircular towers, and though much had fallen, much still stood, demonstrative of the city's command over the whole region in the days of its prosperity and authority vested from Rome. I thought of the dust, and Omar's thoughtful remark that armies had raised dust on that plain centuries ago. From the elevated position of Volubilis the long trains of men and animals and the dust trails hanging in the air must have been clearly visible many miles away. I looked over the broad horizons, stopped only on one side by the Zerhoun hills, and half expected to see such a procession. But no army had been there for hundreds of years, just as the city's streets and houses and courtyards and temples had heard no laughter or voices since its decline. Did the people then living in this beautiful landscape, with a blue sky and a pleasantly cooling breeze, ever think that one day only visitors full of curiosity would come to walk over the sunken paving-stones to gaze at the mosaics preserved among the ruins?

Cicadas were singing as we entered the ruins of the city, but Omar and I had to explore it alone, except for a guide, because the Dutchman was suddenly ill through overindulgence in fruit. We left him and his wife to sit in the shade of some orange trees. Fragments of sculpture had been placed in the garden. A marble Venus rose not from waves but from flowers, more a goddess of survival than of love. A path wound down between trees, passing some gravestones incised with beautiful Roman lettering. It was more elegant and elongated than the lettering on Trajan's Column in Rome, whose inscriptions have always been taken as the model of perfection. The inscriptions at Volubilis had a delicate form, like the flowing lines of English letter-carving in the early eighteenth century.

Silence possessed the landscape. Ancient stones soaked up the sun, absorbing its heat, reflecting its light, their colour lion-skinned, their texture rough with ages of exposure. The Roman city grew up on the site of a burial-mound for a Berber hero, but already by 201 B.C. the Carthaginians had established a trading-post there. Inscriptions unearthed from that period suggest that the inhabitants spoke Punic besides their own Berber dialects. When Carthage fell to the Romans, many refugees fled to this city under the Zerhoun hills. But Volubilis maintained favour in Roman eyes and the Emperor Claudius raised it to the official status of a city.

When Juba II was appointed to the throne in 25 B.C. he chose Volubilis as the seat of power and ruled from there over the whole province of Mauretania. His reign of nearly half a century gave Volubilis much of its royal splendour, for he loved pageantry. So also did his wife, Cleopatra Selene, daughter of Antony and Queen Cleopatra of Egypt. Juba was an accomplished man. He produced a large number of writings in Latin and Greek and enriched his towns with marvellous works of art and notable sculpture. A bronze portrait of himself shows a handsome face, full lips and broad nose, and sensitive, thoughtful expression, different from the hardness depicted by bronzes of the Caesars.

By Juba II's reign, though they kept their own dialects, the Berbers spoke Latin and the Carthaginian language had died out. Volubilis had also acquired colonies of Greeks, Syrians and Jews. The Roman garrison was made up of men from many nations and some of these soldiers were English. Evidence for this came from a tablet unearthed on the site which recorded that it was erected by Nestorea, centurion of a troop of soldiers raised in England and garrisoned at Volubilis in A.D. 190–2. I wondered how the soldiers from England reacted to the heat of the plains. But how did the Berbers from Morocco react to the mists and rain of northern England, for almost at the same time as the English troop came to Volubilis, Berbers were guarding Hadrian's Wall.

Volubilis performed a not-unimportant function as an outpost of Rome's Empire. Far flung, the city enjoyed Rome's continual attention, for it was economically significant if not militarily. This accent on the arts of peace rather than those of war, and the mixture of racial temperaments, may have been partly responsible for the development in Volubilis of the visual arts. They reached a degree of skill unusual in a remote, colonial city. The tombstone lettering, taken from the city's Western Cemetery, was a glimpse of this skill.

Yet, as everywhere in the ancient world, plot and intrigue and sudden death were the coinage of political life. Ptolemy, Juba II's son, succeeded his father, but only for a short period. The Roman Emperor had him murdered. Pliny wrote in his *Natural History*, '. . . under Claudius, the Roman army fought in Mauretania for the first time. King Ptolemy had been put to death by Claudius Caesar and the freedman Aedemon sought to avenge him. It is known that Claudius came as far as the Atlas while pursuing the Barbarians. Consuls and generals appointed from the Senate, as well as the Roman knights who would later govern this land vied for the glory of penetrating the Atlas.'

Most of what could still be seen in Volubilis belonged to the second and third centuries A.D. Christianity had supplanted classical pagan beliefs and churches and shrines were built on saints' bones. Fifteen thousand people lived within the city walls. But the city, without knowing it, had seen its greatest days. In A.D. 285 the Romans walked out. An administrative reshuffle made Volubilis less important in Rome's scheme of things. The province of which it was capital for a time had always been a minor one. The withdrawal from this particular outpost of empire must have been regarded as expedient. Berber raids on the city had been continuous, and presumably the expense to Rome in terms of troops and keeping communications open was no longer justifiable.

For years after this débâcle Volubilis ran under the momentum of Roman life. Well into the seventh century Latin was still being spoken and the Cross still stood on the city's altars. Arabs first besieged the city in 684, but it was not until the Prophet's great-grandson arrived in 788 that the Crescent superseded the Cross. Moulay Idris quartered himself in Volubilis before moving three miles away to the mountain spurs, where he established his own city which later bore his name and contained his tomb.

From then on, though it was by no means completely abandoned, Volubilis ceased to figure as a principal city. Moulay Idris's son founded a city as his father had done, and this was Fez. While Fez waxed, Volubilis waned. Nevertheless even in the sixteenth century Volubilis was still in good working order. A record exists which told how lions came down from the hills to devour bones in the streets. But the splendid marble bones of the Roman city were destined themselves to be devoured by another sort of lion—the architectural megalomania of the insatiable Moulay Ismail. In the seventeenth century he plundered Volubilis for its ready-made architectural treasures. The chiselled and polished stones and fountains and columns were ideal for the Sultan's outburst of palace-building in Meknes, and he had many Roman features dismantled and transported across the plains to his own building sites. The marble monoliths of Meknes's Bab Mansour gateway were one example. They looked strangely different from the columns which still stood upright in the Roman city above the River Khoumane.

John Windus and the British party visited the ruins at Volubilis in 1721 and his book included some engravings of the Roman remains. After this the old capital of Mauretania was forgotten until 1874, when the French Minister Tissot identified it as Pharaoh's Castle. A proper examination of the ruins, and the rediscovery of their importance in the antique world, did not take place until the French Protectorate began in 1912. The excavations and studies then made have since been faithfully and skilfully continued under the Moroccan Government.

A large area was still under excavation, as I saw when Omar walked with me down the intriguing path which traversed a small ravine, crossed a bridge and brought us up to the main part of the city. Besides gravestones, many other incised tablets had been found, some of them recording agreements made between the Romans and the surrounding Berber tribes. There were also many bases upon which statues once stood, although the sculpture itself had largely disappeared or had been taken away to museums throughout Morocco. Rabat had a large collection of art objects taken from Volubilis, including numerous statuettes as well as bigger works which belonged to the inscribed plinths still standing among the ruins. A bust of Cato the Elder was amongst the Rabat collection, a bronze considered by experts to be one of the finest examples in the whole Roman world. This famous work was only discovered in 1948. The bust is unique, for no other of Cato is known. Another bust of a young man was found at the same time and these two are the only life-size cast bronzes in existence.

The ruins of Volubilis would have an added attraction if the sculpture could be brought back to stand in the strong sun of the mountains and plains, where green-pillared cypresses nod forty feet high against the blue sky. Volubilis may always have had gardens, because water was channelled in from the hills and river. Certainly olive trees grew plentifully there on the slopes round about, as they do still today. Olive oil was the basis of prosperity in Volubilis. It was exported to Rome, as were wheat and the valuable thuya wood and a local purple dye which supplanted the famous dye from Tyre. Lions and other wild animals for the arena also went from Volubilis along with the olive oil.

Buildings connected with the pressing of olives and the collection of the oil could still be seen among the ruins. Such an olive press was the first thing the guide took Omar and myself to see, though Omar had been there many times. The grindstone part of the press was still there and I saw grooves down which the oil had run. This press stood on the farther side of the ravine, on the city's highest part, from which the whole surrounding landscape could be seen. Here a broad paved way had long ago been laid across the elevated land, the grooves of chariot wheels had marked the stones which baked in the midday heat. I thought of shade the buildings must have provided and of the cool Roman houses, each with an atrium and perhaps a pool and fountain.

We went to the House of Orpheus. The stumps of fallen walls, unearthed by careful excavators, gave an idea of how the house had been. The reception room's mosaics have escaped destruction. Sufficient remained for Orpheus to be seen surrounded by animals while he played his lyre. We passed on to the Baths of Galius, where the nine-inch-deep baths ran one into another and were patterned with fish. The underground heating-room with fire chambers and duct for hot air were still intact, giving an excellent picture of some dark-skinned stoker below and Roman gentleman above stepping into the steaming fish bath.

The Roman habit of taking steam baths later led to the so-called Turkish bath and to the *hammam* bath-houses which are still popular in Morocco. One of the Volubilis baths had a mosaic floor on which dolphins sported. The city was many miles from the sea and this marine motif might perhaps have been done by a craftsman working to Roman patterns. Cretans lived in the city and I wondered whether the dolphins had been inspired by the remarkably similar ones of the Knossos frescoes, though Knossos became a devastated ruin long before the building of Volubilis.

Like Ahmed and Hassan, the two English-speaking schoolboys in Meknes, Omar had cycled out to Volubilis during school holidays, and no longer found any interest in the kneading-troughs of the bakery, or in the altars of the Temple of Minerva. He wandered on ahead while the old guide, himself rather like a lizard, darted nimbly over fallen stones and broken steps, explaining every building or object in French, Spanish and German, hoping, I supposed, that I would understand at least some of his words.

'*Le Bain*,' he said. '*Baño. Bad.*' And then, pointing at the mosaic fish, '*Poissons. Pez. Fisch.*'

The city's Forum stumped him, for a forum is a forum whichever way you look at it. So he just said 'Forum' and sat on a broken column. His function was not only to be a trilingual, or even a quadrilingual guide, for he also had some English words, but to be a watchdog, too. Souvenir-hunters had carried away important fragments in the past and the guides were there to ensure that no fragment of sculpture or carving ended up in a New York penthouse or a London antique shop.

Moulay Idris I had preached the new religion of Islam in the Forum and made his first converts there. Only the plinths remained from all the statues which once stood around it. But the broad flight of steps leading up to the aisled Basilica, though partly broken, still gave access to the raised platform under whose vaults justice was once dispensed. The Basilica had largely collapsed and its columns were either broken or removed altogether. The surviving walls, the arches, the blocks of stone piled up to form massive cornices, and a row of columns with fragments of entablature still resting on the shafts, were powerful in conjuring the original form of the building. Those stones were aggressive and hard and suggestive of military engineering. Like most Roman buildings they lacked charm and gracefulness.

Two pairs of storks had balanced huge untidy nests on the top of some standing columns. Others were locusting elsewhere among the ruins. Elaborate patterns of migration and definite migration routes worked out by international ornithologists for the behaviour of the white stork, come adrift in Morocco. The white stork did not do what he was supposed to. He was not only partially sedentary as in eastern Asia, but bred up to 9,000 feet above the sea in the High Atlas. Omar stood looking enviously at the big birds which stood on one too-thin red leg. Storks were remarkably tame, but though used to a policy of co-existence with Arabs, who would not harm the sacred birds, they kept a watchful, perky eye open nevertheless, for Berbers were not averse to stork's meat. Omar caught me looking at his expression. He grinned, for stork's eggs are most powerful in procuring children. He was also amused to know that storks and babies had a close connexion in England, though it could hardly be through eating their eggs, for the last hatch laid in Britain was at Edinburgh in 1416.

We wandered about the Basilica, jumping from stone to stone where weeds had sprung up and hare droppings had fallen into crevices. We stood silently then, looking through columns and arches at the golden landscape spread before us and at the Zerhoun hills beyond and the higher mountains still farther, the Atlas, which Roman consuls and generals 'vied for the glory of penetrating'. Many Romans stood where Omar and I did, and discussed possible expeditions into the Atlas. Terror mixed with admiration in Pliny's description of those mountains which had more than a score of peaks over 13,000 feet. Of one he wrote: 'Such is the most fabulous mountain in all Africa. Surrounded by sand, it lifts up towards heaven, rugged and barren on the side facing the Ocean, but covered with thick, shady forests and gushing streams on the side which faces Africa.'

The formidable barrier of mountains dividing Morocco was still no less an obstacle than it had been during the Roman occupation, as I was later to see. Though roads now penetrate the Atlas, the terror of knife-edged precipices could not be less in our own day than they were in Pliny's. Unfortunately, I did not get up to Timesguida Ouanoukrim in time to see an annual ceremony which the people of Agoundis perform on its 13,412-foot summit. A bull was sacrificed up there once a year. But since this is a canicular event, and the days when the dogstar rose and set with the sun in 1964 were just over when Omar told me about this ancient rite, I missed it. I was intrigued to know how a bull was taken up to such a rugged height.

The mountain-top ceremony of today sounded like a ritual performance of 2,000 years ago on the altar of Jupiter at Volubilis. As we left the ruined capital Omar showed me the base of this altar sited next to the Basilica. Then we came to the House of Desulterius. This was once an imposing villa, inhabited now only by lizards scurrying over the mosaics of fishermen and jesters. Volubilis had an Arch of Triumph and this was its most complete building, the weathering of some seventeen centuries being almost its only damage. The Emperor Caracalla built it in A.D. 217, a weighty affair which must have been too much even for the stone-hungry Moulay Ismail to cart away for his ambitious schemes in Meknes. The arch, with a central opening and two flanking pedimented niches for fountains between free-standing Corinthian columns, stood where the main way through the city turned at right-angles, giving a vista up the hillside in one direction, and a vast panorama of the plains in the other. From the arch the city itself looked extensive and the ruined walls, honey-coloured in the blazing sun, evoked the scene as it must have been after the Romans abandoned the place, so depriving the arch of its imperial significance.

Our guide watched my reactions to the bygone architectural glories with a kind of proprietary pride. He made sure that Omar explained how children's memorials were the small standing columns we passed. And he took me through Caracalla's arch to see the House of the Dog, so called because of the magnificent bronze sculpture of a dog discovered in it, removed for safety to the local museum.

Volubilis was not the only Roman town in Morocco. The others were worth visiting also, but none of them had the importance of Volubilis. Also, their mosaics had mostly been taken up and removed to museums, such as Tetuan's intriguing Archaeological Museum. In the garden forecourt there, bowered amongst bougainvillaea, Roman mosaics from Lixus, Tamuda and the Matmoras had been set up, looking curiously like modern abstract art. In spite of such an attractive setting, however, such works lost some vital quality by being separated from their proper surroundings. And this was the reason why Volubilis seemed so rich. A surprising number of its houses and courtyards still had their mosaic floors *in situ*, and were worth going to see for themselves.

It took me more than one visit to see the Spring of Diana, the wild animals depicted in the House of Beasts, the Four Seasons, the many mosaics in the House of the Labours of Hercules, the Ionic colonnade of the royal palace of Gordius, besides practical everyday things of stone like the tanks used for keeping fish, or the cornmills and olive presses, the broken altars and graveyards whose memorial stones recorded not only the names of the dead but the high degree of skill in the arts and crafts attained in one of Morocco's earliest capital cities.

I cut my first visit short when Omar reminded me of the waiting Dutchman and his wife, and also the man going with the van to Meknes who must have been counting the minutes. But I suspected the sight of Dionysus surrounded by sea-nymphs, and a glimpse of Bacchus with Ariadne, had roused in Omar a desire to hurry home to Meknes, where Chedlya was waiting in the house of the hi-fi.

Pliny was right, and still is—*Ex Africa semper aliquid novi.*

6

Ebb and Flow

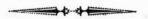

Out of Africa always something new or at least if not new always surprising. I had grown to expect surprises in Morocco. Bowling towards Rabat along flat roads, straight for ten miles or more at a stretch, I refused to be surprised any more at the fertility of the plains. The notion of the country as a barren land of rocky desert and mountains no longer fitted the real situation. Rich prairies spread like cloth-of-gold to every horizon seen from the bus windows. Bales of straw had been built into stacks like aircraft hangars and they dwarfed the tiny straw huts of the farmsteadings.

Undoubtedly these thatched houses belonged to Africa, primitive dwellings often with no opening other than a low door which admitted both the occupants and the light of day. And yet the orchards and vineyards around the straw *douar* villages yielded clementines and wines for the tables of Paris, olives and potatoes for Algeria and England.

The Rabat bus sped for an hour through this uninterrupted land of plenty, whose wheat and barley went to countries the world over. But we were yet to pass through the green twilight of the vast Mamora forest whose oaks covered a million acres and produced cork for export to Russia. But the children's thick fur coats being sold by pedlars at the bus station in Meknes had not, I felt sure, come from Russia by way of trade exchange. Fur coats indeed, in a temperature over 100° F.! *Ex* Morocco *semper* surprises.

We stopped at Khemisset.

'Chemistry set!' exclaimed an American matron on the bus.

121

'What a curious name!' Her comment was a good phonetic rendering of the soft, guttural Arabic.

Khemisset was a delightful place crowded with trees and flowering shrubs, and serving as the market town for the golden prairies. The overloud bus radio was silenced at last by the pealing bells of the water-sellers whose tall conical straw hats looked like replicas of their straw hut homes. Three of these men, wizened and weird, wandered around together and would have made ideal Macbeth witches on a London stage.

Beyond Khemisset we passed several jasmine farms and large tracts given over to mint-growing. Then we hurried through lentisk woods where the North African francolin was preserved against the licensed hunter, though the local wildfowler was prone to poach this fine game-bird. And then came the mighty Mamora whose oaks were more orderly than the unruly lentisks which gave juice used for tinting earthenware. Every fallen twig and branch of the great forest was sawn and neatly piled by an army of woodmen. Wild pear trees had also been cut up and taken to the charcoal yards. The oaks received V.I.P. treatment on account of their cork, which made a considerable and profitable industry. Mile after mile of the oaks had recently been stripped of their bark, leaving the trunks with a brown texture, like stags' antlers in velvet. Wild boar roamed these woods, though most visitors to the glades were picnickers rather than hunters. A seven-mile ride out from Rabat brought the forest within easy reach of the capital, and Sunday was a favourite day for the crowds. And after pleasant hours spent running about in the speckled shade children went back to the city, their arms laden with wild flowers as a trophy of the day's outing. This was perhaps the best area in Morocco for those with botanical leanings. During one picnic there I found a lovely species of sparrow-wort. I could not identify it beyond the fact that local people called the flower *passerine de Mamora*.

The bus hustled on to Rabat and suddenly, it seemed, was slowing down and joining the traffic crossing the bridge over the Bou Regreg. This river emptied into the sea near by and Rabat stood on one of its banks. The enormous Hassan Tower, built on a small hill above the river marshes in the late twelfth century, dominated the approaches with its tall silhouette, a familiar national symbol on bank-notes and stamps, and a favourite on every picture-postcard stand.

As soon as we had left the Mamora forest the air blowing through the bus windows had a different overtone of scents. The breezes were fresher than the heat-heavy air of the plains and had the unmistakable salty, ozone tang of the sea. I had not seen the sea since Tangier and my first act in Rabat was going to be a plunge into the Atlantic. First, that is, after finding an hotel. Coming out of the C.T.M. (Compagnie Auxiliaire de Transports au Maroc), I booked into the nearest and most unpretentious hotel I could find. Most advertising signs were in Arabic and French and by an enamel plate marked 'Pile Wonder' was the Hotel Majestic, which had a room with a view and a balcony.

The view was enchanting, overlooking a corner of Rabat's walled *medina*. A broad modern avenue interposed between the Hotel Majestic and the *medina*, but I could see over the tops of the orange trees to a long wall, pierced here and there by gates and tiny doorways. Above its battlements the whitewashed walls of the *medina*'s closely crowding houses sparkled in the sun. Minarets poked above like fingers. Cats prowled on the walls, tormented by swifts and swallows who sliced the air with their flight. Beneath the wall, on dusty, unmade-up ground by the metalled road, families spread themselves. Women hunched up comfortably against the uneven surface of the wall and watched their children or fussed busily with the bedrolls and bundles and pots and pans which would accompany them on the bus or donkey they waited for. And when the children or household belongings palled the women obligingly searched for errant bugs in each other's hair. Or they slept.

Sleep at midday did not seem to be part of Rabat's general system of life, as it did, for instance, in Meknes. The *medina* hustled and bustled when I went through the wall and up a street surprisingly straight for a *medina*. It gave at its extremity on to a small gate in a wall. And beyond lay a stunning, unexpected spectacle of the Atlantic, immense and shining.

This vantage-point was high above the beaches where rollers crumbled into lacy trains of foam. The ground sloped gradually down a long way to the sea and a wall enclosed this gentle hillside which was a cemetery. Respect for the dead is part of Islamic faith, but this did not seem to mean, as it does in Christian cemeteries, that while within eye-shot of a grave the living have to pretend they, too, are not living. Visitors to the graves of loved ones were not at all upset by people walking among the graves taking the short-cut path to the beach. Boys and girls on holiday from school laughed and talked and swung their swimming-costumes as they threaded a way between the lichened headstones which, except for the absence of crosses and swan-limbed angels, looked like the tombstones in an English country churchyard. Youths played football in bare feet on a lower part of the slope, as yet unoccupied by graves.

The *medina* wall ran along the top of the slope, finally rising to command the approaches of the Bou Regreg River. There were rocks below this fortified corner of the old city, and a sandy beach, sheltered by a massive breakwater curving into the sea. I returned to Rabat three weeks later and saw the breakwater's huge chunks of rock being battered by thundering waves and a lunging swell that sucked hideously in and out of the boulders. On that day coastguards patrolled the beach and breakwater, blowing warning whistles at swimmers who went too far out into the running swell of the river's mouth.

From the end of the breakwater the river could be seen winding inland, passing beneath the fortified wall of Rabat. It was very wide here. On the opposite bank stood the old port of Sale. Rabat's beach and Sale's appeared as a golden crescent, although the river bisected this scimitar of sand. As often by the sea, the light was remarkable, and over the Hassan Tower and the town the sky was edged by a rose hue and over the sea by a tangerine tone. Such colouring was an odd but somehow suitable reminder that this Atlantic was an African ocean.

My first swim at Rabat proved to be one of many, and, like all the others, sharpened my appetite. Drinks and snacks obtainable on the beach were not enough for me, despite complaints from students, who had also been bathing from the not-so-fashionable part of the beach, that I had only spent an hour in the sea. They let me go, however, when I promised to return the following day. They were desperate for practice in speaking English. I was desperate for cheese, and walked up through the cemetery and down through the *medina* and across the orange-tree-lined avenue to the cheese counter of the Galeries Lafayette de Paris department store. Perhaps the French originated the Moroccan genius for cheese. Besides the local cream cheeses of mountain villages, which tasted like crowdie from the Scottish Highlands, there were shops which specialized in all the top-grade European brands. Two Swedish seamen with heavy kitbags on their shoulders were being served by a girl who cut up a large wheel of Gruyère.

Armed with a long French roll and a slab of Gruyère, I walked down the Boulevard Joffre to the public gardens and sat to eat near some dragon trees. Moroccan parks were similar in most towns and cities. Formal in a French way, they always formed part of the modern town sprung up during protectorate days, when gardens and wide, tree-planted avenues were built. But unlike the old college courtyard gardens of Fez, the public gardens did not luxuriate. They looked dusty and tired. Perhaps the lack of trim lawns was responsible, since Kikuyu grass is difficult to cut with a mower, and has the appearance of being experimental planting in a horticultural station.

The Rabat public gardens were well cared for and shady, with palms and bamboo and orange trees. Rows of dragon trees were a speciality, but of no appeal for me. There is something repellent about the dragon tree's smooth trunk and multiplicity of branches terminated by stiff tufts of spiky leaves, spread like a horny umbrella to keep sunlight out. The gardens lay on the way to the Hassan Tower and when my Gruyère was finished and the tougher bits of bread-crust thrown to the perky sparrows, I continued along the Boulevard Joffre, this time walking close to the *medina*'s wall and its square bastions until the buildings stopped and the road swung in the open towards the river, passing the small hill and its astonishing tower.

Yacoub El Mansour built *Ribat El Fath*—the Camp of Victory. It was a memorial to the victory at Alarcos in which his forces routed the Castilians. The *medina*'s ramparts were constructed during his reign, as were the walls of Fez. Like Moulay Ismail at Meknes, Yacoub El Mansour was an ambitious builder. The palaces at Meknes crumbled away with neglect, but El Mansour's greatest work, though constructed five centuries before Moulay Ismail's would-be Versailles, survived. The renowned Giralda in Seville, the beautiful

Koutoubia in Marrakesh and the Hassan Tower at Rabat were all done under his inspiration.

When El Mansour died in 1199 the Hassan remained unfinished. He intended this to be the largest and most beautiful mosque in the whole Islamic world and though the tower stands now almost in the same condition as when the great patron of the arts last saw it nearly eight hundred years ago, the extensive aisled halls of the mosque to-day are no more than row upon row of columns, some shattered, some headless, and none with the arches and vaulting which would have made the mosque a masterpiece of architecture.

The rows of columns stood upon an enormous platform of embanked earth. A thick retaining wall of stone, probably the only one to be completed, ran along the side facing the river. The tower rose from this wall, a majestic structure whose rust-coloured stones were carved on the surface into blind arcading. The tracery of the arcading followed a counterpoint of geometric shapes, one interlaced with the other, the ribs crossing and recrossing in a mesh of arch forms. The richly modulated patterns so created were confined within square-headed panels in a curious anticipation of similar devices which English masons were to employ three centuries later for surface decoration of Perpendicular architecture. It is odd that although twelfth-century Andalusian builders in Spain developed the art and technology of arch and vault construction to a high degree of competence and inventiveness, Spain never produced the wonders of such construction which later appeared in Gothic France and England.

But Gothic architecture was the art of masonry, whereas the Moorish builders used brick and stone together, as I could see from the inside of the Hassan Tower. There were really two square towers, one inside the other, the space between them being occupied by a ramp which wound up from ground to roof. The ramp was supported on a brick barrel vault, springing from stone voussoirs and spanning between the inner and the outer towers. This was an ingenious design of immense strength, displaying a knowledge of engineering and building skill equal to that of the Romanesque builder in contemporary Europe.

One hundred and fourty-four feet above platform-level the

ramp emerged to a spectacular panorama, showing Rabat and Sale and the wide river between, and the expanses of the Atlantic, and inland the hills and plains. On the way up the landscape had been fragmentary, glimpsed, first on this side, then on that, through narrow windows pierced in the eight-foot walls of the outer tower. But from the flat roof the fragments fused together in a magnificent view, showing the whole lie of the land at a glance.

The Hassan was not only popular with foreign visitors but with the Moroccans also. No entrance fee was charged and families could come and go at will to enjoy the thrill of a great height and a sheer drop. On the roof German tourists and Italian sailors worked busily at their cameras, capturing the sugar-icing *medina* of Rabat clustering above the river-mouth, taking a bird's-eye view of the sailing craft dotted along the river, focusing their lenses on the wasteland of ruined columns among the mallow undergrowth immediately at the tower's foot.

But most of the people on top were from Rabat, or Moroccan people on holiday by the sea. Women in *djellabas* or *haiks* sat right on the edge, dangling their legs over the sheer drop. Height did not worry them and quite calmly, though not daring to lift their veils, they bared their brown breasts and gave suck to their babies. One mother nursed a boy who was by no means the youngest of her brood. Other children walked or stood on the edge and old men put their turbans down as pillows and slept on them, mouths open wide, oblivious of the drop only inches away.

Minarets always stand to one side of Andalusian mosque court-yards and the Hassan was no exception. Across the other side of the stone-column forest a new mausoleum was being built in honour of the late King Mohammed V. Tons of white marble slabs were ready for fixing to the mosque's walls and stacks of green glazed pantiles were waiting for the structural roofs to be ready. The new building, though grandiose, looked puny compared with the noble Hassan Tower. But perhaps such comparison was unfair, because Morocco had few other structures either ancient or modern which could rival El Mansour's formidable minaret.

The French decided to build a new town at Rabat. After the 1912 Treaty, Marshal Lyautey settled there. He was a wise and cultured man. 'I shall not touch the Arab town,' he wrote; 'I will clean and enrich, supply water and electricity, but that is all . . . I will also respect the city of the Sultan, enclosed between its high fawn walls, with its mosques, its palaces, its harem, and its royal gardens. But opposite, in the *bled*, I will build another town. There a cathedral, very high and very white; then broad boulevards, planted with palm trees and flowering shrubs. The houses, the palaces of the Residence, the barracks, high school, law courts, and hospitals are to be spacious in the style of the country. Let there be parks, Gardens of Babylon, flowers, running water, fields of orange trees.'

By the Marshal's decrees Moroccan traditions flourished under the French occupation. The medieval architecture of the Almohades and Merinides was not destroyed and neither were the *medinas* sold out to unscrupulous real-estate sharks. Marshal Lyautey built a new town, not only at Rabat, but at Fez and Meknes and every major city of the kingdom. His notion of 'in the style of the country' was difficult to interpret, though most buildings of this period had characteristics similar to the indigenous, cubical, white-walled buildings of the *medinas*. A decade later, after the 1914 War, flat-roofed, cubical, white boxes became the rage of the architectural *avant-garde* and notable Frenchmen such as Le Corbusier in part created this modern movement. But it is extremely questionable whether, as some people maintain, the style was directly influenced by Moroccan architecture. Similarity, however, there certainly was. And by the 1930s such white boxes had been built in England.

Morocco's new towns certainly got their 'broad boulevards planted with palm trees', and the Marshal's command 'let there be parks' was taken up by every municipal council, though the gardens hardly became 'Gardens of Babylon'.

Long wide avenues with lines of trees, and intersections marked by fountains or sculpture had a long history in France. The monumental town plan was well tried and could hardly have been more different from the close-packed, teeming yet haphazard alleys of the *medinas*. To go from Rabat's *medina* and pass through the gates into the French town was to see demonstrated the significance in the Western world of the Renaissance with its accent on axis and perspective.

Sculpture by erosion—southern desert rocks

Sea-scape by invasion—indented coastline

Goats wanted,
dead or alive . . .
for yielding
milk or carrying
water

The Avenue Mohammed V went straight as a die at right-angles from the *medina* wall, stopping only to take a slight bend and continuing (disguised as the Avenue Yacoub El Mansour) by the royal palace up to a hill crest where, through a gateway in yet another stretch of ancient wall, lay a view of the Bou Regreg River below, winding lazily through its plain, past the ancient hillside fortress settlement of Chella.

Such avenues, constructed in modern times, resemble each other everywhere in the world where the Romance languages are spoken. Parts of Rio de Janeiro and Lisbon and Caracas and dozens of other towns on both the east and west Atlantic shores as well as around the Mediterranean's resembled Rabat's Avenue Mohammed V. Yet the crowded pavement cafés and busy shopping arcades had an agreeable animation of another kind entirely from the *medina*'s.

Though none of the buildings was individually a masterpiece, at least none were so hideous as to destroy the Avenue's good urban manners. Even the Courts of Appeal did not disturb the Avenue's architectural respectability, despite being deliberately self-important with some tricks of the Italian Fascist style. The Courts' portico was set back from the other buildings, so making a grassed forecourt graced with some expert topiary. A negro was scything the Kikuyu grass, shaving it as closely as the barbers shaved old men's heads. He was wearing 'Blue Dollar' jeans, yellow tee-shirt and white turban. Another similarly attired gardener was raking the cut grass, while yet another watered the lawn. A woman in a well-tailored *djellaba* walked through the Courts' iron gates, picked up the watering hose, drank from it, and walked out again.

The Avenue's shops offered a selection of fine wares to be found in most capital cities. Smart Parisian fashions filled the clothes shops, men's as well as women's, and there were tailors' shops which might have come straight out of London with their military dress uniforms and tally-ho hunting gear. There were boutiques selling jewellery made almost inconsequentially of diamond clusters and every precious stone imaginable—set, of course, in gold. There were some splendid florists with dewy displays of roses and carnations and birds-of-paradise and all the kinds of floral set-pieces such shops sell from Buenos Aires to New York the long way round. Bookshops kept company with these well-to-do affairs, books in Arabic, in French and almost every other European language and finely produced 'coffee-table' volumes of Old Masters and Impressionists and Japanese woodcuts and Sumerian sculpture and all the art indulged by the sophisticated.

There were photographers' studios with stiff-looking wedding groups and starry-eyed brides and smiling students clasping *baccalaureat* diplomas. The last word in chromium-plated fans whirled in a score of airline offices and pastry shops which had nothing to learn in miniature confectionery from Zurich. It was a sort of Bond Street where you could spend £100 in half an hour without wondering where it had gone.

I turned from the Avenue past some even more esoterically expensive shops and came upon Rabat's smart area where consular coats-of-arms and embassy flagpoles peeped above creepers spilling over white walls of villas in spurious styles of architecture. Marshal Lyautey had also commanded 'oceans of flowers, bougainvillaeas purple and violet, climbing up the azure-leaded houses, flame-coloured hibiscus, rose bushes and geraniums'. The private houses and clinics had all obeyed orders, and indeed exceeded them with a lavish provision of canna lilies, love-lies-bleeding, salvia, oleander and plumbago and Madagascar creeper.

In the midst of it all the grandest fulfilment of the Marshal's dream was the cathedral, dedicated to St. Peter. It was, as the Marshal had wished, 'very high and very white'. Unfortunately the cathedral looked as if, in the process of trying to make it 'in the style of the country' the designer could not make up his mind which country—France or Morocco. I had never seen anything similar and could only classify the style as Gothic-Arabesque. It was a Polonius kind of building, tragical-comical-historical-pastoral, scene individable or poem unlimited.

However, it would be too much to say that in trying to please everybody the architect had pleased nobody. Inside, the cruciform cathedral was much less pretentious than the outside would lead the visitor to believe. A high lantern over the crossing lit the altar, which, on the raised sanctuary faced the congregation in compliance with recent revision in the liturgy. High clerestory windows overlooked the tall, simple nave. So far so Gothic, or almost. But the lantern windows were filled with an extraordinary tracery, like crochet work. Presumably in deference to Moroccan decoration, it was modelled upon the geometric tracery of the kind seen, for example, in the arcaded panels of the Hassan Tower.

As if in compensation for this bizarre extravagance the cathedral's art works were comparatively good, the stained glass particularly. One window alone made a visit to the cathedral worth while. This was the light in the baptistry niche, an abstract design in thick glass with cool ambers and pinkish mauves and charcoal greyish-blues and small blobs of red which glowed like rubies. The sanctuary furnishings were also well designed and the altar itself was a plain slab with six short and fat candles and a simple crucifix. Roman Catholic churches frequently ruin even the best of buildings with hideous, sugary statuary and appalling stations of the Cross. At Rabat these were all good, the stations being a clever kind of mosaic of small coloured pieces of tile.

A large French colony still lives at Rabat, and no doubt the people derive spiritual refreshment from their airy cathedral. The Marshal's grand ideas and good intentions did not, alas, result in a masterpiece, which was an unfortunate thing by a nation noted for its cathedrals. But the two gawky towers at the west end and the odd lantern, when seen from outside, at least had whiteness as a virtue. In Rabat's sunshine and under that blue, lambent sky almost any architectural sins could be absolved.

Jacaranda canopied the avenue, and the trees still had a few late plumes of mauve blossom left over from their springtime glory. If the public gardens had not exactly come up to the Marshal's Babylonian expectations, the new town's avenues justified the French planning. Though it was a pity that the most important of the avenues *had* to be planted with imperial palms, many were planted with planes instead. Their shape and their shade, both dappled yet twinkling with light, looked far more graceful than the dry, dead-looking palms in formal military rows.

Marshal Lyautey had the right idea about railways and stations. 'So that nothing shall be dirtied', the trains had to come into the city centre through tunnels. And this out-of-sight out-of-mind policy has paid handsome dividends, for today the railway station at Rabat sits in the Avenue Mohammed V as respectably and as clean as the Courts of Appeal. It is only in England that grime, inefficiency and discomfort are considered essential to the romantic myth conjured by the word 'railways'. The faintly Art Nouveau station in Rabat was cleaner and more pleasant than any station in Britain. The marble hall, giving access down to platforms discreetly built at the bottom of high embankments would put the Dickensian slums of British Railways to shame. I went back to Tangier by train from Rabat some weeks later, and rode in an air-conditioned coach as if in an aeroplane, quietly, comfortably and with a restaurant service as good as an airline's.

From the station I crossed the Avenue with a swarm of other people, directed by a white-helmeted policeman standing on a smart modern traffic pulpit complete with sunshade. I walked past the 'high fawn walls' of the 'Sultan's city' where soldiers from the Imperial Black Guard were coming off duty in their white, voluminously pleated pantaloons. This part of Rabat had changed little since the Marshal's day, except that the Frenchman's own mausoleum lies in state across the 'imperial boulevard' and that nowadays the royal palace has no harem.

And so to the hillcrest overlooking the inland course of the Bou Regreg River, through the low gateway of the palace-city walls within city walls, and across a plateau of sunburnt wasteland to the slopes above the river, and over the dry scrub to yet another walled city—Chella, city of the dead.

Although this huge sloping enclosure, overrun with wild gardens, bristling with ruined masonry, was a royal necropolis, it became one of Morocco's most enchanted places for me. Long ago the Romans settled at Sala Colonia, today's Chella, choosing this place which had once been a Carthaginian trading-post. The Roman settlement, with its forum and other public buildings, was, as yet, only partially unearthed. Chella's principal attraction for Moroccans lay in its historical and religious association. Until quite recently, the sultans would cross from the royal palace before going on a journey and sacrifice a bull, as the people of Agoundis still do on the summit of Timesguida Ouanoukrim on dogstar days.

Association with religious matters made Chella a forbidden place to Jews and Christians until the beginning of the twentieth century. The walled town beyond the imposing palaces and boulevards of Rabat expressed everything of the past for the Moroccan, and the past swallows even the foreigner entering the Moorish gate with its heavy wooden doors and high vaulted interior. Something inexplicably magical haunted the place. Legend became credible, even the legend that King Solomon's ring was buried in the chunks of the gateway masonry, the finder being rewarded with the gift of speaking the language of the animals and with powers to control even the most powerful djinns.

Inside the gate, confined only by the walls, the gardens full of flowering shrubs and trees began. Immediately to the left a water garden had been converted into the most charming open-air restaurant in Morocco. The old walls here were invisible under masses of Florida liana whose blossoms fell in a gentle pink shower on to the cobbled courtyard and into the pools. Broad banana leaves heaved gently in the breeze like punkahs. Arched openings gave glimpses of the gardens beyond. Though some areas were subjected to the discipline of gardener's tools, the plants for the most part ran uncultured where they pleased, and where trees had fallen morning glory and nasturtiums overtook them, making a trellis of the decaying trunks and branches. And from somewhere in the jungle came the tinkling noise of water and the trilling of hidden larks. Canna lilies started up in lavish clumps, the brilliant red flowers overlaid with a sheen of gold-dust varnish. Bees bumbled heavily through the air, not knowing which exotic way to turn, drugged by the cloying scent of oleander.

A path descended the slope between cactus hedges and at the lower levels, mysterious as Mayan ruins or the jungle temples of Angkor, so entangled with growth that it was difficult to see where architecture began and trees stopped, were the remains of a delicately beautiful mosque and mellowed minaret. A tiled courtyard with a tiled pool and two circular, shell-like basins cool with the plash of water, had been cleared. Steps and half-fallen walls of former chambers ran up and down, appearing and disappearing behind dense greenery, hinting in the beauty of decay and destruction at the beauty their marble columns and mosaics and fine-wrought filigree plaster had when a king was brought here to be buried.

The Merinide king, Abou El Hassan, better known as the Black Sultan, might perhaps have approved of the ruin his tomb now was, for unlike the desolated remains of some places, such as the deserted bone-bare Volubilis, Chella's stones of the dead were garlanded by wild growth, and frequented by the living, seeking an hour or so of shade and quiet. Abou El Hassan, whose reign from 1331 to 1348 was one of Morocco's most enlightened, was a patron of the arts comparable with his predecessor by nearly two centuries, Yacoub El Mansour. Under him, the city of Fez reached perfection. The colleges he built there were still in use, and that, too, would probably concern the Black Sultan more than the ruin of his own tomb-mosque.

Although six centuries have passed, the beautiful cursive script of the tomb can still be read in translation, 'This is the grave of our lord the sultan, prince of the surrendered, and victor in religious warfare in the way of the Lord of the Worlds, who died—may God accept and make him acceptable—in the mountain of Hantata on the night preceding the Blessed Rahia the First in year 752 and was buried in the direction of prayer. May God receive him into His favour and instal him in Heaven.'

I wondered if Mecca, Medina and Jerusalem still possess the fine copies of the Koran which Abou El Hassan wrote with his scholarly hand so many centuries ago. Near his own tomb was that of his Queen, Shems es-S'babi—the Morning Star. From her name some historians have inferred that she was a Christian slave. Female captives often became influential figures, right down to the twentieth century, when a Circassian slave was the power behind the throne of her son Sultan Abd El Aziz IV.

To wander about the gardens of Chella, so surprisingly luxuriant, was to wander in a half-lost, half-forgotten world. The hidden turnings, the secret steps, the ways tunnelled beneath enmeshed trees overhead, the maze of walls, the floors of ancient rooms now half unearthed, sunken below the accumulated soil of centuries, the storks' nests on the top pinnacle of the little minaret and another on the fragment of an Indian-looking carved stone bracket, the gloomy cistern beside a wall from which a giant fig tree had sprung, the patches of sunlight on golden stones, the bracken unfolding fronds like bishops' croziers, the arum lilies thriving in humid corners of pools, and secret zephyrs stealing about the ruins, scenting them with oleander, all these belonged to a dream of a vanished Oriental luxury.

Standing about in the gardens were *marabouts*, square, domed shrines where women sat or prayed. And in one corner, sunken in the ground, overhung by dense growth, the sacred pool. This for many was Chella's main attraction, for the cistern built around a spring not only contained water blessed by seven saints but within it dwelt the sacred eels—or if not *the* sacred eels at least *some* sacred eels, for doubtless even holy eels are not less slippery than their fellows elsewhere. Since nothing is sacred but thinking makes it so, the eels in that pool were saintly enough for the women who brought their children to watch the cod-liver-oil-coloured creatures sliding sinuously through the clear shallow pool.

Like everything else at Chella, the eels had a long history. Their ancestors inhabited the same pool in the 1190s when Yacoub El Mansour was building the Hassan Tower. And some authorities maintained that the eels were part of a pagan pre-Islamic tradition. But pagan or no, the eels were popular with pious Moslems. Those who came to pray at the saints' *marabouts* went also to the pool, taking eggshells with them, for there was nothing the eels enjoyed more by way of a treat than a nice eggshell. They were strangely fascinating to watch as they lurked about the openings in the underwater wall. In the wall above the water candles were lit in niches thick with wax.

The Romans, with their usual eye for practical things and comfort, had also constructed cisterns at Chella, and water still gushed through these underground chambers. There was also a bath, a circular one fifteen feet in diameter with arched niches in the walls of the octagonal room. They may have once contained statues or perhaps were simply used as shelves for jars of aromatic oils while the lordly Romans soaked in the steaming water. The Roman remains revealed a settlement much less ambitious than Volubilis, though there was a forum and buildings with columns and entablatures. Their fragments littered the ground and I saw some carved with the wonderfully plastic design of acanthus leaves, whose flowing curves caught Pliny's attention—*Acanthus lubricus et flexuosus.*

I went to Chella several times, finding its allurements irresistible. Certainly the red walls above the river contained a place more like the Gardens of Babylon than the municipal arboretums were, which Marshal Lyautey brought into being. The Marshal, however, had no fears about art, and he liked what he knew. In political affairs he also knew what he liked and one thing he liked very much was to see the end of an ancient and bitter feud. The rivalry between Fez and Marrakesh was a childish tantrum compared with the backbiting that had been going on between Rabat on one bank of the Bou Regreg River and Sale on the other. An old popular saying goes 'Till the sand becomes raisins and the river milk, Rabat and Sale will never be friends.' The Marshal brought this situation smartly to an end. Today Sale seems to be no more than a sleepy seaside annexe to Rabat. But in the Middle Ages Sale was the greatest African port on the Atlantic. Caravans crossed the desert to it, laden with ivory and gold dust, exotic hides and feathers, wool and honey, carpets and wax.

And waiting for them at Sale's quays would be merchant ships, ready to bear these African riches away in overloaded bottoms to Genoa and Venice, France and England. It may have been just such a ship whose loss upset Antonio in *Merchant of Venice.* Sale's merchants were noted for their honesty and courtesy, two qualities not attributed to them after the Spaniards were forced to leave in 1627, when Sale set itself up as a semi-independent state. The port became so powerful that poor Rabat was reduced to a mere vassal in the Republic of the Two Banks.

It was then that Sale became a household word on seafarers' lips for the city established its infamous School of Pilots and Piracy. The school's graduates became members of the much-feared Sallee Rovers, marauders who swept the Atlantic from the Cape Verde Isles to Ireland. Two years before going to Morocco I had been in the Azores and saw the tiny village church of Anjos, on Santa Maria island, where Christopher Columbus's crew went ashore. The church was deserted and unused, but among its few remaining effects was an old document in a frame, and it read 'The Moors have been here in 1675 to take women and children.' On the church wall was a large whip which the Sallee Rovers used on their captives.

Defenceless little Anjos was only one of hundreds of sea villages where terror filled every stout heart whenever the three-masted xebec appeared on the horizon. All over those mid-Atlantic islands I found nineteenth-century engravings, unintentionally comic, depicting the not-so-comic situation of screaming girls being carried off in the arms of Sallee seadogs. The pirates' cruelties to Spanish friars and English sailors were the subject in London's streets of many ballad-singers' broadsheets.

Eventually, such were the losses to merchantmen on the high seas that a kind of protection racket was set up. At the establishment of the Alaouite dynasty the Republic of the Two Banks was re-united with Morocco. Its sovereigns were only too happy when some bright schemer suggested that European kings should pay not to have their merchant vessels attacked by the Sale pirates. More often than not this protection money did not go to Sale, but to Fez or Meknes. And these cities, as if this first extortion was not enough, claimed the larger part of the booty from the raids which the Sallee Rovers still carried out in spite of the European protection money. The Sallee Rovers did not deal merely with captured goods but in captured people. Moulay Ismail was delighted to get his 15-year-old English wife from them as well as many thousands of her compatriots to work as slaves on the building of his palaces at Meknes.

The Rovers sailed in xebecs, three-masted boats with twelve to twenty-four guns which sometimes carried crews of two hundred men. Their operations were swift and deadly, in small fleets of about five ships. Every man-jack aboard was a tough and experienced fighter. Descending on some merchantman clumsily ploughing through the Atlantic swell, the Sale pirates had easy prey. Not only were their xebecs manoeuvrable and bristling with cannon and armed men, but the merchant ships were comparatively helpless. Built for bulky cargoes, they could not carry cannon effectively. When it is recalled that 25,000 Christians slaved on the building of Meknes alone, some idea can be gained of the numbers captured

over the years. The Sallee Rovers were formidable foes, well organized and operating on a vast scale.

Nor were the pirates all Moslems. Renegades from Latin countries,
escaped convicts and rogues fleeing from authority found profit and
freedom in the wild sea life of the Rovers. These mercenaries probably contributed considerably to the long unbroken success of the
pirate ventures. Among the many British men who sailed under the
Sale flag was 'one Carr' who in 1727 became head of the arsenal and
kaid of the Jews. In 1780 a Scot took over command of a sixteen-gun
xebec, changing his name to Omar. The Court executioner had
learnt his gruesome trade as a butcher boy in Exeter.

And there was the ubiquitous Thomas Pellow. When 11 years
old he rebelled against the 'moft fevere Difcipline' of the Latin
school at Penryn. He persuaded his uncle to take him to sea. They
set off from Falmouth for Genoa with a load of pilchards. On the
homeward journey two Sallee Rovers descended on them and carried
them captive to Morocco. Moulay Ismail gave the young Cornish
boy to Moulay Spha, one of his favourite sons. For several months
the Prince kept poor Thomas in irons and beat him 'moft feverely
baftinading me with a Bull's Pizzle, furioufly and fcreaming "Turn
Moor, turn Moor, by holding up your finger." '

Tom could hardly be blamed for thinking more about the soles
of his tender young feet than his immortal soul. He switched to
Islam, as did thousands of English and Spanish, Portuguese and
French, Dutch, Italian and Greek captives with him. Soon Tom was
free enough to go out fishing, pleasing the Sultan so much with his
catch that he was given twenty gold ducats. Unfortunately this sum
did not nearly buy his freedom and he remained a slave for twenty-
three years before escaping to Gibraltar. His book of slavery under
the Moors told how during those years in Morocco the most common
remedy for illness was a similar branding with red-hot irons as the
people still use today on animals.

'The Holy War by Sea', as the Moroccans termed their naval
activities, brought in heavy ransoms besides the protection money.
Before the British evacuated Tangier they were paying 200 pieces-of-
eight (£50) for English slaves. In 1690 the French Trinitarian Fathers
paid 10,000 dollars for thirty Frenchmen, though they got forty-five

eventually, because Moulay Ismail was so impressed by the way the priests embraced his horse's legs. By 1706 prices had risen and the Portuguese paid 1,000 dollars each for six Jesuits and 475 dollars each for 120 laymen.

In 1725 one Thomas Betton, a turkey merchant, died and left £26,000 in trust to the Ironmongers' Company for ransoming British slaves in Barbary. Several thousand pounds from the trust went every year to Morocco, until 1825 when the grants were given instead to Church of England schools. However, the Moroccans were not alone in their barbarisms. Europeans shipped negroes from Morocco, until prohibited from doing so in 1777, a ban which cost English slave-dealers dearly.

If ghosts of those seventeenth-century xebecs could sail into the mouth of the Bou Regreg estuary today, and tie up at their moorings in the river overlooked by the Hassan Tower and the red walls of Chella, they would find the tables turned, and the once-powerful port of Sale reduced to no more than a quiet suburb of Rabat. But 'suburb' is hardly the word for the ancient port which still, in spite of its decline, has its walls and narrow streets and magnificent beaches of fine sand, more extensive than Rabat's.

Many Sale people commute daily with Rabat, crossing the river bridge by bus, as I did, and going from the one town to the other in less than ten minutes. I did not first go to Sale until the late afternoon rush-hour, when the bus stop outside the Hotel Majestic had the semblance of a queue. From the balcony of my room I had watched the Sale buses come and go every few minutes, a transport which perhaps more than anything had realized Marshal Lyautey's idea of bringing the two towns together.

At Sale the bus stopped outside the brown walls and horseshoe gateways. The Bab Mrisa, now some distance from the estuary, was once a water-gate. Sale not only lost the fortunes of piracy when the sultans took their cut from the proceeds, but it also lost the use of the river for its port when the Bou Regreg changed course. Today Sale's walls, which reminded me of Pevensey Castle in Sussex, are some distance from the water's edge. The old port's buildings survived decline and many sights familiar to pirates and slaves alike could still be seen. The El Mrissi Mosque, the *medersa*, the sanctuary of En Noussak and the aqueduct all date from the Merinide kings, while the Great Mosque had stood there since the twelfth century, roughly contemporary with the Hassan Tower looming on the river's opposite bank.

A velvet warmth lingered in the Sale *medina* after sundown, and even at eight o'clock the cobblers and fruit-merchants, artisans and herbalists, and the dozens of other callings which make the Moroccan *medinas* throb with life, were still busy buying, selling and talking. Talk was the most popular entertainment in the kingdom. Talk between friends, talk between buyers and sellers, talk among groups sitting under trees, talk between the very old and the very young, talk three times a day before, during and after meals, talk over endless glasses of mint tea. Talk and laughter. And there was always time for talk, time existed for talk. And there was always somebody to talk to. Everybody talked, especially to a stranger or a foreigner. And if the talk was comic through misunderstanding, then there was laughter too, especially at foreign tongues trying out words in Arabic. I thought it impossible for anyone of any age from one to a hundred years old to be lonely in Morocco. The mixing of ages was perhaps more startling in comparison with our own teenage-conscious world than the mixture of skin colours. In the *medinas* children became involved and active in everything that happened from their earliest years and seemed to glide into adolescence and out into manhood without the violent emotional upheavals which tear society into factions in the Western world.

Except for the clamour of the *medina*, Sale was a quiet city, dreaming of bygone, wilder days. But once a year Sale broke out into a colourful celebration, and this was at the Mouloud, anniversary of the Prophet's birth. The city becomes a centre of attraction at this big Moslem feast day when, throughout the kingdom, it is honoured by firework displays and when delicacies made from dried fruits are added to the menu. Sale has a spectacular procession unique in Morocco. Centuries before the School of Pilots and Piracy was founded the town had been famous for its wax, which was exported all over Europe and especially to France and England. Wax decorations still form the famed feature of Sale's Mouloud festival nowadays. The waxwork procession is a brilliant affair of miniature architecture carried on poles high above the heads of the crowds, fantastically decorated temples with domes and arches whose openings are filled with gaudy baubles. All the surface of these three- or four-foot-high lantern-shaped models were covered with the intricacy of design so beloved by Moslem artists.

The years of continual wildness, however, were not so long ago. Sale pirates went out to sea into the nineteenth century, when brigs left the Bou Regreg after unfortunate vessels. The city suffered severe bombardment by both the French and English because of the pirates. In 1803 the U.S.A. stormed Sale because of the raid on the Boston brig. Attempts were made to put an end once and for all to the city's marauding crews. Sultan Moulay Sliman made a treaty with France in 1818 and denounced the Rovers. But piracy did not stop. In 1851 two French ships full of corn were plundered in the harbour. Again the French bombarded the town, but this merely drove the pirates out to the high seas again. As late as 1921 two vessels were taken by them and their people held to ransom. And piracy, less romantic perhaps than in the days of xebec and cannon, was still going on in the 1950s, though by this time the operators had shifted headquarters to Tangier. When Tangier became an internationally controlled zone it was an ideal centre for black market operations in postwar Europe. Piracy cases were still being held in the various courts until a few years ago, including that of the American Consul.

The old pirate port at Sale lies beyond the city walls and the tides, as restless as the Rovers themselves, have left it stranded high and dry. Today it shelters craft no more dangerous than strings of coloured bathing-huts, where swimmers can change before racing across the sparkling sand to fling themselves into the powerful but innocent waves of the incoming Atlantic. Brown naked bodies had been on display there for centuries. But the young men who flex their muscles today do so not for slave traders but only for the benefit of the girls in bikinis, or those no less observant ones wrapped in the mystery of *haiks*.

At night the beach was almost deserted, though perhaps then most beautiful. The Atlantic breakers, tide in or tide out, thrashed noisily on to the sand and glowed with borrowed luminosity from the lights of Rabat across the river. The red and white bathing-huts were locked up, giving shelter to nobody but a patrolling policeman who leaned against them for a surreptitious cigarette while on duty. A pack of pye-dogs roamed along the sands where once the packs of pirates swarmed about their swift ships.

I took my sandals off and walked barefoot, letting the fine grains flow over my feet in soft warm heaps. Across the river, Rabat sparkled with light. Part of its ramparts were floodlit. I thought of the thousand romantic tales to be told of these Barbary coasts. But Rabat's *lumière sans son* left them unvoiced except as fancies flitting through my mind. The only sounds were distant barking dogs and the sluggish swirl of the river currents answering the turn of the tide. The river caught the lights of Rabat and broke them into gleaming fragments like a shattered mirror.

Ten o'clock was gone when I got back to the *medina* to inquire about a bus to Rabat. The barber, now engaged in shaving a small boy's head, called out 'Good night, mister,' again when I passed his shop for the second time. He laughed about the bus. The last one to 'the place over there', as he disapprovingly called Rabat, pointing to it with his cutthroat, had gone hours ago. But another customer took me through the town to the gateway where taxis waited to fill up with late travellers wanting to be ferried across the bridge over the Bou Regreg River.

I was the first, and when, after a short wait, five others had been collected, the big American car left the parking-place under the trees, drove round the city walls and went over the bridge. The Hassan Tower, looking bulkier than ever, loomed against the night sky. It was even more impressive than in daylight, a vast shadow in the starlight, rising above the moon-flecked flowing river. And then I realized why the Carthaginians and the Romans, the Almohades and Merinides, the Sallee Rovers and Marshal Lyautey had chosen this site for trading posts—and royal capital—the river.

The estuary was more important than any of the beaches baring their sandy breasts down the long Atlantic coast. Chella and the Hassan Tower, the changing fortunes of Rabat and Sale, had all been born of the Bou Regreg, now emptying itself into the sea between shining mudflats. Running down its valley from the burnt-up hinterland, flowing beneath the crumbling walls of Chella, turning the small craft tied at ancient moorings below the Hassan, sweeping out to sea beyond the ramparts of the two rival cities, Rabat and Sale, one-time Republic of the Two Banks, this river had given birth to them all, had seen sultans and slaves, high and low alike, come and go.

7

Changes at the White House

Under the white concrete cliffs of Casablanca nobody could go pot-holing for Carthaginian or Roman remains, because the skyscrapers had consumed all traces of former civilizations. The disciples of Le Corbusier were not perhaps so much to blame as the Portuguese. In 1469 the Atlantic town of Anfa was captured and destroyed by the Infante Don Ferdinando. A century later the Portuguese returned and built a town, calling it Casa Branca—White House. They stayed until an earthquake in 1755 so shattered White House that once again it had to be evacuated. Then a Moroccan town appeared, phoenix-like from the ashes, and this, too, was called White House, but in Arabic —Dar El Beida. Use of Dar El Beida's harbour was granted to the Spanish, who translated White House into Casablanca. And Casablanca it has been ever since, the French merchants, whose colony after 1830 outnumbered all other foreigners, resisting the obvious temptation to change the town's name yet once more into Maison Blanche.

A terrible slaughter in Casablanca caused the French landing in 1907 and eventually led to the Protectorate Treaty in 1912. The carnage resulted from the clash of old ways and modern development in the city. During improvement works to the harbour the Shawia tribe thought the Moslem cemetery had been desecrated. They swooped down and killed three French, three Spanish and three Italian infidels. Thousands of their own people died before the trouble subsided.

Since those days of modernization Casablanca has never looked

Sacred storks'
whereabouts . . .

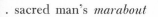. sacred man's *marabout*

Pitcher—skull-
capped Berber
water boy

Tosser—turbaned
tambourine player

back, or rather down, for its new buildings grow progressively bigger and higher every year. The small fishing port of sixty years ago has not only become Morocco's commercial capital but the largest town. Money and the power of money are strong magnets and have attracted to Casablanca most things the modern world associates with them, not least the brilliant gaiety of expensive and exclusive nightlife which makes Casablanca an essential 'must' for Atlantic pleasure cruises.

Modern Casablanca is international, which means that like most international things it belongs to nowhere in particular. Nobody could be blamed for waking up in Casablanca and thinking they were in São Paulo, a city which in many respects it resembles. Even the fifty-six miles of excellent highway south from Rabat are international in that this mileage is done in considerably less than an hour by fast cars with people who look at nothing on the way, itself an international feature of travel. Even the bus from Rabat got there in an hour despite heavy traffic. But I did not mind, for the stretch of fine road eventually led to the international symbols of modern progress —industrial sprawl and destroyed landscape. We rushed through the miles of Casablanca's outskirts of factories and ugly buildings which exposed nicely the advantages of the traditional life which most Moroccans still manage to live by one fortunate means or another.

For the first time in Morocco I saw the sad spectre which stalks South American cities, the spectre of shanty towns. In Venezuela they call them *ranchitas*, in Brazil *favelas*; in Casablanca they are known as *bidonvilles*—'tin-can towns'. A familiar pattern was repeating itself. The higher the concrete apartment blocks went, the greater the city's economic prosperity, the more the poorer people were drawn into the city by the illusion of waiting fortunes. As air-conditioned flats reached for the sky, so more and more oil drums were flattened for the ever-growing *bidonvilles*. I had seen it before. In Brasilia, the brand-new capital of Brazil, a shining symbol of Brazil's faith in the future, two shanty towns sprang up for every one bulldozed away by an embarrassed authority. Moroccan authorities were no less concerned. The Nationalist Movement which plotted the overthrow of the French régime made a hue and cry over the *bidonvilles*, citing them as evidence of the evils of colonialism. The French have gone, but the *bidonvilles* remain.

Even so, faced with the choice between a Casablanca oil-drum shack in the sun or a back-street slum in the grime of Manchester, I know which I would choose. Besides, Casablanca's beaches have something which the Manchester Ship Canal has not. And also, on closer inspection, Casablanca's new buildings were a good deal better than most new ones in Britain, including the factories. What a fascinating prospect the visitor to Britain had until recently when arriving at London airport and then being driven along the industrial estates of the Great West Road with its phoney palaces erected in honour of razor blades and tyres.

Before reaching Casablanca's outskirts the dual carriageway passed through eucalyptus woods and filtered sunlight clearings reminiscent of the New Forest in Hampshire. Thin turquoise strips of sea peeped above the seaboard plains. Occasionally the road ran near the sea, giving a glimpse of sandy bays and neat, bright-painted wooden beach-houses, their colours gone through a magical mutation in the luminous sea atmosphere. Then we passed a pig farm. They were the first pigs I had seen in Morocco, for both the Jewish minority and the Moslem majority abhor the poor pig. But Casablanca's plethora of national restaurants, French, Spanish, Italian and Chinese, needed pork for their cuisine.

From pigs we came to hibiscus, which now separated the carriageways, making a crimson line for miles, right into the city. Even when the first factories began the hibiscus continued, its royal colour a foil to the white buildings. Clusters of sumptuous peach-coloured blossoms opened bell-mouths to show scarlet centres of a deeper red than the riot of singles and doubles that dappled the green river between the traffic lanes.

Comparisons are said to be odious, presumably because one of the things being compared *is* odious. I could not help, however, comparing the C.T.M. bus station in Casablanca with Victoria Coach Station which is yet another of London's transport monstrosities. The C.T.M. station was new and beautifully designed both for use and appearance. Its terrazzo floors were spotless, another reminder of the myth about English cleanliness. The bus station was the best one I had seen anywhere, with the exception of São

Paulo's, which made an un-odious comparison with Casablanca's.

The new El Mansour Hotel near the bus station, a slim elegant skyscraper of blue and white with rows of shuttered rooms sleeping in the midday sun, was beyond my pocket. But I found a comfortably seedy *pension* in the next street and had at least a view of the smart hotel across the flat roof outside my room from which half a dozen lean cats eyed my intrusion with lordly suspicion.

I closed the shutters before going into the town, partly to keep the room cool, but mostly to keep out the cats, for I had a sneaking feeling they slept on the bed when nobody was about. Although Tangier had a Fat Black Pussy Cat Café, most Moroccan cats were lean, presumably because they fended for themselves and kept the rats at bay. On the other hand, though highly independent, cats were not ill treated. Moulay Ismail gave one of his a state funeral, admittedly after dragging it through the streets and hanging it as a punishment for eating his pet rabbit.

Casablanca was still a town of predominantly white houses. Whereas the ancient *medinas* in most cities were tawny and encircled by tawny walls, and most French new towns tended to be principally ochrous, Casablanca was noticeably white, and this again gave it that South American, international tone. Brazil became a copy-book during the 1930s under the Vargas régime. Following Le Corbusier's visit in 1936 and the building of the famous Ministry of Education in Rio de Janeiro, a whole generation of architects converted the face of Brazilian cities. The creations of Oscar Niemeyer and Affonso Reidy and the Mindlin brothers made a new vocabulary for building in hot countries, and Casablanca took on something of this character.

Yet much still remained of the city's pre-modern French protectorate period, as well as its own original *medina*. Casablanca's centre was the large and busy Mohammed V Square, and from it a wide, palm-lined boulevard ran down towards the docks and the nearest beaches. This was the Hansali, a place to stroll and savour Casablanca's peculiar atmosphere of thriving business. Dock gantries at the end of the boulevard showed through the palms, signs of the city's source of wealth. And all around were shipping agents and consular offices and naval colleges, ship-chandlers and scrap-merchants. The railway passed near and freight trains went clanking by, grinding under the load of precious cargoes like phosphates, an export second only to agricultural produce. Casablanca, one of the world's most extravagant entertainment towns by night, was seething and serious during the day. International playboys there doubtless were at the swimming-pools and beaches and in the night-clubs, but there were plenty of work-boys, too.

Being a favourite port-of-call for cruises, Casablanca had learnt to cater for the one-day tourist. Boulevard Hansali provided a row of shops with goods likely to catch the novelty-hungry eye of people who next day would probably be in Madeira or the Canaries. Such tourists are connoisseurs, not of taste or value, but of the quality things have of being uniquely expressive of a particular country, expressive, that is, to their friends back home. The best objects of this kind in Morocco were the beautifully hand-made craftsmen's things from the *medinas*. Alas, the Hansali's shops mixed these fine wares with machine-made goods, execrable imitations of the real thing which can be found in similar places all over North Africa.

How could people buy the stools shaped like camel saddles complete with brass knobs, and the hideous outsized pouffes, and the garishly dyed sheepskin rugs, and outrageous machine-stamped brass trays and silver teapots, and badly done overvarnished boxes and tables of marquetry, and carpets woven with Victorian oleograph representations of camels in deserts and love scenes of sheikhs with veiled girls? Most Moroccans would not be seen with such trash, for they can, and do, get the real thing at quarter the price in the *medinas*.

I sat on one of the back-to-back benches on the boulevard and consulted my street map, and found that since its printing ten years before many of the street names had been changed. Shoe-shine boys came with their boxes and sat in front of me and with expert subtlety tried to make me feel ashamed of my sandals, by now well ingrained with the boys' native soil.

'Spik English? Look, mister! Why you no shoe-shine? Good shoe-shine! You give me dollar?'

Cajolery, threats, resignation. And failing all else, they would sit on their boxes just out of arm's length, imitating me to their friends, knowing that in the end I would laugh, too, and give them money, whereupon they would fly after their next victim.

My map was out of date largely because passages between the newest skyscrapers needed a name suited to their new importance. So now there was United Nations Square and the Park of the Arab League, the Avenue of the Armed Forces, though the Forces could do nothing about the American invasion by John Wayne in the cinema and Elvis Presley on the postcard stands which also sold arm-badges of Venezuela or Monaco, Paris or Berlin, Zurich and Copenhagen. A dozen of those sewn on a windcheater sleeve would make an experienced traveller out of anybody. There was never any need to do it the hard way like the German hitch-hikers clumping down the Hansali in hobnail boots, overburdened like Bunyan's Pilgrim by monstrous rucksacks. And in order to carry that symbol of status, now gone out of fashion in England, the airline bag, it was certainly not necessary to have travelled by air. Many shops specialized in airline bags and Moroccans carried them like Danes carry briefcases.

Quite the most fascinating place for me in Casablanca was the Central Market. It was a heavenly place as clean as heaven. The astonishing variety of fresh foods catered principally for the large European population. I could imagine fabulous French menus appearing on hundreds of French dinner-tables that night. The white marble halls of the fish market were loaded with turbot, soles, red mullet, dolphin, green pollack, sea bream, whiting, gurnard, frog fish as well as hog and dog. Besides ordinary lobsters there were langoustes and langoustines. There were crabs of every size and shape, shrimps and prawns, and the extraordinary *pieds-biche* which had indeed delightfully delicate shells shaped like a hind's hoof at the end of the black, leathery tentacles. The sea eels were enormous, brown and white mottled creatures, resembling snakes rather than the slender black eels exported from Ireland's River Bann to London street markets.

On the fruit and vegetable stalls I saw a cornucopia of luscious things from several continents and the meat market looked so good and free of flies that even a vegetarian mouth would have watered. Or perhaps not, for I halted, suddenly upset among the festoons of ducks and guinea-fowl, hares and turkeys, the Barbary pigeons Mary Queen of Scots so longed for in prison, and there, laid sadly row upon row in white enamel trays, were tiny bare bodies. The skylarks selling at four shillings a dozen were big and expensive compared with the ortolans. I turned away from the pathetic sight, experiencing unusual sympathy with vegetarians who feel the same way about all dead animals. I suspected the tiniest birds were really rock, cirl and corn buntings which bred over a wide area of Morocco, despite the market trays being labelled 'ortolans'. These small creatures were a delicacy to the French palate, of which Benjamin Disraeli would heartily have approved. 'Let me die,' he wrote, 'eating ortolans to the sound of soft music!'

But was it Aldous Huxley who showed that even green plants feel the pain of being picked or cut? Perhaps the pedlars in the Boulevard Hansali may have thought me insensitive for consuming the sweet small shrimps I bought in the market to eat in the palm-lined avenue. But the pedlars may not have been gifted with such sensibilities, nor did they seem to be very imaginative. What could I do with long waving fronds of pampas grass? Could the persistent man with a pile of beautifully tooled leather book-covers not see that while eating shrimps people just don't want to look at book-covers? But, in fact, I did glance at the traditional craftsmanship like the grand Moroccan bindings in eighteenth-century libraries. The real reason I tried to drive him away was because I had already overspent on such luxuries in the *medina* at Fez. Street pedlars follow the tourist like his shadow, close on his heels they pursue him everywhere from the restaurants of Tangier to the brothels of Marrakesh.

'You like handbag for the lady? You look see.'

'No.'

'A nice big pouffe for your mama?'

'No. Mama doesn't like pouffes.'

The unstuffed leather seat looked more like a huge sombrero for American tourists in Mexico. In the end I had to get up from my bench in the boulevard, hoping to find a beach where I could finish my punnet of blackberries in peace. Since no beach was visible from the boulevard, I asked a French matron of a doubtful fifty years which would be my best way. She stood listing to one side with her full weight on one foot while her diminutive toy dog did its little business. Then, when it had finished, Madame inspected me, clutching the dog under her arm, patting it with a podgy hand whose nails were painted the same scarlet as the dog's nails. She told me of the glamorous beaches of fashion, Kon Tiki, Miami, Tahiti, though she always went to the Lido on Ain-Diab. But choosing was difficult because they all had good swimming-pools.

Oui, Madame very difficult to avoid those sort of places with their elaborate dressing-cabins and smart bars. The conversation was listened to by the persistent shoe-shine, who, philosopher that he was at 9 years old, knew, as he had shrewdly guessed my nationality and state of pocket, what sort of beach I wanted. He told me, at the price of having my old sandals resuscitated, to go out to Ain Asbaa. He also showed me where to get the bus in Mohammed V Square, and I leapt on to it after a dash through an onrush of mopeds and scooters. The bus was being milked by beggars. The blind and the halt pushed through the standing passengers, waving horribly maimed stumps in the travellers' faces.

On the whole, I decided, as the bus covered seven miles of Casablanca's suburbs, the shoe-shine philosopher, right in everything else, was wrong about going out to Ain Asbaa. The industrial sprawl and wastelands *en route* were too much the opposite of snobbish lidos, though the wealth of datura around some of the *bidonvilles* was most impressive. Andre Gide had thought so also and called the great white thorn-apple blossom by the old French name, trumpets of Jericho.

I began to think the 9-year-old shoe-shiner had put me on the wrong bus by way of a joke, but eventually the industrial suburbs stopped and the sea came into view and we were in Ain Asbaa, confronted with miles of sand, crowded near the village and thinning out towards the farther beach. Boys swarmed around the beaches like wasps at mint-tea glasses, and made a furor of excitement under the public shower-baths. Youths played football and did handstands or wrestled. Others strutted up and down, showing off to the girls. Veiled and tattooed mothers watched toddlers playing in green rock pools. The sea was blue and inky towards the horizon, where ships were dark silhouettes plying to Casablanca. Long bamboo fishing-rods stuck up against the sky like a forest growing on the offshore reefs.

Besides the soft roar of the sea, the noise of voices continuously filled the air. Lying back to sunbathe was like sinking into a warm timeless sleep. In fact, it turned out to be an hour's sleep and I only woke then because of the sand-flies—or what, at first, I thought were sand-flies. I swatted one and found, instead, that I had caught a tiny brown hand. Gulliver, waking to find himself tied down by the Lilliputians, could not have been more surprised than I was. At least thirty boys and girls, some of them teenagers, broke from the circle surrounding me and ran when I sat up. They had been staring at my tattoos, which must have seemed much more outlandish than the herring-bone patterns on their mothers' noses and ankles. The small brown hand had been touching the tattoo on my arm.

Nightfall had stolen over the city and the sea by the time I got back to Casablanca. The blue of the sky had seeped away and in its stead was a luminous turquoise of many tones and intensities. Complete darkness, which made the stars so sharp, came only slowly in Morocco. And in the lingering twilight I went into the *medina* which bordered one side of the neon-flashing Mohammed V Square.

Being part of Casablanca, the *medina* was also part of the city's tourist itinerary. I was pleased to find the *medina* so little affected by the tide of liner cruise passengers which swamped the place throughout the year. If I had not been into the web of alleys in Fez and Meknes and had not seen the real thing in small places like Chaouen, perhaps the subtle differences of the Casablanca *medina* would have been unnoticeable. But I could detect a difference, perhaps of tempo, perhaps in tones of voices, in the glances given the stranger which here were not so much curious and friendly as they were mercenary and friendly. Also, cars nosed their way through Casablanca's *medina*, which they could not do, for instance, at Fez. Alternative tours through the streets were signposted for those visitors who like to see as much and understand as little as possible. And many of the *medina*'s shops were filled with inferior goods from the docks, and not with craftsmen's work.

Nevertheless, the *medina* was a better place to spend the evening than the world-renowned night-clubs of modern Casablanca, whose hostesses stood outside beckoning with uninviting gestures, all hip and torso squeezed into the tightest of French dresses, the implication being that sooner or later they would be squeezed out of them. The more exclusive and thus more expensive night-clubs were also more discreet than their less particular rivals. Yet all were alike in an excessive artificiality. Night-club was, of course, synonymous with striptease joint.

Resisting a temptation I did not feel, not even for the hearties of the various 'horse-riding clubs', I wandered about the *medina*, happy to look at the strange assortment of things for sale, happy to talk with passers-by, happy to peep inquisitively into half-open doors. I discovered the Union of Moroccan Workers. Their youth-club gymnasium was in a disused workshop whose door I pushed open to be met with an enthusiastic invitation to 'come right in'. Normally, I supposed, the gym never saw a stranger. They had fitted it out themselves for wrestling and weight-lifting, the leader told me, and it was open to young men between 17 and 27. So far they had about fifty members. Some of them were climbing up the ropes fixed to the wooden roof trusses and doing press-ups on benches, all obviously determined to become like the muscle-men depicted in murals they had done themselves and in photographs of weight-lifting and body-building champions which were pinned on the walls. The only evening when they did no training was Sunday.

Probably because the French had adopted *le weekend*, Sunday was much more like the Christian Sabbath in Europe, and businesses closed, though most Moroccans went to prayers in the mosque on the Moslem holy day on Friday. A third Sabbath, however, was noticeable in the *medinas* when the Jewish shops closed. Casablanca, like most other cities, had its *mellah*. Here, the Jews were strictly segregated behind high walls and were forbidden to buy land outside them. The *mellahs* were often overcrowded and through the centuries had frequently been pillaged. During the 1912 troubles in Fez the *mellah* went up in flames when Moulay Hafid panicked in his suspicion of French moves against him, just as a few years before the Shawian tribesmen marched on Casablanca's *mellah* after the massacre on the Europeans in the harbour. But to pillage the *mellah* was always the first action in any civil unrest.

Although the Jewish minority controlled a considerable amount of commerce in Morocco, the *mellah* was nearly always the most poverty-stricken quarter of the town. The idea of bloated Jews waxing fat on the community whose blood they sucked had nothing in common with the old bearded Jews walking about in long robes and skullcaps I saw in Casablanca's *mellah*. Both Jews and Moslems told me that they lived happily enough. On Moroccan national occasions, rabbis and Jewish leaders would send letters of congratulations to the local governors and even the King. Only when boatloads of Jews decided to leave the narrow confines of the *mellah* and sail for Israel was embarrassment caused. As a member of the Arab League boycotting the state of Israel, Morocco sends delegates to Cairo's conferences and they have some explaining to do as to why their country allows Jews to emigrate and thus strengthen Israel.

Jews had settled in Morocco long before the Arabs, and they claim to have gone there initially after the Fall of Jerusalem. Jews were certainly blacksmiths and carpenters to the Romans in Volubilis and elsewhere. They were prosperous silversmiths when Moulay Idris brought Islamic teaching to Morocco in the eighth century. And under the Sultan Moulay Ismail, Jews were forcibly made Court jewellers, having to present gold rings set with pearls to all the hundreds of princes at their births.

Today some of the best and cleanest shops are in the *mellahs* and Jews have a high reputation as herbalists, especially for the making of love potions. I had made friends as easily with Jews as with Berbers and Arabs. When nothing caused irritation of the normal easy-going friendliness of Moroccans, Jews seemed to fit into the live-and-let-live atmosphere as happily as everybody else. But it would be wrong to ignore the presence of tensions. Moroccans are emotional. An ordinary conversation can sound like a violent quarrel, and a real disagreement between two Arabs can be mistaken for the outbreak of a fight to the death. Such flames die as soon as they flare up, and it was always odd to see men who had been exchanging the most terrible noises at one moment walking off down the street hand in hand the next. I was a little saddened, therefore, that the only street fight I saw in Morocco was between a Jew and an Arab.

This was in the shoe market. But before this, I saw other things in Casablanca which were sad, even if inevitable. Behind the bright lights and dim plush interiors of the famous night-clubs a quiet disintegration of traditional life was going on. Perhaps, in itself, this was not serious in extent. But it was an ominous portent as to how the infiltration of the modern Western world could, like a chronic disease, destroy the age-old way of life which makes Morocco's distinctive character. Being a great port and business centre, and being constantly exposed to Western ways, Casablanca would be remarkable indeed if it did not pick up some of them. For instance, though I saw them nowhere else in Morocco, not even in Tangier, I did see drunks in Casablanca falling over beggars in the streets.

Moroccans were a handsome people, perhaps the most handsome I had seen anywhere in the world, including Brazil. They were not only handsome but immensely dignified. The shepherd on the hill, the cobbler in the *medina*, the mint-seller by the roadside, the student from the *medersa*, all had an inborn dignity of bearing. Dignity was perhaps the characteristic which made Morocco seem without the division of class. But this dignity was fragile. Its green leaves could be blighted when touched by Western-style corruption. And in Casablanca I saw how the blight could, so easily, set in.

Corruption, of course, is not an absolute. But what is acceptable in one context may not be so in another. I could not see what good would come to Morocco if all its cities began to lose their character as Casablanca had. What will happen if television usurps the ancient entertainment of talk? What will happen if the bright gewgaws of the Western world create teenage consciousness, so destroying the ancient harmony among different age groups? What will happen if the Moroccans should become affluent and lose their dignity and charm, friendliness and gaiety in the undignified scramble for possessions, and worse, the scramble for more possessions than their neighbour has. The Koran, like the Old and New Testaments, does not scorn riches. But it places the good life and the intellect above riches. And Koranic teachings became ingrained and produced a people welded together in a harmonious existence. In Casablanca I heard discordant notes.

But, on the other hand, who could blame the youngsters for being attracted by Western comics and magazines? Who could blame them for hanging round juke-boxes? Who could blame them if they thought less of praying in the mosque than of imitating the heroes in 'Christian' films who drink and make free with women and shoot a man as soon as look at him? What possible purpose could the American Cultural Institute serve in Fez, when the cinemas showed all too clearly the American ideals of toughness and hardness? Who could blame the Casablanca youngsters for thinking the Koran old-fashioned with its *There is no God but God* when clearly in the Western world there is no God but Money—money which could buy glittering cars, an entrance to the night-clubs and smart lidos, and even the almost unattainable life in paradise which the tourists from the liner cruises so obviously enjoyed?

Nobody could blame the youths for wanting to wear jeans and tee-shirts instead of the *djellaba* as they streak along the roads on Italian and Japanese scooters and make love to any available girl on any available beach to the accompaniment of jazz on transistor radios. Sons no longer kissed their fathers' shoulders in respect, and drunkenness broke much more than a Koranic law. A chain centuries long was broken, whose links were harmony.

For the moment, however, the catastrophe was far off, and perhaps the change to modern life would be gradual enough for the best of the old life to be absorbed in the new. There seemed to be nothing explosively dangerous in boys staying up to all hours playing billiards in pool rooms. Curiously, though the disciplines of Islam and ancient customs had been thrown off, the less-attractive qualities of prejudice had not, and anti-Jewish feelings was one of them which flared out in the market.

The shoe market was like a fair, with hundreds of pairs hung up on strings like puppets. I was indulging in some further William Morris-type moralizings, prompted this time by the predominance of plastic sandals over leather ones by craftsmen, when suddenly the whole lot went flying as two rival shopkeepers started fighting. One of them was wearing the Jewish skullcap. In the end forty or more people were involved and only the timely arrival of a woman in a nightdress, with hair flowing free, stopped further blood from spilling. The incident was forgotten almost the moment it ended. But it had happened between Jew and Arab.

A few hours later a gun-fight took place in the city. In July 1963 there had been a plot to overthrow the monarchy. Twelve men had been sentenced to death in their absence. One of them was traced to Casablanca during my stay there. His house was surrounded and, observed by Egyptian police visiting Morocco, a gun-battle ensued which ended when the wanted man fell dead. The siege made national news for a week.

Casablanca's *bidonvilles* appeared in the city centre as well as on the outskirts. Reflection from the blaze of light given out by batteries of neon signs partly illuminated the desperate poverty of the tin-can slum I found down the Rue de la Concorde, past the Kosher butchers. A tiny boy of 5 or so came out of his shack to water a chestnut horse tethered to the solitary street lamp whose dim glimmer helped further to show the plight of the Casablanca poor. When the horse finished drinking the little boy sat on the brown dusty earth and used the water tin as a drum. To this tin rhythm a drunk, throwing grotesque shadows, came lurching down the Rue de la Concorde. The boy fled into the tumbledown shanty of tins and old boards he knew as home. The sack curtain over its door was lifted wide and a woman looked out. Then the curtain fell again. At least it was not *her* man.

My irregularly circular walking tour through the *medina* had brought me via the *mellah* and *bidonvilles* back to the Boulevard Hansali, where now the tourist shops were taking in their displays of brass pots and pans, copper kettles and leather pouffes for the night. The underdressed German hitch-hikers had found youth hostels, the overdressed seamen had found high spots in the night-life and the oversexed dogs ran in an erotic herd through the grand avenues.

The night was comparatively young. Yet already Casablanca was empty, the night-clubs had drawn the tourists and the wealthy off the streets and prudence over early working hours had drawn the dockers and factory workers off to bed. This was the first and only place in Morocco where I felt lonely. The atmosphere was anonymous.

I sat on a bench in the boulevard and watched three naval police-men patrolling the streets. They marched single file in immaculately white uniforms, complete with white gloves and white batons and helmets, and looked like surgeons going to an operating theatre.

When they had gone, their steps automated by some military compulsion, I was alone, except for beggars sleeping in doorways and other human flotsam floating between the white cliffs of streets.

The neon signs flashed frantically as though signalling a desperate S O S and getting no response. On. Off. On again. Then off. An inane semaphore. Green, blue, red, yellow, white, their meaningless messages went out casting light upon the wonderful works of man, the Berlitz School, Wagons-Lits, the British Bank of the Middle East, the Polish Consulate, the Seventh Day Adventist Chapel, the Russian Orthodox Church, the Swallow's Nest Restaurant, the Balmoral Hotel, the American Express, the Sacred Heart Cathedral, the Jockey Club, K.L.M., Air France, the curled-up shoe-shine boy in the Rotary Club's doorway, the beggar with the whole wide Avenue of the Armed Forces to himself where he could spread a rag over the pavement on which to kneel, turning to Mecca, for his prayers. And his prayers were better said by night, for by day the *mouddhin*'s call from the minaret was drowned by car horns and ships' hooters and pneumatic drills and the high priests of Mammon calling over the intercom of their skyscraper temples.

8

Pavilion'd in Splendour

Marrakesh lay 150 miles away, deep inland at the foot of the High Atlas Mountains. Unlike me, the millionaires who went from all over the world to winter in the grand La Mamounia Hotel did not travel by bus across the plains to the southern capital. But I was not attempting to tread in the steps of the Aga Khan, Sir Winston Churchill, Barbara Hutton or the Emperor of Ethiopia. Apart from a difference of income between the famous and myself as well as our mode of transport, there was a difference of season, too. I was visiting Marrakesh in the summer. This was a feat considered by some as being equivalent to Shadrach, Meshach and Abednego going into the fiery furnace. These people, as usual, were the kind whose ideas and conventions were those of the gossip columns. So although they prophesied impossible temperatures in Marrakesh I went undaunted to the Casablanca C.T.M. bus station. And, naturally, I found a number of people like myself, including a dentist from Leeds, trying to get a place on the Marrakesh express.

A young Berber who sat next to me held a pair of donkey blinkers on his lap. He was grinning at my battle. I fought the same battle on every bus and this time I looked like winning. The boy, whom I supposed to be about 14, was amused because I managed to keep at least one window open. Moroccan bus travellers preferred tightly closed windows and curtains drawn against the sun and were immune to the stifling heat and atmosphere.

The Berber boy also grinned because, along with the Leeds dentist, I featured in an incident which enlivened the journey. A police road-block halted the bus just outside Casablanca and a search took place for which the dentist and I were singled out. The spectacular gun-battle earlier in the day against the 1963 royal plotter had revealed trafficking in firearms. Road-barriers in the vicinity held up cars and buses and the passengers had to produce identity cards. The young Berber, in a sense, needed no identity card. His skullcap, different from the Jewish black type by being knitted in brilliant red with white and green geometrical designs, gave evidence enough that he was a Berber.

Having neither a Jewish nor a Berber skullcap nor an Arab turban, the dentist and I were persons of interest to the police as well as the boy with the donkey blinkers. I felt slightly less conspicuous when Moroccan passengers had to show their identity cards. My canvas bag was searched twice, my passport pored over, and the poor dentist had to open up his suitcase, which had been put under the big luggage net on the roof. The police spoke no English, the dentist no French. He could not describe the object which a policeman pulled out of the case. String vests were wrapped carefully around a long gun-like shape. Breaths were bated, the suspense terrible. Then everyone except the dentist laughed, as much from relief as comedy, when the last string vest revealed a telescopic tripod.

Casablanca and its modern paraphernalia dropped behind us with no regrets from me. I gladly exchanged it for the flat lands stretching inland where the hard brown earth shimmered unsheltered in the sun. We passed mules pulling carts crowded with farming people. The carts trundled along shining, mirage-wet roads where presumably no local buses ran. Only an occasional cactus hedge or forlorn castor-oil bush broke up the landscape's foreground, varied at intervals by petrol stations and Shell signs. Telegraph poles inclined at drunken angles, and the railway's overhead cable pylons accompanied the road for most of the way, emphasizing both the monotony of the endlessly straight road and the emptiness of the brown land whose colour even the stubble-hunting sheep and cattle copied as though in camouflage.

In some places along our route camels were more numerous than donkeys. These strangely beautiful animals were at once dignified and cumbersome, and unlike other beasts of burden seemed to be born for nobler things. Though free to roam the fields, the camels and horses had their forefeet tied together. The sun had left little foraging, so the animals were prevented from straying miles away by the rope round their front feet. As the camels hopped they reminded me of kangaroos. Sometimes a white camel could be seen, perhaps standing alone, his head raised high as he surveyed the scene. Others were harnessed to long ropes and drew water from deep wells.

Although the sheep looked like cinnamon dumplings in the dusty earth, much of the land was arable and constantly under the plough. The hirsels were large, and some with new lambs, though there was little heart on all the herbage floor for dam or lamb. In this open landscape the only protection afforded the animals lay within the mud-walled enclosures of the steadings, walls which also enclosed the farmhouses.

The farms resembled fortresses on a miniature scale. The marauders to be kept at bay were foxes and jackals and the terrible, swoping lammergeiers. Shadows of this bearded vulture's seven-foot wing-span swept swiftly over the flocks as it snatched up a lamb. Besides their habit of dropping tortoises from great heights to smash their shells open, lammergeiers swallow bones as big as a lamb's femur. Such a successful war was waged against the vultures by the farmers that now they themselves are protected to stop their complete extinction.

The bus began to pass through higher, rocky country, but we saw no vultures, even though large flocks of pin-tailed grouse wheeled about like pigeons, flying off towards the coast. This higher land gave further evidence of the large-scale attack made in Morocco on the problems of a barren land. Machinery and modern transport had been yoked to combat mile upon mile of bare land. The intense ploughing over vast acres had been a revelation to me. And so also was the highly organized and extensive afforestation.

Roads in many parts of Morocco ran through miles of recently planted forest, which must, in twenty to fifty years, transform the face of the country not only by prevention of erosion but also by the collection of moisture and even by changing the climate as large areas of forest are known to do. Here, in the scree hillsides, large regions had been planted with trees. Up in the foothills white canvas villages of roadmenders' tents stood out as brilliantly in the clear air as the whitewashed *marabouts* of the local holy men.

Now the landscape became bold, full of noble forms. Gigantic sweeps of hill rose up to whalebacked skylines. Walled farms, camouflaged like the animals, nestled under the slopes or stood in isolation half-way up the flanks. Thin trails wound their way up into the hills like veins leading to heavens-knows-what lonely settlements. We passed a fair. Dust raised by the hoofs of hundreds of animals hung over it. The day's business was already done and the country people were dispersing. Patient, delicate-footed donkeys bore their masters away, moving at a slow trot, while in front loaded camels plodded in their aloof dreamy way. These little caravans dotted the road and away through the fields smaller dust-clouds betrayed others as they followed the tracks into the hills. It was a timeless sight, moving and beautiful. I hoped that no harsh progress would come to destroy this harmony of land and people.

We left the last silhouette of donkeys dark against the gilded stubble of the harvested wheatfields. The horizon opened again, but this time agitated by distant, serrated hills, a rippling of the plains' still waters that must eventually become the giant white-crested waves of the High Atlas Mountains. After a stop at Benguerir we began the last lap to Marrakesh, running speedily through yet another great stretch of plain. On both sides dust devils eddied in whorls from the ground, racing across the brown earth in high spirals like tornadoes. They looked sinister, for their source of power, though invisible, drove them faster than the bus, so that they overtook it before suddenly disappearing into thin air, for all the world like a djinn.

We reached Sidi Bou Othman at the foot of a ridge called the Djebelet—the Little Mountains. We passed an eyesore camp, presumably American, marked with double-think signs. 'Peace Is Our Profession'. The young Berber beside me was hypnotized by the camp. I wondered how many atom bombs, if any, were stored underground ready to stir up dust devils of a more lethal kind than those rushing across the plains. But professional peace reigned on that afternoon over the hazy land where, in an unsuspecting moment, I saw a faint blur lying in a hollow of the plain many miles away. From the blur a solitary grey smudge stood up. The scene was astonishingly similar to York Minster seen from the hills to the north, a mirage-like vision of a far city with a high tower. And so, now, lay Marrakesh.

Perhaps for me, even more than Fez or Meknes, those two cities steeped in Moorish history, soaked in association with the days when the Crescent and the Cross confronted each other with bloody blades, Marrakesh was a symbol of Islam. And, moreover, Islam coloured with the mysteries of an old Africa, of mysteries hidden in an almost-forgotten past. The idea of seeing Marrakesh excited me, and I was pleased that I first glimpsed it from twelve miles away, a distance which properly enhanced its magic. The dark smudge standing vertically was, I realized, the tower minaret of the famous Koutoubia mosque.

The High Atlas, rearing up behind the distant city, were themselves like a mirage floating in the sky, for the nearer we approached the farther they withdrew. But as the bus fled across the Plain of the Haouz, Marrakesh itself took on form and colour, and by the time we passed through the wide belt of palm groves encircling the city the colour took on deeper tones of red until, at last, as we drove into the boulevards of the ex-French sector I could see why it was called 'Marrakesh the Red'.

Quite unexpectedly the boulevards gave on to a huge open square crowded with robed figures, surrounded by low buildings and opening on one side to another space beyond which the pink tower of the Koutoubia mosque dominated the scene. The C.T.M. bus station was directly on this square, the Djemaa el Fna. After disembarking I had to look no farther than the bus-station roof for an hotel. Somebody with much imagination had built a single-story hotel on the flat roof. This not only allowed all the rooms to open on to an inner patio, but also provided a terrace giving an excellent grandstand view of the excitements in the great square below.

Two youths were washing the tiled patio when I climbed the stairs and asked for a room, which, like the rest, opened from the arcade round the patio. It was pleasant and comfortable and for an amazingly low price boasted a private bathroom with a shower-bath and the indispensable and inevitable bidet. From the bed I could look into the cool patio shaded by bamboo screens laid on wires across the top. Despite the bamboo canopy, birds came into the patio and flitted happily among the shrubs and palms which stood about in pots, faintly reminiscent, though not disturbingly so, of English sea-side winter gardens. The birds despised the bread I threw them because the roofs of adjoining houses were covered with golden grain drying in the sun. I had scarcely ever stayed in such a pleasant place. Part of its fascination lay in the knowledge that this oasis of quiet was in the very middle of Marrakesh's bustling life, and that just down the stairs was all the thrill of the Djemaa el Fna—the Meeting Place of the Dead.

This translation of the Arabic name referred to the days of former glory in Marrakesh when enemies of the Sultan were silenced by the simple process of having their heads chopped off. The heads were salted and displayed round the square as a deterrent to others. Who-ever named the square as the Meeting Place of the Dead had more than a touch of irony in his humour. Modern Marrakesh is unchanged in many respects, but completely so in that one. The absence of salted heads in no way detracted from its air of urgency spiced here and there with a nice dash of barbarism.

Djemaa el Fna was the meeting-place of the very-much-alive, an enormous and popular fairground where, instead of roundabouts and switchbacks, much more exotic entertainment drew the crowds, who never tired of listening to the story-tellers, watching the glass eaters, or of shouting encouragement to the frenzied snake-charmers, or of eating and drinking from the rows of booths before going back to follow the conjurers and dancers. I never tired of it either, for each of the groups in the square contained first-class performers.

People went to Fez to study and pray and listen to Islamic scholars in the cool tiled spaces of the amazing Merinide architecture. But they descended on Marrakesh to enjoy themselves, to abandon themselves to the rhythm of African drums and African enchanters. The noise of the drums beat in the air, a non-stop throbbing whose summons to join the thronging square was irresistible.

I joined a circle of people, nearly all in *djellabas*, intently gathered around a group of tumblers. The inner ring where they performed was made by children sitting on the ground, attention rapt, faces solemn and laughing by turns. They gasped or clapped as the tumblers went through permutations and combinations of balance and speed. Behind the children rows of older boys and men stood, their eyes following the lightning movements of three men and two young boys in pink satin shirts and yellow pantaloons who somersaulted and stood on each other's heads and climbed to each other's shoulders to make pyramids, and who sped round the admiring circle in cartwheels, all to the music of three drummers and two flutes. The chief tumbler carried on a stock patter with the crowd. He stopped in the middle of a fantastic gymnastic feat and shot a question at the audience. Back came the answer in unison, the children shouting at the top of their excited voices. They all knew. They had seen it all before dozens of times. And they all loved every dazzling minute of it.

Behind us two blind youths sat on the ground chanting poetry, but the story-tellers had bigger audiences. These clever men were not so much story-tellers as actors, being both narrators and characters. Again, the childen sat inside the circle of adults, mouths open with suspense, little hands clasping and unclasping as the hero or villain of the piece lived out their destiny in the story-teller's various voices. Usually, a foreigner was an attraction that children could not resist. But they did not even notice me at the fringe of the story-teller's circle.

Most of the stories were old and well tried and had possibly been told for generation after generation in the square at Marrakesh. Tiny girls with boot-button eyes and old men shaking with age sat enthralled at the tales of love and death, of ancient princes poisoned by rivals, stories of fiery steeds and brave deeds, and even stories of modern travellers lost in snowdrifts up in the mountains seen from the square. Certainly one of the story-tellers would be relating yet once more the tale about the Battle of the Three Kings when Dom Sebastian of Portugal put up a puppet sultan against old Abd El Malik and all three were killed.

This historical tale also fascinated European authors at the time. British dramatists seized eagerly on the famous sixteenth-century battle. George Peele wrote the *Tragicall Battell of Alcazar in Barbarie*. Shakespeare and Ben Jonson were most contemptuous of the play, though Dryden found it useful a century later when he came to write his own *Don Sebastian*. In 1673 Elkanah Settle (the Doeg of Dryden's *Absalom and Achitophel*) wrote *The Empress of Morocco*. Although both Dryden and Duffet tore the play to shreds, it had good success in London. Duffet even went to the length of writing a parody on the play. He called his parody by the same name and the concluding lines from this second *The Empress of Morocco* have given a jingle known to every generation of British children since:

> *Rosemary's green*
> *Rosemary's green*
> *Derry derry down,*
> *When I am king*
> *You shall be queen,*
> *Derry derry down.*

Some of the stories the children listened to in Djemaa el Fna were read from tattered books which looked like seventeenth-century copies, but which were probably much more reliable history-wise than Settle's subsequent *Heir of Morocco* which had a long run at the Theatre Royal in London. Ahmed the Golden, who ruled Marrakesh after the famous battle, was far more distinguished than the three kings who were killed and earned their fame in European dramas. Ahmed was a better subject for stories because he was a powerful king who also bore the name El Mansour—The Victorious—as did his predecessor of the same title who built the great Koutoubia near the Djemaa el Fna.

Although I could understand nothing, I found myself listening with intense fascination, my attention drawn by the rise and fall of the voice and by its inflexion, its warmth or anger or cajolery, all of which came across perfectly well, though I could follow no thread of story. That was how I had heard Karen Blixen talking at a friend's house near Copenhagen. This great story-teller had not realized I knew no Danish and so she told tales in her own language to the company, and though I could not follow, I sat under the spell of her voice and expression. The story-tellers of Marrakesh held me in the same way, and I remembered Karen Blixen, who was dead by the time of my visit to Morocco.

I think she would have loved the story-tellers, whose magic even made the water-sellers put their wobbly goatskin bags on the ground and forget about ringing their bells as, once again, the brave tale was told of Ahmed el Mansour going out to conquer Timbuktu in 1579, when the red city of Marrakesh was a royal capital swarming with slaves who carried back the spoils of war, gold and precious stones, silks and ostrich plumes, besides lion cubs to be trained as guards for yet more slaves.

But the dark-skinned water-carrier would never tire of hearing about his ancestral homeland far beyond the High Atlas Mountains, south even of the great *sahara*, the desert. Perhaps it would all seem a little mythical to him, because for centuries now there had been no racial divisions in Morocco, nothing to make the negro different from the Arab sitting with pride and elegance on a fine horse caparisoned with embroidered saddle-cloths behind us. Nothing, that is, except appearance, for the negro's full features and dreamy, far-away expression contrasted with the aquiline face and sharp eyes of the Arab. And many Berbers in the square had yet another racial influence, for their cheekbones were high and prominent and their smoky eyes were almond-shaped, strongly hinting at Mongolian origins.

Many of the boys listening to the story-tellers had their heads completely shaven, a great number of others had their hair cut into an extraordinary kind of topiary, part shaven, part left but cut into shapes. Boys with this Mohican hair-do looked like first-year students in some Brazilian universities who were barbered in this way to prevent them by force from putting on airs. Humiliation was not the reason for the Moroccan children's haircuts, but superstition, linked with religious beliefs and the saints of the *marabouts*.

A small boy with only one ringlet behind his ear on an otherwise shaved head, or the small girl likewise shaved except for a tuft sprouting from the crown of her head, did not think their hair comic at all, especially when compared with the blond wigs worn by men dressed as women who entertained their uproarious audience by contortions and female impersonations of a bawdy kind.

Quack doctors squatting about the square had busy practices, judging by the number of consultations they made and the amounts of queer-looking powders and potions they dispensed. Many of their prescriptions were simply written charms. The doctors' tinsmith assistants made small flat containers from thin sheets of metal and before the patient's very eyes enclosed the charm in the container which the patient would then wear on a string round his neck. Other charms consisted of amulets made from old rags. Horoscopes did a roaring trade, though these were already printed on a piece of paper, and had merely to be folded and kissed by the astrologer's assistant into yet another flat brass locket for wearing round yet another brown neck. Women fortune-tellers had as many clients as the quack doctors and horoscope men. Their art involved the pretence of half-trances, the hearing of inaudible voices and a peering into amber stones which were turned round and round in the seer's hands to catch the sinking sun and to study the reflection of the person being fortune-told. This done, sentence was pronounced, but in a whisper privately delivered into the client's ear, for others were waiting their turn.

But nothing was better than the snake-charmers, not even the incredibly skilled bicycle acrobat who performed amazing feats of balance and judgement of eye and muscle and who concluded his act by standing blindfold on the saddle while the bicycle free-wheeled with gradually decreasing speed round the inner circle of children. His was a skill I had not seen even in the great European circuses. But neither had the great circuses any animal acts comparable with the Djemaa el Fna's snake-charmers.

Far from being a phoney affair specially got up for tourists, the snake-charmers' main appeal was to Moroccan audiences. Foreign onlookers rouse little curiosity. The charmers drew their audiences from the Berbers and Arabs, old Jews and tall Sudanese. They also engaged in mumbo-jumbo peculiar to their calling, but I had to change the earlier, sceptical view I held in Tangier about snake-charmers. I could not then believe that the snakes were not emasculated, deprived of their fangs and poison sacs and drugged prior to the performance. But in this cynical and suspicious approach I not only underestimated the charmer's art but his audience's intelligence, too.

'Do you think we would watch harmless serpents?'

Blushingly I confessed that I *had* thought that. But the indignant young Moroccan who was in Marrakesh on vacation from university in Switzerland put me right. The thrill of the snake-charmers lay precisely in the danger. There was always a chance that they would be bitten. They used the most deadly snakes, the hooded cobra capella, the small *gartita*, the puff-adder, and the much-feared *ausat*.

'If you don't believe me,' smiled the student, 'go to the Christian cemetery.'

There lay, he said, the remains of other doubters about the snakes. One of them had been a German actress who died after proffering her hand to one of the snakes in the Djemaa el Fna. I was not prepared to test my scepticism. It was much easier to take the snake-charmers in good faith. After all, the audiences kept their distance from the reptiles, and even the charmer never let his brood out of sight until they were safely shut in their boxes.

Moroccan snake-charmers were, in fact, much more than wandering showmen who had picked up a few half-dead animals to do tricks in the market-place. They drew the largest crowds because they were Aissaouas to whom Allah had given the great honour of dealing with the serpent which brought about man's expulsion from the Garden of Eden. The snake-charmers' patron saint was none other than the same Sidi ben Aissa whose followers cut themselves and danced to a frenzy, the sect which so fascinated my friend Omar in Meknes. The tribesmen who were selected as snake-charmers were also distinguished by long, wild hair, for most Moslems kept their hair extremely short.

For all that Allah gave the Aissaouas protection from these creatures made in the devil's image, the snake-charmers took extra precautions themselves, just to be sure. Slashing your limbs with a knife while in a frenzy and drinking boiling water were one thing. Snakes were another. And so the charmers immunized themselves as far as possible against the effects of snake-bites, which occur far more often than might be supposed. Certain herbs afforded partial safety and after a number of years snake-bites themselves induced a degree of immunity. A bite which would be fatal to somebody not so immunized merely made the snake-charmer unconscious for a day or two.

The snake-charmers always had their own bands. The drums rattled out exotic rhythms, and flutes played weird snake music to the accompaniment of a medieval-looking lute. The snakes did not appear to be particularly charmed by the music. With great solemnity, not altogether surprising under the circumstances, the leader described a circle in the dust and one by one released the snakes from their boxes. He dared anyone of the audience to step inside the ring. But nobody did. As he stepped into it himself he uttered a prayer loudly enough for all to hear: 'May Allah protect me and Mohammed assist me.' Like one voice the audience responded '*Amin*'—may it be so. It was so, when I saw it.

Djemaa el Fna hummed and throbbed with music, not only from the groups of snake-charmers but from the bands accompanying the buffoons and the Chleuh dancers. There were singers also, playing for themselves on strange stringed instruments with the softest, sweetest, most haunting wisps of melancholy sound. But most of all the drums vibrated in the warm, darkening evening. As the whole sky flamed with the glory of the westerly sun, turning the pink buildings into glowing coals, the square reverberated with the cross-rhythms of the endless drumming. And the drums went on when the stars came out like diamonds on black velvet. The drums' notes were carried by the faint breezes which nightfall brought when the men pulled the high-pointed hoods of the *djellabas* over their heads as they moved among the performing monkeys and unwearying story-tellers who could go on for a thousand and one nights.

In the gathering darkness flares were lit on the booths and stalls where sticky cakes and sweetmeats were stacked, where smoke from the kebab grills hung darkly on the air, and where mountains of freshly cooked snails appeared, piled like pebbles in huge pans. The charcoal fires glowed under the boiling-pans and the piles of delicacies were subjected to the probing pins of rich and poor alike. I went to my patio room at eleven o'clock, long before the food stalls closed down, and as I took a shower and slipped between crisp sheets the noise of drums filtered faintly in and finally lulled me to sleep. But when I went on to the roof terrace at nine the next morning they were still going and crowds had already collected around what appeared to be the same groups of dancers and story-tellers.

The Meeting Place of the Dead was L-shaped and the *medina* bordered its rows of booths and colourful projecting sunshades.

PAVILION'D IN SPLENDOUR

Above the low, dense mass of pinkish-brown-red buildings cypresses and jacarandas reached up in unexpected splotches of green, and everywhere the asterisks of palms punctuated the landscape of jumbled flat roofs. From the C.T.M. terrace I could see all the morning activities of the square. Just below me old buses were being loaded up, the usual odd assortment of luggage and animals being fastened on the top. In contradiction of the age-old aspects of the place, more mopeds and bicycles than donkeys weaved among the crowds. Live chickens and pigeons were tied to the handlebars. Even the hand-barrows were rubber tyred and some of the barrows were mounted with huge lurid placards advertising the latest attractions of the Marrakesh cinemas. And though most men wore *djellabas*, there was a complement of jeans and tee-shirts, and the postmen went about their deliveries in khaki uniforms and flat blue caps. The High Atlas had withdrawn behind low, hazy cloud, but a line of foothills remained clear, a reminder that Marrakesh sits at the footstool of the great mountain throne.

No high buildings could be seen from the roof terrace, though five minarets projected from the jostling houses of the old city set within its wide fringe of palm groves. Because the French had kept their modern town well away from the ancient one, the giant presence of the Koutoubia mosque could be felt, a mighty symbol of Allah's all-pervading presence. The tower looked down loftily upon the writhing snakes and the tireless drummers and upon the blind men chanting for alms, as it had looked long ago on the grisly salted heads displayed in the Meeting Place of the Dead.

But the great minaret also reached up to heaven, a salutary reminder of judgement to come and of the light by which intellect may conquer the darkness of pagan superstition. Mathematics again informed this tower's design, which ascended in seven stories. The red sandstone walls were panelled and indented with geometrical designs and the interesting blind tracery associated with Moorish architecture. The Koutoubia tower had been built roughly contemporarily with its sister towers, the Hassan, which I had seen in Rabat, and the Giralda in Seville. Christian slaves built the Koutoubia 800 years ago, working at its pointed arches, laying the massive stones course by course until the topmost level, where a white mast,

171

threaded with three golden spheres, pierced the glaring African sky.

The masonry was not as regular as that of the Hassan, but the curiously Gothic character was similar. In spite of the Koutoubia minaret being complete and still used in connexion with its mosque, and although it was taller than the Hassan, I was not so imbued with a sense of power and grandeur as with the mighty remains overlooking the river at Rabat. Perhaps the setting for the Hassan Tower and its suggestion of former splendour increased its monumentality. Seen from a dozen miles away the Koutoubia was also a dramatic sight. But from close at hand it lacked some quality which the Hassan possessed.

Nevertheless, in its own setting of Marrakesh, the Koutoubia presided over the city with magnificence. Its designer had mastered not only the technical difficulties of tower-building but the subtler difficulties of aesthetic design. In this sense the Koutoubia proportions were perfect, giving a sense of rightness, neither too slim nor too squat, neither too heavy nor too light. This just, nice balance between the technical and visual demands, between the need for stone to be expressed as a heavy solid material and the contrary desire that a tower should soar, distinguished both the Koutoubia and the Hassan. And it may have been in this that they were Gothic, rather than in their use of decorative motifs which later appeared in medieval northern Europe.

The Saadian kings also made Marrakesh their royal capital and graced the city with fine architecture. Arts of all kinds flourished under their patronage and one palace was especially splendid, El Bedi—The Marvel. Unfortunately many of these wonders were wilfully destroyed by order of Moulay Ismail. He was jealous of them. When he succeeded to the throne in 1672, a throne which Moulay Ismail's brother had won from the last Saadian king some years earlier, he had their principal buildings in Marrakesh pulled down, including the marvellous El Bedi. The African Sun King could not bear that Marrakesh should possess finer buildings than his own new ones in Meknes. Though the new walls and palaces at Meknes, deliberately intended to rival Louis XIV's megalomania at Versailles, were extensive and impressive, none of them was as fine a work as the beautifully carved and decorated courts and arcades and ceilings the Saadians brought about in Marrakesh.

Moulay Ismail's intemperate jealousy might well have left not a stone of the marvels standing but for his religious fear of disturbing the Saadian royal tombs. While wrecking almost everything else, he merely had the tombs and their beautiful mausoleums walled up. And so they remained, first forgotten, and then entirely unknown for over two centuries, until 1917, when they were discovered again.

Although the Saadian tomb pavilions represented only a fraction of the original palace buildings, their excellence suggests that if the same high art invested the whole palace complex it must certainly have been one of the world's masterpieces of architecture. As it is, the pavilions, opened up by skilful restoration into the walled gardens, are one of those great works, small, precise and jewel-like, which breathe an ineffable beauty through the centuries, as fresh today as the day they were built. The temple of the Wingless Victory on the Acropolis is one, and so is Ange-Jaques Gabriel's Petit Trianon at Versailles, with the chapter house at Southwell Minster as yet another. Though sharing nothing in terms of ideals or motifs, such works have in common a timeless perfection.

The Saadian tomb pavilions belong to this elect company of art works which are in the same relationship to the major monumental architectural masterpieces as the quartet is to the symphony. Like other buildings of this illustrious kind, the Saadian tombs seem to be a conjunction of all that is finest in the art and craftsmanship of a particular style, period and place, and yet, paradoxically, by the very means of the restrictions, to take on a universal and ageless quality.

I found my way to the tomb pavilions through a narrow passage beside the huge El Mansour mosque, close to the city walls. The mosque was caged in scaffolding and undergoing repairs. High doors stood ajar in the long blank wall topped by deep, corbelled eaves, but I could get no more than a glimpse of the courtyard. Access to the tombs was normally through the mosque, but this being an impossible route for infidels, a passage had been cut through the enclosing walls to by-pass the mosque. The way had been specially cut for Marshal Lyautey to visit the tombs after their rediscovery.

The narrow passage gave on to a delightful formal garden enclosed by high walls. Projecting into the garden were the tomb pavilions, plain outside but rich inside. They opened by means of elaborately moulded Moorish arches directly into the garden court, so that it was possible to stand on a garden path and peer into the high chambers. When my eyes adjusted from the dazzling sunlight I could see the exquisitely wrought surfaces so beloved of Moorish craftsmen, and a fine, strong sense of spatial proportion not always found with fine carving and decoration.

In the first pavilion I saw square domes supported on four free-standing columns. These were marble monoliths with subtly tapered shafts. Other chambers opened from the pavilion, revealing further complex geometrical decoration through two side doors with carved panels. The ceilings were coffered with intricate miniature vaulting resembling stalactite formations, an impression reinforced by the dull glitter of gilding like the glint of minerals in living rock.

Each of the tomb pavilions was different, though similar in that they were all lofty, pierced by arches and crowned by fantastic ceilings. The most fabulous of these was of cedar, composed of small pieces most skilfully laminated and jointed. I never knew which to admire more, the cedar ceilings or those with miniature vaulting whose myriad concavities were gilded or painted white and blue and green.

John Bentley's Westminster Cathedral came to mind as I wandered about the Saadian tombs, for their profusion of marble worked in delicate reliefs was similar to much of the vigorous pseudo-Byzantine which Bentley employed in his great church. Although architecturally not dissimilar to Westminster's cathedral, the Saadian tombs were positively *dis*similar to Westminster's abbey. The tombs of the English abbey are not only monuments to their occupants but to their creators also, the whole effect being akin to a chamber of horrors, not in a wax-works but in a marble-works. By contrast the actual tombs of the Saadian kings and their descendants were modest in size and sculpturally sparse, being merely moulded slabs set in the floor. Yet somehow their simplicity was more eloquent than Westminster Abbey's monuments. The Saadian kings rest beneath delicately carved marble only a few inches high, decorated with nothing more than Koranic inscriptions. The glory was in the lofty, airy chambers over them.

In the Hall of the Three Niches the royal children lay, a sad story of early deaths told movingly by the grave slabs which were shorter than those of the royal parents. Looking at the ivory-coloured marble I could almost see their beautiful young faces as pale as the marble, their bright boot-button eyes dulled in death. Birds flitted through the Hall and I was glad that Moulay Ismail's wall had been removed, letting in scented airs from the garden.

Ahmed the Golden himself lay in another pavilion more splendid than the rest. His tomb slab resembled the others, but was railed off by a simple wooden bar on which some tattooed women sat chatting in subdued voices. Birds flew in here also, and from the garden courtyard the garrulous chirping of sparrows vied with workmen's hammers going about the careful business of preservation and restoration. No doubt the royal children had chased the sparrows which then, as now, were probably a mixture of the house sparrow with the Spanish and Italian species. It was difficult in Morocco to distinguish between them in certain areas and this gave reason to suspect a widespread hybridization, although in many places Spanish and house sparrows could be found breeding locally, maintaining separate habitats and behaving as entirely different species.

The garden courtyard and pavilions of the kings' tombs would alone justify a visit to Marrakesh. The Koutoubia tower and the market-place excitement of the Djemaa el Fna were the city's most famous attractions. But to see the Saadian tombs was an experience that vibrated in the memory long after the din of the market-place's drummers ceased to throb in the inner ear. The tombs, though built for death, spoke clearly of life, for they proved that the finest feelings of humankind may spring up and blossom anywhere in any age, no matter what darkness or horrors swamp the rest of the world. The gardens, walled on one side of the old bastions of the city, induced such contemplation. Their atmosphere was cloistral and calm. Even the workmen with their wooden mallets, carefully tapping the green and white tiles of tombs scattered among the trees and rosemary hedges and the agaves shrouded in spiders' webs, seemed to know that this place was different from any other.

I left the way I had come, going out into the *medina* by the narrow passage where cupolas over the tombs peeped above the walls. The birds inside the courtyard were luckier than those I saw outside in the *medina*, where captive live ones were for sale. I could not tell whether the greenfinches were being bought as songsters or as food. The boys buying them seemed concerned only to spread their wings to see the amount of yellow on the plumage. They cost less than a penny each. On my return to London I spent a Sunday morning in Club Row, Bethnal Green, where unringed chaffinches fetched £3, white-throats £2, when the R.S.P.C.A. inspector was out of sight.

Wandering slowly along the twisting streets, I saw an increasing number of men wearing black skullcaps and from this I knew the Jewish *mellah* must be close by. Here also I saw plenty of birds, but dead ones this time, hung in various states of decay round the doors of quack doctors' booths. Rotten heads of vultures hung between great-crested lizards, horns of gazelles and wild sheep to be burnt for curing boils and scabs, fennec and macaque skins, ground-up crickets and powdered grasshoppers, camel hoofs and many magical owls, besides dried chameleons used as a snake-bite antidote, and anti-leprosy tortoise meat, iris roots for ulcers, Jews' mallow powerful in love as well as curing cravings for hemp, and squills called Pharaoh's onions. There were nameless powders and seeds all waiting for customers whose amours needed the stimulations of love potions and ointments and those in despair of getting a child or lover. I thought of Omar and Chedlya in Meknes. These concoctions displayed in heaps and jars and boxes and bottles were an unbelievable survival from primitive times. I was told that the ingredients must always include dried snake to ensure that any baby was a boy.

One street in the *medina* specialized in old rubber tyres. With the skill of hand which seemed to be a Moroccan birthright, the thousands of worn-out motor tyres were converted into horse harness and sandals and hundreds of three-foot-high water jars complete with rubber lids like Jersey jugs. The sickening stench of rubber was more than I could bear, and though invited in to see the rubbery conversions I tactfully but firmly declined and instead availed myself of another invitation, this time into a room opening from another street.

Brown cubes—a village in the west High Atlas

White squares—Rabat, capital by the sea

Dismounted nomads
near the Sahara

Mounted tribesmen
near Khemisset

Fifty children, between 3 and 7 years old, sat cross-legged on the floor. They all smiled or waved when their schoolmaster, in a Berber blue gown and yellow cap, beckoned me in. Some of the children tried to catch my special attention by winking or pulling faces or gesticulating when they thought the teacher was not looking. Most of them held wooden boards with Arabic lessons on them like eighteenth-century hornbooks in England. Others were writing with a bamboo stylus dipped in sepia, and I saw their beautiful Arabic calligraphy. They penned a few words and then handed it to the schoolmaster for approval. Their writing done, they began to recite from the Koran, swaying to and fro to the rising and falling cadences of the Holy Book's wild, flowing poetry. I stepped over their white plastic sandals piled up near the door and departed with the Koran chorus following me down the street.

Sounds from the *medina*'s streets stayed in my mind as well as sights. Later that night, when I came out from the last performance in a travelling theatre near the square, I was caught in a procession winding slowly through the *medina*. A long snake of people were doing something like an Afro-Brazilian samba in Rio de Janeiro's carnival. Behind the dancers eight small boys pulled a cart on which a live sheep, on its way to a sacrifice, was held down by other small boys. Also on the cart was a large silver tray full of oranges spiked with incense sticks. Another tray bore three or four dozen lighted candles, and elaborate silver dishes like goblets with domed lids. One of the boys gave me a candle to light. Holding my lighted candle I joined the procession and went with it a short way. But although we collected other people along the way, I discreetly dropped off.

I had no idea what the celebration was all about and it might be embarrassing to find myself at the door of a mosque or involved in some religious ceremony in a private house. So I slipped away unnoticed and went back to the C.T.M. roof terrace.

I felt like a Saadian king as I surveyed the city by night. The kings' sleep had been a long one. I hoped that mine would not be. I had fallen in love with their red capital and wanted to see it again in the morning before going farther south, into the regions Ahmed the Golden passed through to wage a holy war on the Niger.

9

The Flowering Desert

Ouarzazate was reached by the most dramatic road in Morocco. Between Marrakesh the Red and the Berber town 130 miles away on the edge of the Sahara the immense barrier of the High Atlas intervened. Normally the same distance across the plains by the miles-long stretches of straight road would have taken three or four hours. But with the mountain peaks to negotiate we did not reach Ouarzazate until 9 p.m., even though we left the C.T.M. station in Marrakesh punctually at 1 p.m.

From the beginning the journey was auspicious. Quite early on I saw my first roller. The large jay-like bird was sitting on a telegraph wire displaying his magnificent light azure plumage and his bright russet back. We passed six of these beautiful birds at various points on the way. They all chose telegraph wires as a fine perch from which to spot juicy grasshoppers. When they swooped on their prey there was a burst of colour as their vivid blue wings bordered with black flashed through the air. The bee-eater was even more sumptuous, though the brilliant yellow and blue-green feathers were not so seldom seen this side of Marrakesh as in the palm groves on the Casablanca road.

Whole landscapes were as exotically hued as the rollers and bee-eaters. Slowly we left the plain behind and came into a mountain world of ochre and sulphur. Villages were poised on promontories, and donkeys struggled up the long twisting roads, carrying their masters to some absurdly balanced settlement on the edge of a precipice. The bus engine ground slower and slower, the gears growled more frequently as we came laboriously into still higher and steeper hills. At these cool heights so many trees flourished that the landscape was like Christmas gift wrappings. Many of the flanks in the red sandstone and black schist were covered with old forests of ilex and thuya. From such forests as these the Almohades had taken thuya for the roofs of their mosques and palaces in Spain. Thyine wood was listed amongst the riches of the earth in the Revelation of St. John the Divine, and was the *arbor vitae* of Theophrastus. A table made from the enlarged trunk base measuring ten hand-breadths wide was worth its weight in gold to the Patricians.

We came into the rugged heart of the High Atlas. Here aeons of eruptions and erosion had faulted and formed the rock masses into fantastic shapes. Long ago the rock was scooped and swirled, scarred and swooped up into cones and pinnacles. The flanks, dotted with thuya and firs and juniper, were littered with gigantic boulders fallen from towering heights. Here also the rock changed colour and a dirty yellow suffused the laminated strata.

Shuddering and straining, the bus pulled several hours later into Taddert, a brown mountain village with brown hills rising above it. Some of the passengers knelt at the roadside to say their prayers. I was the only one unaccustomed to the sight. A peculiar gracefulness attended the saying of prayers, when the worshipper, kneeling on a mat or cloth opened his hands, touched the lobes of his ears with his thumbs and pronounced 'God is Great.' With solemnity and humility the hands were folded and a recitation of the Koran's first chapter was begun privately to themselves. Rising towards Mecca, whose direction everyone seemed to know instinctively, they muttered 'The perfection of the Lord, the Great.' I watched the travellers at Taddert discreetly, not wishing to intrude or disturb them by my curiosity. They made a final prostration, face to the ground, where hens fought over the eggshells from our meal. With a glance over the right shoulder and the words 'Peace be unto you' and a repetition of this over the left shoulder, the prayers were concluded.

Taddert's highest building proudly possessed a stork's nest. Most of the village was of single-story houses, built of stone, with iron bars or grilles instead of glass in the windows, and roofs of thatch overlaid by dried mud. It was a cool and charming village like a film

179

set for an adventure story. The village elders sat on the rough pavement raised above the road, drinking mint tea and gossiping or playing draughts. They were friendly, but we could not talk because they could speak no French or English. Blue rock thrushes and subalpine warblers were singing clear, liquid music. The birds probably bred as far up as those heights. I was reminded of whitethroats by the warblers' song, but it was without the hard, scolding notes. The pink breast and white moustachial stripe of the cock did not show itself until we left the village and passed along the maize terraces by the river.

After Taddert the hills became red again, and green shelves with rich crops ran along the crimson mountainsides. A damp sulphurous scrub here and there showed hidden springs trying to seep through. The country was wild and the road wound for miles round a continuous series of hairpin bends, one leading directly into the next, each more treacherous than the last. Stupendous views opened on all sides, but I did not care to look downwards. The Tizi N'Tichka Pass, at 8,380 feet, was the climax, and from a narrow tendon of mountain no wider than the road and with sheer drops on either side, we commanded a grand, barbaric landscape. Rays of the setting sun pierced through gaps and gorges in the scoured rocks, striking through with straight beams bright as swords of silver. Although the fresh and sweet mountain air blew in the bus windows, storm-wrecked oaks showed how the hot, suffocating simoom rushing in from the Sahara ravaged these valleys.

Across the skyline the cables of a ski-lift drooped between its pylons like fine-spun fibres. But as we drew nearer I saw that this was no ski-lift, though in winter the snow-covered slopes became a haunt of skiers. Rich deposits of manganese were mined on these lonely heights and the cables belonged to the overhead chain of buckets which carried the ore from mine to transport for the coast. I caught a glimpse of a miners' camp, and the road, now tilting gradually downwards, betrayed the presence of modern technology by its signs and prefabricated buildings. At several stops along the way, boys came to the bus offering coloured crystals of minerals for sale.

Our grinding climb was done and now the driver speeded as if in relief at our safe progress round the horrible hairpins and precipitous drops. Now that we were descending the long southern flanks of the High Atlas the land formations changed again. Whole valleys had been terraced and planted with maize and barley. In imitation of the layered landscape, villages were terraced also. The houses, flat-roofed and square, joined homogeneously together, their roofs making a flat pattern of planes, interrupted here and there by open, internal courtyards. And in this stretch also the mountain ridges, red against the late afternoon sky, were terraced by geological formations which curiously resembled the humanized landscape of the lower slopes.

Fortress-like shapes and long rows of serrated rock ran for miles along these ridges, giving them the appearance of castellated battlements. It looked as if the Crusaders had been up there building great walls. I thought of their castles in Greece, and how similar the hilltop walls at Argos and Corinth were to these natural forms in the High Atlas. The terraced fields seemed to be protected by these castles of rock. Women were herding in the fields below, and in their wide straw hats they looked like ancient Mexican Indians, so that the rock castles became Aztec temples in my fancy.

But more was to come, as if perception was drug-stimulated. The mescalin visions of the Aztecs could hardly have been more fantastic than those I now experienced simply by peering through the bus window. We had come at last to the flat barren expanses leading to the Sahara. This was not sand but sun-baked earth and rock, running flat to a red-hot horizon where the sky was molten gold gushing from the crucible mouth of the sun itself. The world was in flames. But only for a moment. The sun hovered in its west-bound trajection and suddenly solidified into a cool ball of gold suspended in a void. Then a slow transmutation began, a magical transformation of this pro-Saharan region into a monochrome of crimsons where vermilions melted into carmines, where flamingo pinks flushed to *couleur de rose*, where the deepest magenta merged with the reds of a cardinal's cloak. The barren earth, buildings, rocks and hilly outcrops, gullies and dried watercourses floated in a crimson continuum.

The most striking characteristic of this dry region was the architecture made of mud bricks in age-old traditional ways by the people themselves. Walls were thick, pierced only by tiny openings which kept out the worst heat of the day and retained heat during the cool night. Each house consisted of a collection of cubes and prisms, and each group of buildings, whether a farm or a whole village, was a large cluster of these cubes. The walls were battered, diminishing towards the top, where the parapets were worked into miniature battlements. Such an effect was not accidental, for the tiny settlements were fortified and used defensively until quite recently, when marauders and enemy tribes swept plundering across the plains.

The first sight of this oddly abstract, sculptural architecture had occurred in the mountains when the bus stopped by a roadside farmhouse like a miniature castle. Thinking back afterwards, I could see that the mountains there had given a hint of the strange sunset, for they were the reddest so far seen in the High Atlas. But at that stage of the journey the land was still fertile and a river ran through the valley. It was dry with summer drought and children walked home to their villages, picking their way among the litter of boulders. But once free of the mountains down to the fringes of the Sahara the curious architecture was everywhere, unchanged since Biblical times and entirely different from Morocco north of the Atlas.

The villages merged into the sun-baked plains, for the mud bricks they were made of was the ochrous earth itself. Their forms stood up from the earth as though eruptions of it, strangely echoing the ranges of scarred hills which stood, similarly isolated, on the plane of the half-desert like objects in a Surrealist painting. Trails of green cultivation lurked in hidden indentations in the parched earth, flourishing only near the castle clusters of the villages. I could hardly believe that any water could be found in such a sun-blasted place.

Ouarzazate's twinkling lights showed up for miles, and at last, stiff and tired, and thinking principally of food and bed, I got out of the bus. I found the night unexpectedly warm. The town was small and full of Germans and Frenchmen, straw-haired and straw-skinned, slightly absurd with their exaggerated Hemingway sort of toughness. Their cars and trucks showed they had either just crossed the Sahara or were about to do so.

Ouarzazate was one of the last outposts of comfort and civilization before the desert rigours began. Because it was one of Morocco's first towns on the north side of the Sahara an army camp had been built there. Three small hotels by the camp were all full of hardy Hemingway heroes and one-night-stand tourists, and reluctantly I climbed a hill to the posh Grand Hotel du Sud run by the National Tourist Board. This, too, was crammed, mostly by French tourists. On the way up I had spotted some caves in the roadside rock. Thoughts of a troglodyte night came into my mind, but before I had time to dispel them Mohamed Zouak, the Grand Hotel manager, appeared. I was tired, frustrated and touchy and in quite the opposite mood to the charm and concern of the young manager. Would I care to have a drink, he suggested, while he tried to sort things out. Coca-Cola rushed icily over my parched larynx. Perhaps, I thought, he will let me sleep in this arm-chair. Five minutes later I was shown into a magnificent suite reserved upon the strictest priority for V.I.P.s.

'*La chambre du Roi*,' said the old negro major-domo as he put down my shabby canvas bag, which was still bloody from the bus accident.

Though this was the V.I.P. suite, I washed some nylon socks and was amazed to find them dry in half an hour. Dryness, I was to discover, was the secret of Ouarzazate. Dehydration was the secret of its land, its architecture, its bearable heat of 120° F. or more. The slightest suggestion of humidity would have rendered the climate quite insupportable. But the dry air saved the blazing sun from being a killer—at least in the shade.

Shade was what I mostly sought in Ouarzazate next day. I walked carefully, plotting my way from tree shadow, to shadow of wall, to dappled shade of an avenue to the comforting shade of a café awning. I sat in the shady lounge and talked to the manager, Mohamed Zouak. He was only 24 years old, already experienced in hotel management. Besides his own native Berber and Arabic and excellent English, Mohamed was fluent in French and Spanish, and was learning German. He had a staff of thirty and still found time to talk to guests, answering their inquiries about journey routes and accommodation prospects in other towns of the region. Young Mohamed, who was a lighter-toned reproduction of Harry Belafonte, certainly knew how to make a big hotel tick over with a machine-like efficiency, and yet be friendly and intimate at the same time.

The Dra region in which Ouarzazate stood had been called the Valley of Olives by old Arab historians. The Saadian dynasty came from the Dra, and it was not impossible that the unusually fine sense of architecture those kings had, derived in the first instance from contact with the amazing kasbahs and fortified houses of this southern area. There were so many of the mud citadel villages that in some places they almost joined together. If they had any influence on the taste of the Saadian kings, it would have been in clarity of form and richness of texture rather than in motif, because the Dra architecture is unique in Morocco, owning to no influences other than its own long tradition. The villages have a kind of barbarism about them, a wildness of primitive desert life which was old when Volubilis and Fez were new. They belonged to times contemporary with earliest Biblical history, when Moses and Abraham counted riches by herds. This architecture recalled Sardis rather than Athens, for the kasbahs around Ouarzazate have the same quality as the acropolis of the kings of Lydia rather than the mathematical precision of fine marble in the Athens of Pericles.

Olive groves there may well have been in the days when Elizabeth I of England addressed Ahmed the Golden as 'Our Brother after the Law of Crown and Sceptre', but these have since given way to date palms and the tamarisk. This feathery, dusty tree was put to more use than merely fuelling the bakers' ovens as elsewhere in Morocco. I saw women collecting the autumn *takaout* from the tamarisk. *Takaouts* were galls made by a fly which injected its eggs into the leaves, and they contained a high proportion of tanning dye used by the men on leather and by the old women on their leathery faces and feet.

I went elephant-hunting after breakfast—not the big-game sort but the elephant shrew, a small creature whose name refers to its long thin snout rather than its mere ten inches of length. These odd creatures had misproportioned hind-legs which resulted in a kangaroo appearance. Such shrews had been displayed in a Marrakesh herbalist's, where I had learned that they were used against fever, a story no more incredible than the thousands of people going through life with pieces of paper round their necks for amulets like those I saw for sale in the Djemaa el Fna.

Some of these writing-medicines were eaten, especially if a holy man had scribbled the name of God or a Koranic text, and this could cure illnesses resulting from a neighbour's Evil Eye besides simple indigestion. Such writers were often hereditary saints descended from the Prophet. Since, however, Morocco is the Sherifian Empire, being a hereditary saint was not difficult. A small place like Moulay Idris had 2,000 Sherifs, descendants of Mohammed through his daughter Fatima. I could not accept the fire-doctors so readily, for, besides branding mules and asses as I had seen in Fez, they were still consulted for cauterization of the human body with weirdly shaped irons for different diseases.

Ouarzazate's people had more of Africa in them and had a more sultry complexion than their compatriots across the Marrakesh side of the High Atlas. Women carried water-pots and bundles on their heads, as much for shade as for carrying. A strong racial influence here came from the Haratins, a dark people whose origins were as much debated as those of the Berbers. From their appearance, Haratins clearly have strong connexions with both Berber and negro, and it was through his homeland of the Dra Valley that Ahmed the Golden returned with his enormous army victorious from the Niger war, bringing captives to be sold in slavery. Ouarzazate had always been on the important caravan routes going to and from the deep Sahara and had a slave market for Berber merchants.

A curiosity of Ouarzazate's light and atmosphere was its intense brilliance and clarity, due probably to the absence of suspended moisture and dust. Often in countries subject to fierce sun all colour and form drains away during the midday period, returning only with the sun's evening decline. But at Ouarzazate the sharpness of light and intensity of colour remained constant, producing a weird supernormal sense of perception. The scene was like a pre-Raphaelite painting where everything is just *too* real.

On the Sunday morning of my visit only the faintest of cooling zephyrs moved through the still air like ghosts of a breeze. But suddenly, in the afternoon a strong, warm wind sprang up which threshed the palms and tamarisks to and fro, and whistled through the hotel where, in my V.I.P. suite, I resorted to a long siesta. Shutters banged and dogs barked and dust flew like steam off the earth.

At half-past six the wind went as mysteriously as it had come, the palms were metal-stiff again and the dust vanished. Long shadows lay like bars over the barren land as I crunched across it to the kasbah.

Because this Berber architecture plays tricks with scale, and because the atmosphere's extreme clarity destroyed any sense of distance, I could not tell how far away the kasbah was. A long-robed figure walked beneath its sloping walls, and I was surprised to find myself much nearer than I thought at first. This upsetting of normal judgements was oddly disturbing. None of the previous evening's extraordinary crimson luminosity occurred again, though the kasbah walls turned pink against a background of olive-green hills whose hue merged with that of the green patches in the landscape. Narrow passages and open spaces and irregular houses piled up like sugar lumps hid behind the kasbah's rough protecting wall. Square towers and turrets stood up against the sky. Blank walls blinked with tiny slit windows, whose actual size was quite impossible to guess. All this barbaric forceful architecture was mud-made. Crude and vigorous patterns in relief filled the upper parts of walls and towers. On a swelling outcrop of rock opposite the kasbah's main gate was a threshing-floor and near by some cave-dwellers were tethering their donkeys for the night.

Back in town I shared a table at Chez Dimitris Restaurant out on the pavement with a Siamese couple on a lengthy world tour. They claimed the Dra Valley as the most spectacular landscape they had encountered in all Africa. I believed them. Unfortunately I could only spend as many days in Ouarzazate as an Englishman before me had spent months in the Grand Hotel du Sud. Like many British people, he fell in love with the town and had just stayed on and on, so Mohamed Zouak told me over a last drink together.

'You must come in the winter,' he said. 'Ouarzazate is even more beautiful.'

On the day of my departure I left the town at 5 a.m. by the dawn bus bound south-west to Taroudant. An old and toothless, brandy-slugging Frenchman wearing soiled khaki sat opposite me. I had first seen him at Chez Dimitris's the night before. The beret worn at a jaunty angle was as black and as shiny as the young Moroccan wife beside him. Her dignity was aided and abetted by heavy jewellery and long, pendant earrings in seven tiers like Chinese wind bells. Day had already arrived, bright but not yet hot. In the military cantonment soldiers paraded for physical training, their dazzling white singlets making the surrounding pampas blossom look tawdry.

Two hundred miles had to be covered to Taroudant along the road which kept on the southern side of the High Atlas, though luckily no more terrifying precipices had to be negotiated. At first we came on to long stretches of desert dunes in which nothing living appeared except ground squirrels which chased one another across the road. Mounds of stones had been piled up in places where holy men once stopped to pray. They resembled the funeral cairns still built in Western Scotland today. The desert was ideal holy-man country, bare and inhospitable, perfect for ascetics, appropriately furnished with occasional wayside *kharrob* trees bearing John the Baptist locust beans. Some of the mounds were markers of floodwater level or were signposts of routes up into the mountains, and each was dedicated to a saint who could protect the traveller from drowning or getting lost in snowdrifts on the mountain pass dedicated to him.

Here and there a lonely, naked sacred tree that had defied wind and sun stood up from the desert, bearing a load of votive offerings hung from its branches, tin amulets, locks of hair, strips of clothing and mysterious parcels. Apart from locust trees, there were huge gnarled thuyas under which shepherds and herds sheltered during storms. People also came to tell the revered trunks of relations' deaths, a custom similar to the one in Ireland where, until not so long ago, country people would run and tell the livestock and bees of a death.

This was no desert of sand, but a wasteland of rock more like the endless expanses of the lava *hraun* in Iceland. Brooks threaded through it, attracting oleander and tamarisk. But even the paradise luxury of the oleander could not disguise the harsh oppressiveness of the sterile wastes. Yet occasionally I saw villages marooned in the stone wilderness. The bare surroundings conditioned their architecture. Stones and rocks were not so easily worked as the mud of the Dra Valley kasbahs, whose elaborations and scale these villages lacked.

It was curious to find good, straight roads running through this god-forsaken country. But gradually the hard desert yielded and widely spaced clumps of vegetation ran for miles. A tawny, withered landscape succeeded this, flecked with the green of dwarf palmetto. We stopped and an oil can full of water was passed round like a Baptist holy communion. Then we came through the mountain pass of Taliouine, and once again the landscape changed completely. All the hills and mountains laid bare the bones of the terrain. In places there was vegetation, but it began and stopped abruptly like unfinished petit point. Other hills were grained and veined like marble and others like wood, yet others were lined and scooped like empty sea-shells and toffee-whorls, and others ran with fantastically moulded ribs like Gothic vaulting and piers. The swirling forms of Chinese wood engraving appeared in some places, and elsewhere fine fluted forms were gathered in delicate folds like the marvellous carved drapery of the Winged Victory in the Louvre.

To reach Taliouine we had crossed a broad river-bed and arrived at the small settlement near the natural sculpture in the hills. The driver climbed out of his cabin.

'One half of the hour, please.' I had not suspected he spoke English.

The break allowed many of the passengers time to do business at Taliouine's big fair, for this, bright and bristling, was the week's event of the district, and the event of my journey, because the fair was wonderful as only real country fairs can be. Farming and mountain people had come in from many miles around, and must have set off from their homes long before dawn. Hundreds of mules and donkeys were tethered in adjoining fields. And at the fair itself row upon row of tented booths were set up in front of a permanent market building of stone. Within its cloisters, vaulted diagonally by semicircular arches which produced a perspective illusion of pointed Gothic architecture, many merchants sat, selling marvellous silver jewellery set with semi-precious stones. The air was redolent with the fresh scent of mint tea. Groups of men sat under the arches, listening to talk and smoking hashish in thin wooden pipes.

As with the ancient Arab cities, the market building seemed perfectly designed, the architecture in harmony with the people and their activities. This was folk architecture of great charm, as much charm as the pedlars and women and children who squatted in groups along its double aisle, enjoying a rest in the cool breeze which flowed round the crudely hewn stones and under the rough wooden roof. Children swarmed happily everywhere in the market, but particularly in the stone arcade. Boys as well as girls wore one earring. Most of the men were in blue Berber gowns, and carried beautifully tooled leather shoulder bags in lieu of pockets.

These were tall, handsome people, bearing the rugged marks of mountain life, faces weathered by storms and the hot simoom as much as by the sun. Many of them were negroes, more than six feet in height. In flowing robes they might have been the Prince of Morocco going to choose the caskets for the hand of Portia.

Facing the crowded arcade at Taliouine, equally crowded tents had been pitched, in neat rows. Piled on the ground outside, a motley of merchandise waited for weighing and packing and scooping and loading finally into donkeys' panniers or on to bus roofs. Heaps of almonds made the finest sight, and it looked as if every other tent dealt in these nuts. Where could so many hundredweights of almonds possibly go, and where indeed in that stony landscape had so many come from? Heaps of minerals rivalled the almonds. This part of South Morocco was riddled with mines and commercial companies worked the rich deposits of mica, asbestos, lead, copper, cobalt, molybdenum, tin, antimony, graphite, gypsum, besides the magnesium I had already seen high up in the Atlas Mountains. Even the peasant farmers worked away at superficial lodes, and many came to Taliouine market with half a sack of rock salt for sale. The bus-tops bore huge lumps of mineral in addition to the usual load composed of trussed-up sheep and goats and cloth bundles. Other heaps outside the tents were for incense crystals and the powerful scents of these overpowered all other smells except the appetizing one of roasting kebab meat.

Such a confusion of activity moved about the market that I could not absorb it all. Negro women put their shopping in a bundle which they tied behind them like Victorian bustles. Meat cut from sheep killed only a few minutes previously was carried unwrapped in the hand or on a strong piece of grass. The market jewellery had been produced locally and the semi-precious stones probably came from the surrounding country. A piece of jewellery loved by women on all sides of the Atlas Mountains was the fibula with its chains and pendants. The design of fibulas in Taliouine's market tents closely resembled those made in ancient Greek times, and brooches I saw could have been sent there and then to shops in Oban for sale as kilt-pins.

Many of the people buying garnet rings and silver amulets were themselves pedlars from remoter mountain regions, where they would return later in the day, some of them not reaching their homes for several days. They were loading up their donkeys with fascinating mixed loads of incense and almonds, Indian hemp and wild apricots, tree bark and dried henna, tamarisk galls and dried peaches, cow hides and cotton, and, inevitably, dates, which have been a staple diet for these mountain and desert people for centuries. Years of experience had taught the Chleuh mule-drivers how to pack their oddly assorted merchandise carefully into the goatskin panniers, the *tellis*, so that nothing would be spoilt should a storm occur on the way home. So loaded, they would make for the most inaccessible of mountain passes, where only a donkey could get along the dizzy ledges, and there resell the wares bought down in the *souks* of Taliouine.

Of the twentieth century these regions showed hardly any trace, except in the form of plastic sandals and false teeth from the mule-drivers. Life there was still lived according to the ancient Julian calendar as it affected the small barley-fields. The seasons all related to tilling, the time of ploughing, the sacred time of Nisan in May, when rain was the greatest blessing, the festivities of harvest and the autumnal death of the earth, which only resurrects at the coming of the October rains.

We left Taliouine and its fair. The driver had difficulty in coaxing the bus over the river-bed back on to the main road to Taroudant. Hunger had been catered for by huge loaves and bunches of luscious grapes on which the passengers now set to with a proper disregard of table manners so far as noises were concerned. Propriety was reserved for more important matters, such as that the women should keep their faces covered. They lifted up their veils like trapdoors and shovelled handfuls of food in as though stoking a boiler.

THE FLOWERING DESERT

After a few miles the landscape went through yet another complete transformation. This time a plain appeared again, melting into a misty blue horizon from which a mighty spur of blue mountains rose nobly into the sky. The change of character was as complete as it was exhilarating. Scattered lotus trees (jujube) covered hills and steppes. In springtime this passage of landscape must have been wonderful with the blossom. But spring was long ago burnt up and I saw only the plum-sized fruit hanging on the lotus trees, waiting to be gathered by herbalists for making into cough mixture, a less romantic use of the fruit which is traditionally famous in Europe as a means of making wanderers forget their homes.

The great grey shrike was everywhere on the thorn-bushed steppes. But it was not content simply to feed on rotten grasshoppers which it had impaled on the jujube bushes until 'ripe'. Out here in the semi-desert he became a confirmed predator, not confining his taste to ground squirrels and snakes but seizing wheatears and buntings and bigger prey in his talons. Locally, the shrike was known as 'the pilgrim', because it supposedly followed caravans to Mecca and back. Few of the country people I was able to communicate with had any interest in birds and they were ignorant of their names. The blackbird was suitably termed the garden-slave, and turtle doves were *dhukr-Allah*—praise God. The wintering lapwing got its name *bee-beet* from its cry, and the reputation of having once been Jewish because of his wispy crest, a black skullcap he still wears, in spite of being an early convert to Islam on Moulay Idris's coming to Morocco.

No natural feature characterized this part of the southern provinces more than the argan tree, the Moroccan iron-wood. Tourist propaganda material thrived on the argan forests. Hundreds of photographs have been taken of goats perched on its low-spreading branches eating the leaves. These billowy, top-heavy trees, with gnarled and twisted trunks, were rather like olives, though their foliage was not so silky in texture. Argan wood was much sought after for charcoal and the yellowish timber formed the basis for the popular marquetry furniture. A very fine oil could be extracted from the kernels and used in cooking. Attempts to transplant the argan in other parts of Morocco have failed, yet here in the south it flourished over an enormously wide area, right down to the Atlantic seaboard and as far up the coast as Essaouira and beyond.

In the midst of this upland scrub zone the old Frenchman and his young wife got off after enthusiastic handshakes all round. She placed a sack of meal on her beautiful head with all the grace and dignity of a second Nefertiti, and walked away down a mule track through the thorny jujubes where not a house or domestic animal was in sight. Everybody laughed, not in scorn of the young negress with the old man who was a perfect stage Frenchman, but because even as they vanished among the trees the man turned once again to wave and made us smile with a music-hall mime he had used all the journey.

Although I did not realize it, we had been in the bus over ten hours. At Taroudant in the Sous Plain I climbed out feeling as fresh as when I had climbed in just after dawn. The mysteries of the Julian seasons had entered my bones, beguiling the two-hundred-mile journey south-west. The Atlantic coast itself was not now more than fifty miles away.

The Sous was that vast plain lying between the High Atlas and the Anti-Atlas, and Taroudant had been fortified by the Merinide kings in the fourteenth century when they made the town capital of the Sous. Because of its connexion with the Saharan routes, the city's prosperity had been founded on trade with the Sudan, a trade all too often in human livestock. Although many Moroccan towns still retain the walls built so long ago, most have since spread beyond them. Taroudant had not. The walls confine the city today much as they did originally. Our bus had to stop several times outside the walls, while farmers drove their cows home for milking within the town. I was watching something unchanged in centuries.

A dusty air of pleasing decay coloured Taroudant, a town which in 1550 was described as being as large as Seville. Now it was an easy place, not densely crowded and intense like Fez, nor grand and pretentious like Meknes, and it was very much cooler than Ouarzazate in spite of being on a plain hemmed by mountains. Perhaps the sea's proximity had something to do with this. Once again I resolved, as I had done as a result of my travels in other countries, never to take notice of what other people said. 'They' had said Marrakesh and

Wayside market on the Tizi N'Tichka road to Ouarzazate

Kasbah—last stop before the Sahara

Ouarzazate would be unbearably hot in August. They were not. 'They' also said that hotels in the southern regions during the hot season would be closed. They were open. Some of the larger and more expensive hotels closed a part because tourist numbers dwindled until the cooler season. But I found the Taroudant Hotel within five minutes of leaving the bus. And the doors were wide open as I approached it from behind a herd of shaggy goats.

From the street the place looked like a small bar only, but beyond was a long, arcaded courtyard filled with a profuse jungle of tropical plants. Thick tangles of fleshy leaves and flashy blossoms hid the other side of the courtyard, and grew up to twenty feet, well above the open balcony on the first floor from which my room opened. Morning glory and Florida liana covered the walls. Birds flew in and out of the banana and orange trees in the court gardens, trying to filch fish from the ponds.

Through my window shutters, which reached to the floor, I could look down to the narrow street and almost shake hands with the tall house opposite. This had obviously seen grander days, for now its mud walls had crumbled and the green earthenware pots set on the roof parapet were cracked and chipped. The hotel, too, was an old house, its rooms lofty, its staircases well worn. I wondered if the pretender El Hiba had lived in it when he made the town a centre for his 1912 campaign to win the Moroccan crown. Perhaps he had lounged, as I did after a most tasty meal, in that same courtyard with a basket of figs and grapes like the one placed before me.

Most women wore the *haik* in the street instead of a *djellaba*. But the voluminous, winding robes here were black instead of white, as though they were all in mourning. I had come to the town hoping to see the Blue People who inhabit the south as lords of the desert. For centuries the tribe wore nothing but blue clothing in the belief that this was the chosen colour of the sun and afforded the wearer all kinds of protection. Much of the indigo clothing was dyed locally. But since the colours were not fast, their bodies became blue also.

Although I missed the Blue People, I did, however, finally discover the secret of other blue forms which had puzzled me many times in Morocco. Shops in the *medinas* and the modern sections of the towns sold mysterious parcels wrapped in blue paper. There could have been candles inside, for the parcels were shaped like truncated cones, about nine inches long and three inches wide at the base. At Taroudant I saw one without its blue wrapper. It weighed several pounds and was a solid lump of sugar moulded for sale in that form.

A country atmosphere pervaded the little town. Its mosque was like the parish church in an English market town, not so big as its city equivalents and a little broken by time. The mosque's outer wall was blank and whitewashed and I peeped through a crack in the door and saw a central court and white colonnade. The minaret was panelled with tiles and topped by a sugar-icing of white decorated crenellations. A dwarf in a large turban sat before the main door like a medieval jester. Children played in the dust and made sand castles. Others stood in the doorways of dark houses and ate pomegranates, while others hurried by clasping fresh bunches of mint for evening tea.

Before dark I walked outside the city walls. Deep dust of a rutted track deadened my footfalls. I might have been a ghost. Compared with the grandeur of the imperial cities, Taroudant's walls were humble. But in their day no doubt the castellations and the towers saw enough blood and death. Indeed, in the sunset, they were the colour of blood. But that evening the peace was profound. Only cattle and donkeys went silently through the gates to get safely in the town before nightfall. The asses' panniers were laden with cut grass for their night fodder.

Crops grew right up to the base of the walls. In the surrounding country, palm and olive groves thrived richly, and there were orchards heavy with lemons and oranges, figs and pomegranates, plums and apples. I passed a man making mud bricks, mixing them with straw like the Israelites under Pharaoh. He placed the grey mixture in a double mould and left the bricks in rows ready for drying in tomorrow's sun. Beyond, I found a full water channel, a coursing of the dry land's life, for though the rivers ran dry in summer, plenty flowed in the network of irrigation channels. Yet on one side of Taroudant lay the big dried-up bed of the River Sous. This was the major river of the whole Sous Plain, a region perhaps more fascinating on account of its birds than any other in the whole of Morocco. Hoopoes were everywhere on mint beds and orchards, hunting spiders and cockchafer grubs. From the earliest recorded times the hoopoe has been hunted by man, especially in Europe, because of its high aphrodisiac value. Yet, ironically, in Morocco, where people were so concerned about their love life, the birds breed and flourish freely and widely. Next morning, when I returned to the thick peppery white dust of the main farm track, blackcap and warblers, including the olivaceous, were singing on every side with larks and buntings, each trying to outdo the other.

A slow darkness overcame the last embers in the sky and the dogs tried out the first few yaps for the night-long session of barking. Cicadas' high-pitched vibrations began from still-warm walls and tree trunks. Arches of the city's gates echoed to the clip-clop of donkeys picking their delicate way along. Now the moon's silver light was unrivalled, because the lingering amethyst on the horizon, where silver clouds floated, had changed to the unfathomable colours of night. Camels quietly munched at the leaves of overhanging trees, both as sharp in silhouette as the ragged peaks of far mountains. But in the moon's light the mountains vanished and silhouettes were only a blur. Soft darkness invaded the city also, for there was little street lighting. Passing through the old gateway and along the smaller streets, as I did going back to the Taroudant Hotel, was to pass back into bygone centuries. Essaouira had been built 160 miles away on the coast in the eighteenth century, and as it grew, stole Taroudant's prosperity. So far the twentieth century had not restored the little town's commercial importance, but neither had it destroyed the pale tempo of life behind the crumbling, haunted walls.

10

Sea Symphony

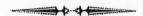

Agadir. This name still sends shivers through those who remember 29th February 1960, when disaster brought the Miami of Morocco to total ruin in fifteen seconds. The earthquake was the most destructive ever known in Africa. Within a quarter of a minute the fashionable resort ceased to be. In its place were ruin, rubble and corpses.

Among the many French and English holiday-makers was 17-year-old Richard Luddington of King's Lynn. He had been staying at the Saada Hotel with his parents. 'When the earthquake came,' he said, 'the hotel shuddered, then collapsed like a pack of cards. I was fortunate, I suppose, because I was under only six feet of rubble and they got me out in six hours. My father was sixteen feet down. It took twenty-two hours to free him. My mother was farther down. She was dead when they got to her.' At the very least, 12,000 other lives were lost in that quarter of a minute. Two weeks later children were found under the rubble, still alive. But hope could not go on, and for fear of epidemics, the Government finally ordered the complete demolition of the ruins. And that was the end of Agadir.

Four years later I was there. I had read in a French paper that the town had been completely rebuilt. Getting out of the bus from Taroudant, I found myself half a mile from the sea amid a wilderness of wasteland and temporary buildings. I could not imagine that the heart of the African coast's Miami once stood there. But at least new roads had been constructed, though they did not follow the destroyed roads' routes. Agadir's brave attempts at resurrection came into view as I walked in search of the Hotel des Dunes. But there was not much. Some housing and a cinema, petrol stations, a few shops, a string of bars. A new Miami had yet to appear.

On a rise overlooking the sea I found a quiet village of temporary buildings. The hotel occupied a group of the single-story houses among the gardens. I told the German-speaking manageress what I had read in the French paper about Agadir's reconstruction. She laughed. Her own story of survival from the earthquake must have been typical. She said that accounts of the disaster in European newspapers were not correct. The only safe place had been the beach, where thousands of survivors rushed, and had done during the months afterwards when tremors continued to shake the site. But the manageress insisted that there had been no 'large tidal wave' as widely reported at the time, including the British Press. On the other hand, she put the number of people killed at between 25,000 and 30,000. Her nerves had been on edge for long afterwards. Even today tremors disturb Agadir, making investors reluctant to bring business in.

In my ozone-scented cabin the earthquake seemed unreal. I felt I was being deceived about the whole thing, and that my comfortable bed, the sideboard and chair and the washbasin, all new, really belonged to a seaside country place, just being opened up for tourists. I could not believe there had ever been a sophisticated resort there at all. The lonely splendour of sea and sand-dunes seen from my window confirmed this.

Agadir's shoreline rose quickly to high sand-dunes, a mountain range in miniature which ran for miles round the wide bay. The sand was fine and ideal for bathing-beaches. The sea came in lazily. The thundering swells which pounded the rocks at Rabat seemed to miss this part of the coast. Its soft sound played a ground bass beneath spectacled warblers' notes and the song of crested lark from the thorn scrub.

From the hotel I wandered down through the wasteland and over the coast road to a wood. The wood also served equally as a changing pavilion for bathers and as a paradise for lovers. Through the trees lay the last dunes and the sea and a panorama of the whole empty bay. A spur of the hills jutted as a headland cliff into the sea at one end of the town, which was still no more than an embryo conceived in a womb of rubble. The hills around were dotted with scrub and looked like leopard skin. At the other end of the bay the sand-dunes lost themselves in the mist of spray blowing from a froth of slow white waves. This mist swallowed the horizon and melted sand, sea and sky together.

For a swim I undressed on the warm, therapeutic sand which winds had blown into drifts like snow. Birds' spoors and the zigzag trails of thin lizards with bright green tails imprinted the sand. This part of the bay was not the smart part. That lay farther down with a complement of soft-drink stalls and changing tents with the pencil-sketch lines of dock cranes beyond. I thought it all rather sad in view of what must have been there before 1960.

I let the sun dry me after my swim and then went back to book on a bus for the next day to Essaouira farther up the coast. Agadir's sands were unrivalled, even by those at Tangier. But the 'town' was still only a building site with completed buildings few and far between. And at last I saw one of the Blue People, a woman in an indigo gown. She had three children with her, whose heads were shaved except for a narrow tuft running over the top like the crest of the hoopoes following in the wake of the bulldozers. Like others I had noticed, the whole family were holding bunches of mint under their noses because of the dust from passing lorries, many of which were crowded with veiled women going to work in new factories.

I walked through a big group of single-story houses which were simple and white walled and arranged round small squares where cars could not come. The design was good and done with recognition of Moroccan town tradition. The children playing in the little squares certainly looked as if no disaster had ever hit Agadir. Playing games or sitting solemnly to watch the men playing draughts, they were as happy as Moroccan children everywhere.

Shops with shutters hinged at the top and lifted up to make sun canopies were small and similar to booths in the ancient *medinas* elsewhere. No windows overlooked the quiet paved ways between the houses, for they all looked inwards to internal patios, again the traditional pattern of Moroccan living. Only gaily painted doors gave access to the street. By one such door I saw a plate bearing the name 'Dr. G. J. B. Bergesio of New York'. The dentist himself was not there, but his dental mechanic, who saw me through the half-open door, took me in and showed me all over the place in the magnanimous way Moroccans have with strangers.

Summer is not made by one swallow, nor could this excellent housing make Agadir the resort it once was, a 'must' in the tourist directory. Long before such modern ideas as mass tourism put Agadir on the map the district had been famous for sugar. The surrounding land was so successful with cane that a story tells how Ahmed the Golden, when in need of marble for his palaces in Marrakesh, paid for it with sugar, pound for pound.

Next morning a chorus of bulldozers and earth-moving machines and pneumatic drills woke me in good time for the bus to Essaouira. Outside the town such mechanical things were forgotten again, for camels were pulling the ancient wooden plough and turbaned figures walked behind broadcasting corn from a bucket. The coast unfolded as a series of delightful sandy coves and bays fringing a blue-green sea, an emptiness interrupted here and there by fishing villages. Where the cliffs became too rocky and too high and too indented with bays for economical road-building, the road turned inland and we hurried through a landscape of Arcadian character, at least when compared with the sun-baked country round Ouarzazate. We passed over moderate mountains and came to a land of argan woods and dry, white villages where bearded, leathery old men got on and off the bus. Boys were selling green bananas and pomegranates from family farms. Goldfinches swayed on the seeded spears of asphodel and crane's-bill.

'Past the gates of the sun and the home of dreams they went and came swiftly to the fields of asphodel.' I recited these *Odyssey* lines to myself as I gazed at the beautiful country rolling by. Here, the orderly olive groves, the domed *marabouts*, the herds of goats, the flowers and the trees (excepting the argan) all belonged to Attica. Trees were dotted about the green country and low hills, making it into a parkland where Pan might be discovered playing his pipes in the shade of a tree.

Farms along the last few miles to Essaouira were given over to the cultivation of sisal agaves. And as we neared the town everybody in the bus stood up to glimpse what looked like the wreck of a wooden ship's hull lying on the sands. The country people exclaimed excitedly about it, though I did not discover until the following day that the ship was, in fact, an old stone fort undermined long ago by invading seas. Essaouira was full of magic and the moment I arrived I knew my stay would be longer than a mere day or two. The walled town occupied a low promontory and its bathing-beaches curved round the bay to one side. The town's grandest hotel was situated there, outside the walls.

But I saw another, the Hotel du Tourisme, actually *on* the walls, among the white houses which topped the old fortifications. I did not hold much hope of having a room facing the sea and harbour, for I imagined the place would be full of holidaying Moroccans and tourists. But luck was with me, and for the unbelievably small sum of seven-and-six a night I had a room just where I had wanted it. Perhaps the tall, cool house had seen better days, and no doubt during the protectorate expatriate French people had gone into the narrow side-street entrance and climbed up its wide stairs in a brief spell away from colonial duties.

My window opened on the bay, whose waters came in to an esplanade below, and on the harbour moles, and I could see some of the stone marine buildings which lent Essaouira its distinctive air. And beyond, I could see islands and the curving bay with the destroyed, ship-like fortress. If ever heaven had been bought for seven-and-six, this was it.

Film companies plunder Essaouira for its ready-made film sets, and these were no canvas affairs on wooden frames but solid chunks of masonry on which two centuries of tides have made no impression. And it is partly in its stone that Essaouira differs from most other Moroccan cities of Moorish and Andalusian influence, where walls of mixed rubble and mud were covered with marble, or tiles of fine plasterwork. A French architect was almost certainly responsible for the layout of Essaouira. His name was Cornut and Avignon was his home town. In 1765 he found himself a captive of the Sultan Mohammed Ben Abdallah. An old book by Bidé de Maurville says that Cornut was given to the Sultan by the English, who were anxious for trading rights. The Sultan commissioned his prisoner to design a new town upon the site of the Phoenician city of Thamusiga.

On the Pizziani map of 1367 the town was marked as Mongodor. Until recently Europeans called it Mogador after the patron saint Sidi Megdoul whose tomb is just outside the town. Old tradition holds that Saint Megdoul was a Scottish sailor named McDougall, shipwrecked on the coast there, while others say he was a Danish captain. What the French captive architect conceived was truly *Essaouira*, which means 'well drawn', its old Arabic name which has become official since independence.

Hardly any changes have occurred to Essaouira since the eighteenth century and consequently its unique character survives. It is remarkably more French than even the modern towns which were built under Marshal Lyautey's direction during the protectorate. Not only the style, which is a sort of French provincial classical, differs from Moorish architecture, but the buildings' disposition. Large open spaces between the city walls and the harbour buildings resemble the *place* in small French towns of the same period. Such space rarely occurs in Moorish towns.

Part of the Frenchman's job at Essaouira consisted of providing defence works, which he did cunningly and in a way which suggests experience in this special technique. I wondered if he was, in fact, a military architect and had been captured by raiders. Speculation about him was fascinating because the town bore the indelible print of one man's work. His architecture was dominated by the sea's nearness and it had the massive simplicity and plainness of walls and quays and bastions which the sea always demands. Marine architecture the world over and in all ages has similar characteristics and Essaouira was a fine example.

That Cornut was a Frenchman could be seen also within the town walls. Instead of the traditional *medina*'s haphazard meanderings of narrow streets, Essaouira's plan had a number of long, perfectly straight streets laid down like the grand axes of a French town plan, streets as straight as the araucaria pines which rose above the jumbled flat roofs of this seaside *medina*. No doubt the captive architect had no books with him and had to rely on his memory for the exactness of proportion and detail for his 'well-drawn' town. Many of the tall narrow houses had would-be classical doorways, but somehow the mouldings got mixed up with Moorish motifs, no doubt

201

at the hand of well-meaning Moroccan craftsmen. Nevertheless, strengthening arches across the streets were round headed and not pointed in the Moorish manner, and so were those of gateways into the city.

Part of Cornut's problem was to make the promontory impregnable to attack from the sea, and it is still possible to see the skill with which he placed the various cannon-bristling ramparts. The Marine Gate was a beautiful and ingenious design, for it was on a spit of land projecting into the sea and the nearest point of defence against any raiders. Two squat, battlemented and turreted towers straddled the end of the spit. Between them stretched lower ramparts with rows of bronze cannons protruding through the castellations. In the centre was a fine gateway giving access to more ramparts behind and the walls of the city itself. The Marine Gate's stones had weathered and eroded in two hundred years, but the stone was hard and neither sun nor sea had destroyed them. The low and wide semi-circular arch of the Marine Gate, its classical pediment and fluted attached columns had kept their forms almost as crisply as they must have been when left by the mason's chisel. To one side squint arches ran under the ramparts and green water swirled through from the sea along the spit of land's side.

The fishing harbour lay in front of the forts and ramparts which stand behind it like a stage set. Against this beautiful back-drop of blue sky and honey-coloured stone the fishing fleets returned during the afternoon. So many boats came in that they were jammed one against the other. Their crews were able to come ashore simply by jumping across from deck to deck and then on to the quay. The afternoon catch consisted mainly of tunny with occasional white shark and sea-fox. As they were unloaded gulls circled round, mewing and crying frantically. Other boats were preparing for night fishing. The sailors baited large hoops, each of a hundred barbs, with sardines.

It seemed odd to see their fleet, which was not unlike its counterpart in any British fishing port, being manned by youths in brown *djellabas* or crews in yellow oilskins but with Berber skullcaps, and young sailors taking off their wellingtons and getting down on deck to make obeisance towards Mecca. Over open-air charcoal braziers, fresh-caught fish were being cooked on grilles to feed the hungry fishermen. The boats looked up to date and seaworthy and all had radio aerials slung like hammocks between their masts. They were trim and painted but except for being mainly motor-driven they could hardly have been much different from boats which muzzled in under the big cannons when the bronze guns were first hauled into position on the ramparts.

Once there, the cannons had never been moved and I saw them still resting on their original wooden carriages, though some of these were beginning to crumble away. The cannons were some of the finest I had ever seen. Tapering, eight feet long, the bronze cannons' modelling was as good as new. The lifting handles on top had been formed into dolphins, sculptured with high arched backs, with a scroll for a tail and acanthus leaves for fins. That classical plant also appeared at the closed end of the cannons, its delicate foliations cast in relief over the knob and domed end of the barrel. Also on the barrels the coats of arms of Spain and Castile were cast with a flourish of heraldry. A band of fine Roman lettering gave the date and birthplace of each cannon, such as 'Barcelona 22de Febrero de 1781'.

From the walls above the Marine Gate I could see the offshore islands. The Isle of Essaouira was less than a mile away and I wanted to visit it. Even this largest of the islands only had 500 acres, but it was big enough not only to support the remains of Phoenician and Roman occupation but something, to me at least, much more interesting. The island's cliffs were the habitat of the rare Eleonora's falcon. A few nights spent on the uninhabited island would be my idea of bliss. But after five days of trying to get across I gave up the attempt. Or rather, Abdallah Oubraym gave up trying to persuade one of the fishermen to take a small boat across to the island. Trade winds made Essaouira one of the coolest places on the Atlantic coast of Africa in summer. But the same winds also made the sea restless. The island had no quay and from the Marine Gate on the mainland we watched great swells crashing mightily in high sprays of foam against the island cliffs. Even if a fisherman could navigate the channel, we would never be able to land on the home of the Eleonora's falcon. Sir Francis Drake visited the island in 1577 and wrote:

'It is uninhabited of about a league in circuit, not very high land, all overgrown with a kind of shrub breast high, not much unlike our privet, very full of doves, and therefore much frequented of goshawks and such-like birds of prey, besides divers sorts of sea-fowl very plenty.'

I did not conceal my vexation with the sea, and my new friend Abdallah looked most concerned. He was another boy learning English and desperately anxious to practise speaking it with a native. But Abdallah was most intelligent and well informed on many subjects, not least upon the past and present life of Essaouira. In compensation for the loss of a trip to the island of falcons, Abdallah said I must see the Château des Sables which lay farther round the bay.

Next morning when I looked from my window Abdallah was sitting on the harbour wall opposite the hotel. He was much too shy to call for me. I waved and mimed the motion of drinking coffee, but he signalled back that he would wait. Big seas were still breaking on the island. Large fishing vessels anchored in the bay rolled from side to side, their mastheads moving like inverted pendulums. No falcons and rock doves would be visited that day. I sat down for *petit dejeuner* to lay a foundation for the Château des Sables. The hotel's bedrooms opened from a wide gallery which overlooked a well which originally went right through to the ground, though this was now covered to make a lounge on the first floor. I wondered if at one time the well had been open to the sky. Potted trees stood about the gallery and outside each room a table was placed and I breakfasted here on coffee out of a large bowl, rolls and home-made preserve as though taking afternoon tea at the Reform Club. Down below the old Frenchman who owned the hotel was shelling beans among the palms.

Abdallah hailed a horse-taxi which creaked and swayed along the coast road, where crocodiles of happy holiday children were going to the sea. Some were singing and some were clapping their hands in the extraordinary rhythm I heard everywhere in Morocco. It was a kind of lively dance rhythm, like a South American samba, a syncopated two-part percussion of hand-claps cleverly woven together in a complex pattern. The sound carried unusually far, for the clap itself was made by the palms of the hands being held stiffly and slightly cupped and then brought smartly together. It was a spontaneous expression of happiness. I heard it in the country and in the *medinas*, in the Djemaa el Fna at Marrakesh, by the sea, in hotels, the smallest street urchins did it, and so did groups of students wandering singing through the streets. More than the drummers and fiddlers and reed-pipe players, this syncopated clapping was for me Morocco's music.

Our antediluvian horse carriage branched off along a track into dune country and when the track disappeared under sand and broom Abdallah and I descended, paid the man a minute sum which sent him into paroxysms of gratitude, and struck off through *les dunes blanches*. Except for the coolness and the distant hum of the sea, this might have been the Sahara. But the sands were prevented from blowing away altogether by lentisk and broom which barely kept their roots anchored in the wastelands. We came to a broad stony river-bed which only had a trickle running to the sea. In winter, Abdallah said, the waters rushed down from the mountains, but in the summer's long drought the stream was sluggish. An old man in a turban, with his *djellaba* tucked up into his baggy pantaloons was washing clothes by jumping up and down on them in the river. His drum-stick legs flew as though he were an Aissaoua in a trance frenzy. Brilliant tangerine butterflies fluttered about, robbing even the gaudy ice plant blossoms of their colour.

We found a ford and managed to cross the river without wet feet. Our movements put up waders and egrets and several hoopoes. Trade winds blew strongly that morning, particularly in the exposed sandy wastelands. Birds were flung about the sky as though they had lost control of their wings. I remembered a summer in Madeira some years previously when people complained of strong Saharan winds, the *leste*, which brought herons from the African mainland to rob Madeira's pools of goldfish.

Trudging through the sands, our faces stinging with wind and sun, we came to the half-buried palace of the long-since-departed Sultan Mohammed Ben Abdallah. Sands had drifted high against its walls and had invaded its courtyards. No wonder they now called it the Château des Sables, for it was indeed a sand castle. But in its heyday, when the Sultan's power and wealth were at their summit, the palace had a great courtyard surrounded by a wall with pavilions at each of the four corners and another in the centre of the court, all built of stone.

By building this palace and Essaouira itself the Sultan had ruined the trade of Taroudant and Agadir, and old tales record that the grand palace was overwhelmed by the shifting sands in answer to the curses showered on it by the deprived tradesmen of the Sous. Some curse, whether theirs or merely the winds', had certainly fallen on the place. Not a sign of life disturbed it now. Only lizards slithered along the top high walls protruding from the dunes. Pigeons flew in alarm from the towers, and that was all.

Ignoring an official notice saying that entry was forbidden, we scaled the walls and slid down another dune to the court. Abdallah said the notice-board was put there because treasure-hunters came to the palace and frequently damaged the ruins by undermining what masonry still stood. He showed me the corner pavilion in whose cellars pirate gold is certain to be found one day. No door gave access to the treasure chamber. It could only be approached from above. I sat in the room over the treasure. Four segmental arches looked out over the sea and the dunes and the white cubes of Essaouira in the distance. This pavilion must have been most beautiful in its original state.

Fragments of delicate plasterwork still clung tenaciously to the stone walls, a section of moulded reliefs here, an architrave there, and above sections of a frieze laced with Koranic inscriptions. The floor tiles had subtle glazings of viridian and ochre, iridescent blacks and ivory whites. The arches gave on to balcony belvederes where perhaps the Sultan's ladies may have sat looking seawards, waiting for yet another ship to come in laden with jewels. Of the palace's gardens and avenues no trace remained. All had disappeared under sand-drifts where only alfa grass grew in the stony hollows. In spite of the 'keep out' notices, the Château des Sables was obviously popular, because signatures and names and drawings had been scribbled on the walls. Somebody had written '*Où est Monet, Gauguin, Cezanne, où est Rodin?*'

Although the architectural style was different, the whole atmosphere reminded me powerfully of Downhill's ruins, a palace which the architecture-minded Earl Bishop of Derry built on the cliff-top of Derry almost at the same time as the Sultan's palace. Outside the château's walls I saw the triple blind semicircular arches under the belvederes, behind which the treasure is said to be. Some of the arches were broken and weather had worn the stones, but not a chink penetrated to the chamber behind. The Sultan built his sea-side palace and the city of Essaouira on the proceeds of captured pirate ships like Captain Kidd's. The pirates robbed around the Carribbean and the Sultan robbed them on their way home. Fair enough, I suppose, particularly as the winds and the sands finally robbed the Sultan.

He built his palace on a commanding rise. To reach the other ruin, the great fort like a shipwreck I had seen on arriving at Essaouira, Abdallah and I had to find a way through thick groves of Spanish broom. It was like a jungle with sand underfoot. Several times we lost our way and in the end climbed the palace knoll again to spy out a route. Much of the dune-land was covered with mesembrianthemums which flourished in their wild state much better than in the form of carefully planted lawns such as those outside the town walls. When we got near the broken fort, walking across sand left wet and hard from the last high tide, I saw how huge the fortress's chunks of masonry were. Originally, the fort had been built as a gunnery commanding yet another sea approach to the city's harbour, presumably having a navigable channel within cannon range.

At some time, as the result of an astonishing undermining process by the sea, the whole structure had been split into gigantic chunks, leaving high, narrow chasms and fissures between. In a kind of Piranesian composition, stone steps and stairs and vaulting and arches and gaping windows and shattered walls jutted out from the massive blocks of rock and masonry. There was the sharp, salty smell of the sea which ran into the fissures when the tides came in and out, leaving behind a litter of seaweed and sea creatures. Instead of crumbling away, much of the fort remained intact, despite being split into the separate chunks.

The original roof platform was still complete, though in several sections, each tilted like the deck of a wrecked ship. Abdallah and I sat up there and ate a picnic lunch of cheese and tomatoes and crisp, fresh bread, followed by some creamy *pâtisserie* and grapes. The strong winds and salty air had made us ravenous. We ate without conversation and gazed instead from our vantage-point over the shining sands which curved round to the white and distant Essaouira. Figures moved across the sands. And inland camels plodded ponderously, carting stones away in panniers. The platform provided an excellent view of the Isle of Essaouira, and from there, too, it was plain why the fishermen did not want to row me out. The wind seemed to be blowing harder, and beyond the tide-line the sand was flying like blown snow. A line of ermine trimmed the island cliffs with a plume of foam shooting up as breakers hit projecting rocks.

The returning tide had crept in imperceptibly. But now its tongues began to lick the rocks beneath the riven fort. Abdallah came back from climbing dangerously in the gunnery's yawning caverns and together we made our way down steps and over lumps of stone and rock to the sands once more. A group of street urchins searched for sea urchins and crabs in the rock pools and mussel-scalps. Walking along the foreshore back to town, I thought we could easily have been in the Sahara, for the wind whipped the surface sand into a fine spray which hissed as it hurried. For days afterwards sand was still coming out of my hair and ears and clothes. But it was exhilarating, and although the only shadows from the enamelled blue of the sky came from wheeling gulls and terns, it might have been a walk along an English shore, because it was cold enough for me to put on a sweater. Abdallah only had a thin shirt and denied that he felt the cold, but I saw goose-pimples on his arms.

Our way back to town lay across dune-lands where the stone-laden camels had imprinted huge depressions in the wind-packed sand from their enormous feet. Their legs were Brobdingnagian compared with the fragile twigs of legs on which the little stints sped along, outrunning the cumbersome camels. The presence of this smallest wader in its winter plumage was a sign that the autumn migration had already begun and that the palaearctic little stints were here only *en route* to South Africa. Human waders were less energetic in the long lagoons left by the last outgoing tide. In these sandy shallows the smaller children played, preferring them to the bay itself, which the sea churned into a muddy red ribbon along the shore, though beyond this the water was green-blue. But near the town the wind seemed far less strong and it was warm again. I looked from my window in the hotel and saw that the sea had once again surrounded the ruined gunnery.

I liked my window. The view could be any in Dufy's delightful Riviera repertoire of too-blue seas white with yachts, with prom and palm-fringed beaches. At least the sense of heat and light and intense colour were the same and I wondered what Dufy would have done in the harbour when, whatever the weather, the fishing fleets went out and half the town flocked at their return to buy the big fish, or, more likely, to fill buckets and baskets with fish which slid off the mounds being transported in lorries. Though Dufy's world was one of racecourses and regattas, as decorative as the decorative bourgeois life he depicted, his eye for bright colour could hardly have resisted the harbour scene at Essaouira when the sardine boats came in at morning.

But perhaps the scene's confusion may have offended his sense of simplicity. The flurry of movement and colour, the goings to and fro, the mesh of masts and rigging, the sea architecture of hulls and wheelhouses and decks, the sea sculpture of anchors and ropes and buoys, may have proved too much for his small canvases. Buckets of sardines, catching the sun and shining like pirates' silver from Peru, were passed by chains of men, from the boats' holds up to the quay where lorries waited. The men worked rhythmically without breaking the continuous flow of baskets, full ones up, empty ones down. They sang Berber songs in a rhythmic kind of antiphon as they worked. The spilled fish were snatched up at once by barefoot children and old men. But such a plethora of fish could not be completely taken and unwanted sardines lay like silver lichen on the quay stones.

While the catch was unloaded to music and rhythm the crews recovered from the night's work and began to make preparations for the coming night. Cabin-boys pulled off sailors' rubber thigh boots and strung the night-fishing clothes to dry among the plum-and-custard-coloured nets whose floats were like ostrich eggs. As the work proceeded the men unloading became progressively covered with silver scales like mermen. After the last lorry had departed and the holds were empty, the cabin-boys hosed the men's brown, muscular legs and torsos, and this done turned their hoses on to the decks, leaving the ship spotless for the evening departure.

A man walked over to me and introduced himself as Bou Rhim-Abdelkrim, the master of a boat I had been watching, the *El Bahar*. The captain told me the night's catch had been twenty tons of sardines, for which they had taken the *El Bahar* out, as every night, between four and seven miles. He had twenty-one men in his crew. Most of the fish was pressed for oil which went to France and Germany and the rest was made into fish meal. As he talked to me Bou Rhim-Abdelkrim ignored the half-dozen urchins who were filling their plastic buckets with the sardines he had caught. When the overfull lorries moved away yet more showers of fish fell and there were always more empty buckets at the ready.

One of the *El Bahar*'s crew said he had been a soldier at Innsbruck during the war and was amused when I told him that the highest British naval title was 'admiral' which came from his own tongue— the Arabic *amir-al-bahr*—lord of the sea. In *Paradise Lost* Milton had spelt the word as 'ammiral'. And that evening I saw a trawler setting out in a choppy sea. The master stood before the mast, a tall, commanding figure with a strong-boned, fierce-looking face. A *djellaba* flapped in the wind and on his head was a snow-white turban. Here was a lord of the sea who would have put the fear of God into Simon Danz himself.

Some of the fishing crews wore the traditional Arab clothes, others were in oilskins and many were in shorts and singlets, or red shirts with blue jeans and some in the more familiar dark blue fisherman's jersey. The whole harbour sparkled with colour, orange oilskin, blue and yellow masts, blue and white superstructures and pitch-black hulls, the jazzy hues of children's clothes, the metallic glint of fish, the foamy whiteness of women's *haiks*, and even splashes of blood when pedlars, selling to the crews, slit the throats of chickens and ducks and let the scarlet blood spill into the water. A Franciscan friar, rotund and benign, added a sombre note, and boats with buoys on board added a Spanish note, for the buoys had red flags on sticks like bull-fighting barbs.

Life was hard for the fishermen. But they obviously enjoyed it. Besides the hectic atmosphere of energy there was also one of happiness. When a pause in the work occurred, and when the holds emptied at last, they played with each other and wrestled like boys, or they lay spreadeagled on the decks sun-bathing and sleeping. Order and rhythm and colour pervaded the harbour, so that it became an entrancing ballet to Berber music.

On the quays as much activity went on, because tractors brought fish meal and oil back from the processing factories, ready for loading into lighters which then plied out to cargo boats anchored in the bay. Other tractors brought corn and wheat, adding to the mountains of sacks on the far quay. Children climbed on the sack cliffs and ran helter-skelter in the dark tunnels between them. Near by an ancient sail-maker sat cross-legged, his turbaned head askew as he went over a great sea of canvas sail looking for tears. Other old salts, complete with pipes and serge trousers and armfuls of tattoos, sat gazing vacantly out to sea, contemplating eternity or nothing. A horse carriage brought a captain back from his sleep at home, and he boarded his boat now spanking clean and shipshape. Other sailors went off, carrying special prizes from the catch for their families, perhaps *hoot Mûsa*—the fish of Moses, or red mullet—the *Sultan el hoot*, the king of fish, a name as romantic as that given the lovely butterfly orchis—*sultanat en Nooár*, the queen of flowers.

Essaouira's harbour had its attendant boatyards, where boats were not only repaired but new ones built. I saw two ship-carpenters using adzes on a new boat being made of cedar-looking wood. The redolence of the wood mingled with the sea smell, as the chips flew from a huge baulk. This yard was guarded by an old sea wall with a little pepperpot turret. Hundreds of gulls in orderly rows along the stone mole watched the proceedings with suspicious superiority, or perched precariously on the ships' rigging like crotchets of a scherzo. Enormous black lighters had been drawn up slipways and their wooden hulls were being caulked and pitched.

Although Abdallah's long summer vacation would last until October, he spent some time every day studying. He knew I would loiter happily about the harbour for hours and needed no guide. The *medina* was more difficult to explore. But in the *mellah* I found a marvellous old-fashioned general store. They sold everything. The aged proprietor sat in a corner presiding over the proceedings like Michelangelo's Moses. Open sacks gave out the rich sacky-cornmeal smell of such shops. Sailors and women in *haiks* wandered in and out, roving round the shelves. A good bottle of local red wine went at one-and-ninepence and I got one of these on several occasions to drink down at the harbour while I ate delicious fresh fish charcoal-grilled in the open air by the Marine Gate.

The Frenchman Cornut's town had some small squares within it, unlike most *medinas*. Trees grew in these, in some cases old and thriving rubber trees which must have been planted soon after the town was built. But the captive architect's finest work was the Scala. These defences, protecting yet another side of the town's promontory, could only be approached from the town side by chasm-like *medina* streets threaded between the walls of tall terrace houses with shuttered windows. In places the streets were buttressed by semicircular stone arches and houses also stood on these, making long dark tunnels. But reflected light fell brilliantly in the open light-wells between, and these, open to the sky, also acted as ventilators drawing draughts upwards, so making the streets continuously cool.

Below and behind the high Scala platform was a straight narrow street which gave on to semicircular vaults under the ramparts. Joiners and cabinet-makers specializing in marquetry had their workshops there. I stopped to see the tables and bibelots of thuya ingeniously inlaid with veneers of lemon wood and ebony, argan and mother-of-pearl.

The magnificent Scala was a long wide platform of sea-pale stone built on rocks along the town's vulnerable side. I walked up a ramp to a three-arched entrance and turret on top. From here, the Scala revealed itself as a fantastic stage set, perfect for La Scala Milan. There was a circular tower and then a circular, cobbled platform with seven-foot-high battlements and eight slots for cannons. General Lord Heathfield had taken one of these guns during the famous siege of Gibraltar, afterwards presenting it to the Sultan of Morocco in exchange for a shipload of corn, duty free. I peered through at the Atlantic raging over the sharp, chocolate rocks below. The winds whistled in the openings and musket slits. Above, the blue, blue sky showed up the white, white spume on reefs and islands. Buffeting winds and the sea's unrelenting surging and roaring made the most romantic sea castle I had ever seen, more romantic even than Denmark's Elsinore.

I wandered down the long, lower platform, where fifteen more bronze cannons poked their noses seawards. The atmosphere was more like two thousand years old rather than two hundred. Ironically, just as Sultan Mohammed Ben Abdallah had ruined the trade of Agadir and Taroudant by building the new Essaouira, so the Roman Juba II had ruined the ancient purple trade of Tyre by building a dye-works at Essaouira which produced a much cheaper deep crimson purple made from purpura shellfish. Then the twentieth century suddenly reasserted itself. Sirens wailed and screamed as fire-engines, ambulances and police cars raced towards the harbour. I thought a ship must have caught fire and I hurried to join the converging crowds. A sailor from one of the trawlers had fallen overboard and drowned between the closely packed ships.

Thousands of people stood silently on the quays watching divers search for the body. Children lined the quay edges and people pressed behind them. I wondered that more were not drowned that day. A soldier stood beside me, carrying an old-fashioned box-iron in one hand and the trousers he was going to press in the other. In the *djellaba* hoods hanging down behind, men carried melons and vegetables. And as the araucaria pines cast long evening shadows on the white walls, and it grew suddenly cold, I wished I had such a warm garment. Abdallah arrived, still dressed only in a shirt and slacks. He drew me away from the sad crowds, insisting that I should buy a woollen *djellaba*. We soon knew that not all the towns-people were down by the harbour, for as my head finally emerged through the ankle-length garment I saw another, though smaller crowd had gathered to watch the pavement performance. There was laughter and, thinking of the drowned sailor, I was suddenly grateful for being alive.

11

A Chain of Hearts

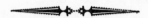

Nearly a hundred miles along the coast north from Essaouira was Safi. For me, worlds separated them, and this should not have been, because the two towns had much in common. Both were fishing ports, both had unique monumental buildings from their past. What the Frenchman Cornut did at Essaouira, the Portuguese had done at Safi. Although the Lusitanian occupation only lasted thirty years, it left behind the finest Emmanueline architecture to be found anywhere in Morocco.

The guns of the Château de Mer secured the city's sea approaches in the same way as those on Essaouira's Scala. Built by the Portuguese in the years 1510–40, the castle survived in a remarkably whole state. It is carefully looked after today, though the Sultan Mohammed Ben Abdallah tried to destroy Safi as he destroyed the trade of Agadir by moving all its merchants to his newly created Essaouira.

Before going to Morocco I had been in Crete. And while archaeological care was lavished on Knossos and similar remains, the beautiful Venetian and Islamic buildings on the Greek island had been completely neglected, not only by the authorities but by tourists, too. In Morocco the interest in historical architecture of all kinds was much livelier. No buildings of interest or beauty, irrespective of who built them, were allowed to fall to pieces. Like Essaouira's old stone fortifications, the Château de Mer at Safi had been most skilfully kept in good condition. The castle, rising directly from the sea rock on huge inclined foundations, was planned around an open central courtyard whose stone paving and walls would

214

make an ideal place for open-air drama, or *Son et Lumière*.

The castle's entrance was on the landward side. High crenellations crowned its towers. Cusped Gothic windows blinked narrowly from the chambers inside. Rampart platforms for cannons and protective cross-fire had been built on the courtyard's sides, giving fine views of the sea and the city and country beyond. Immediately below, the Atlantic swirled over the rocks. Round towers at the corners connected with ramps from the gunnery platform. Passages and stone stairs and vaulted rooms with slots for firing burrowed in a maze through the honey-coloured masonry. From the top of the towers, the rest of the city walls and bastions could be seen extending like outsize stone dikes across the hills.

A *marabout* shrine had been built in one corner of the court and veiled women came into the castle, not to romanticize about its swashbuckling past but to reverence the saint. The white domes of other shrines showed on the green hillsides round the town and two stood just beyond the castle wall. The Château de Mer was as fine a castle by the sea as any traveller could hope to see, and, its original builders notwithstanding, this was due to the Moroccans' care over such things.

I felt disappointed, afterwards, in Safi town itself, where the same sense of civic awareness had somehow gone awry. Though the castle dominated the town's seaside, the same eye that could delight in its strength and massiveness, or look to the sunset over the sea through a tall pointed arch between two towers, also had to look at Safi's unfortunate industrial sprawl. Compared with Casablanca, there was not much of it, but enough to spoil the place. A headland enclosed the bay. There should have been a splendid promenade there, or palms, or some way of bringing the town's landscape and beaches into active service. Instead, near the harbour end of the town there were dock cranes and huge, ugly silos. And nobody could stroll by the sea, because the railway to the harbour had been laid there, cutting off the shore.

Industrial infiltration had also affected Safi's *medina*, which was not quite a traditional *medina* and not quite a modern town either. No doubt the mining of phosphates in the interior and the export of them was good for Moroccan economy. But why did a charming city

A CHAIN OF HEARTS

have to be scarred by the grinding up and down of railway trucks in the one place of the city's greatest amenity, the sea? At Essaouira the sardine fishing fleet blended skilfully with the people's life and with the old buildings. At Safi, the fishing had become part of the industrial squalor. And behind the Portuguese walls the *medina* was beginning to suffer in the same way. Barbicans and a deep moat survived and at one point were possibly the most dramatic architectural composition in the kingdom. Both the moat within its sloping masonry chasm and the road passed beneath high pointed arches. Yet the noble effect was spoilt by a concrete factory beyond.

Safi's townspeople seemed to be devout as well as industrious. Besides the *marabouts* scattered about, elaborate green and crimson panels of texts from the Koran and pictures of holy places in Mecca were being offered for sale by street vendors. Most important among the local shrines was that of the famous proselyte Sidi Ahmed bou Salah, known in the East as 'Master of the Yard-arm'. While travelling to Mecca he was refused a bed in Alexandria, and confounded the Egyptians by resting on top of a large pole. Recognized at once as a holy man, he was implored to come down and not visit the country with plagues because of their inhospitality. The saint took his shoe off and threw it into the air. He demanded that an inn should be built for Mecca pilgrims where the shoe fell. Sidi Ahmed became highly venerated throughout Islam and settled with his two wives at Safi in 1050.

My disappointment was not so much because Safi lacked character, but because everywhere else in Morocco had been exceptionally good. But my mood was hardly made less hypercritical by an uncomfortable night spent in a seedy *pension*. But that was my first and only uncomfortable night. Perhaps I should have broken my golden rule about avoiding expensive hotels as I had done at Ouarzazate. I may not then have fled Safi as early as possible next morning, after a restless night, disturbed alternately by groaning phosphate trains and the vociferous arguments, in the alley beside the *pension*, between ladies of the town and their military clients. And when, towards dawn, these stopped, the *mouddhins* began their calling from the minarets.

Safi's first inhabitants were said to be Canaanites, who also had

216

been obliged to flee, though probably with more reason than I had, since the invading Israelites were bent on cutting off their thumbs and 'great toes' as the Bible puts it. And this was an old tradition. A Roman writer, Procopius of Caesarea, recorded that in his day two white stone columns existed outside Tangier. They bore a Phoenician inscription, 'We have fled before the face of Joshua the robber, son of Nun.'

I felt no guilt in fleeing, however, when my ears were threatened with splitting by pneumatic drills on the road immediately outside the *pension*. I did not stop for breakfast, but got on the first C.T.M. bus going up the coast to El Jadida. The route was an inland one and longer than the coast's eighty-nine miles. But I enjoyed the ride, because once again I saw what different faces Morocco shows to the sun. We passed through plains shimmering with almost continuous mirage effects. Trees and villages were mirrored by the heat, their reflection a perfect inverted image, so that they looked like lakeside villages. The idea that water surrounded the bus was so strong that I kept checking with my map to make sure that we were not, in fact, going through a region of lakes.

Another part of the road lay through country which reminded me of Denmark in summertime, although, Vikings excepted, no Dane ever looked quite like the mad woman who came a-begging at one stop, her head shaved and tattoed breasts bared. Her madness was laughter.

El Jadida succeeded in all the things where Safi failed. I grew to like the town so much that it ran neck and neck with Essaouira for first place in my affections. Its story was as fascinating as Essaouira's and began when the Romans made a town there. The place proved ideal for defence and trade many centuries later when, following a fort built on the Roman site by a party of shipwrecked sailors from Portugal in 1502, the Lusitanian Government established a proper town. They called it Mazagan and held the town for most of three centuries. A great wall flanked by five bastions surrounded Mazagan, which became known as the 'rampart of Christianity in Africa'. The ecclesiastical architecture, especially the sixteenth-century Church of the Assumption left eloquent evidence of those centuries.

But even the Portuguese, experienced and tenacious colonialists, could not hold out against the Sultan Mohammed Ben Abdallah. He raged against this vestige of the Portuguese Empire within his kingdom, the last remaining 'stone of scandal', as he called it. Under persistent attacks from the Sultan, the Portuguese decided to evacuate their outpost. Like the British at Tangier, they mined the principal buildings before leaving. Unfortunately, the explosions did not occur until the Moroccans had moved into the town. So many died under the falling debris and ramparts and buildings which collapsed that Mazagan had to be evacuated once again, and re-entry forbidden to all inhabitants. Nobody returned there until 1821, when a number of Jews were given permission to occupy the old town. A condition imposed on them was that they must call the city by its Arab name El Jadida. Grave penalties would be imposed if the Portuguese name ever appeared again though the name has been used by Europeans until recently. By 1872 the first Europeans received permission to reside in the town, though it was not until the twentieth century that houses were allowed to be built outside the old Portuguese walls.

One of the first houses to appear along the front overlooking the harbour was that of a prosperous Jewish merchant. The tall building of three stories covering a whole block between four streets, looked much older than it was, perhaps because of a reticent classicizing in the design which, though markedly Latin, did not indicate a specific place and time of origin. Warehouses and shops occupied the ground floor and the rooms above had, over the years, been turned into hotels, of which the Hotel de France was the one I chose for my stay in El Jadida.

A wide staircase went up from a tall hallway and stairwell and I climbed up to the first floor, where an aviary of tropical birds greeted me. And on the next floor I had a room facing the sea, a cool shuttered room, with an iron balustrade across the window on which I could lean to look at the beach or the buses below. No covering graced the wooden floorboards and the wide cedar planks of the ceiling were innocent of plaster and paint.

The old Portuguese town smiled golden in the sun, unaware of past violence, sleek and sleepy as a cat. Within the walls two-story houses had been built in the Portuguese manner, with shutters closed on windows set in the wide stone surrounds which distinguish Portugal's home and colonial architecture. Down one street a house had been formed in a round, battlemented fortification. Behind it rose a minaret, white against the radiant sky. But unlike most minarets, its corners had been rounded so that reflected light caressed its surfaces. A carriage and pair could drive through that part of the town. Sunlight penetrated these Portuguese streets as it seldom did in the Arab *medinas*.

Because of stone defensive works, flights of steps and platforms, and sheer drops from immense bastion walls which were so well preserved, El Jadida was popular with visitors and tourists. Boys from 6 to 16 waited to earn a few coins by guiding strangers about the maze of walks and ramps and passages. A 12-year-old attached himself to me and stayed, limpet-like, refusing to leave until I had seen everything.

'*Portugais*,' he said about everything we looked at. Then '*Citerne! Citerne!*'

I knew about the Portuguese cistern, and was glad when the boy took me there. From what I had seen of the cistern in photographs I was not overexcited, though to visit the building seemed the thing to do in El Jadida. I was quite unprepared for the dream-like wonder of the real thing. The subterranean cistern had supplied the six-teenth-century Castillo Real with water. During the town's changes of fortune its entrance was walled up and only found a few years ago when a shopkeeper decided to enlarge his premises. When knocking a wall down he made his startling discovery.

Occasionally it happens that one stumbles on a building which contains an architectural space of great genius. Not all famous buildings have this quality, and not all unknown buildings are with-out it. Such spaces have a majesty independent of actual size. C. F. Hansen's church built in 1817 at Hørsholm in Denmark is an example of a work of genius known only parochially. The Portuguese cistern at El Jadida is another. It was certainly one of the most unusual buildings I had encountered anywhere in the world. Again, the Moroccans' interest in and careful preservation of this four-centuries-old treasure, impressed me.

Basically, the cistern consisted of a single stone chamber, about eighty feet square, covered by quadripartite vaults springing from rows of squat classical columns. The cistern had no windows, but an eye in the central vault let in a dazzling shaft of sunlight, as powerful in the submarine gloom as a searchlight.

A simple wooden walkway had been constructed against the cistern's walls, so that visitors could view this amazing sight from various angles. Profound, uncanny silence prevailed. Profound because no sound percolated from the outside world, and uncanny because the dripping of water, the creak of the walkway and the guide's voice were multiplied by a hundred echoes which scampered among the vaults like imprisoned mad things trying to escape. I sang and a heavenly choir answered in sonorous harmony. I shouted and an army shouted back. I whispered and all the shades in limbo chorused.

The cistern was flooded and the water reflected not only the dramatic effects of light and space, mirroring the columns and their webbed-hands of vaulting, but sounds also. A sense of suspension in a cage of stone was the water's principal effect, because it rose no farther than the column bases, causing the whole structure to be reflected upside down on its surface. Age and dampness had given the yellow stone bronze green-browns. On the enclosing wall a line of discoloration eight feet above the walkway showed the original water-level when the cistern had been used. The cistern undoubtedly ranks as one of Morocco's wonders, a fact of which film companies were not unaware. Orson Welles's Othello had found his way down there.

My uninvited boy guide did not come into the cistern. Without much conviction about my chances, I hoped he would have disappeared by the time I came from the watery catacomb into the reassuring warmth of the street. But he was there, grinning and pleased to see me. In the interval he had planned the next part of my itinerary —an old round-headed sea-gate that once opened on to a part of the harbour, more fortifications, and the mole's long enclosing arms, all glowing in the sun. As he was hawking me from pillar to post I suddenly realized why I had not sent him packing. His comic roguish manner alone would not have saved him, for all Moroccan boys who hope for a dollar from the tourist have similar wit and charm. My

12-year-old guide was genuinely proud of El Jadida. I could tell by the way he patted the bronze cannons or pointed out a view or stroked stone mouldings or risked his neck by leaning over high battlements to show me the sluggish water of an old quayside below. He had affection for his town and this pleased me, because in Safi nobody had seemed to care. There the atmosphere struck me as harder and less friendly.

Dozens of boys were swimming in the harbour, diving from rocks on which the mole stood. They wriggled through the calm water like tadpoles. Older boys curved through the air with lissom grace as they displayed their diving prowess. Their shouts and laughter rang about the harbour. But my guide pulled my sleeve and took me off to see the mighty walls above another part of the harbour behind which houses jostled white and sun-bleached in the sea. Across the harbour, the shell of a church stood up, its scroll-pediments clear in the sky.

A small brown hand tugged once more at my sleeve and we were off again, this time on a tour of the ramparts. I marvelled, as in Fez and Meknes, at the prodigious scale of the works, at the enormous expense of human effort and suffering which must have gone into the making of these monumental piles of hewn stone. El Jadida's walls had decayed more than those farther down the coast at Essaouira. Their cannons were not so well preserved and their wooden carriages had rotted and some had disappeared altogether. Children played on them and no doubt had done for generations. A more ideal playground than the El Jadida's walls would be difficult to imagine. Scrawled writing and drawings, not always of consummate politeness, covered the walls with a rich sgraffito.

As we went along my young guide supplemented his history of El Jadida with the history of film companies who used its walls so frequently for locations. He mimed various scenes he had seen and seemed disappointed when I failed to recognize the impersonations. Going down to the harbour we passed a woman with a child held in the back folds of her *haik* and a large wardrobe balanced on her head as she chatted animatedly to another woman laden with vegetables.

Alongside a quay the *Alfonso Gino II*'s crew was unloading seaweed by hand. The sea harvest nets hung from the masts like Chinese lanterns. Barefooted and wearing nothing but shorts, the eight brown young men were possessed of the same geometrical perfection in action as the Discobolos of Myron, except that they flung armfuls of the purple-brown seaweed on the quayside instead of a discus. The Spanish ship *Fito* from Bilbao, a larger vessel altogether, was taking corn and wheat on board. During my stay in El Jadida lorries and tractors passed continuously through the town, carrying grain to the docks. Autumn had brought heaps of apples to the streets alongside the prickly pears.

Seasons did not affect El Jadida's year-round ritual of sun worship and sea worship. Stretching along the bay, from the town walls, past the newer parts and so on to unfrequented country, the beaches were a spectacle. Low outcrops of rocks occurred in the soft sandy reaches at wide distances apart, so making particular beaches. Those nearest the town buzzed with life and movement and colour. Between sun-up and sun-down they were never empty.

Besides all its other allurements, Morocco added that of perfect sea swimming, a kind of diadem in its crown of wonders. All those Atlantic coastal cities offered swimming in warm waters, which rolled over shallow, sandy bottoms. Rio de Janeiro's Copacabana beach, before fashion moved farther round the bays, enjoyed its fame somewhat dishonestly. In reality the beach was too hot, too crowded, frequently dangerous for swimming and hemmed in by stacked concrete-box hotels. El Jadida's and Essaouira's beaches outstripped Rio's, though they enjoy little fame outside Morocco.

But El Jadida's beaches conjured Brazilian ones for me. Here on Moroccan sands the same enviable mixture of racial groups showed the beauty and strength of mingled bloods. Skins went through every shade from beech to ebony all varnished by a deep tan. As in Brazil, barefoot football raged like an epic battle across the sands. When seen from the Portuguese walls the battle was a mêlée, but close-to separate skirmishes could be distinguished. At midday and early afternoon only a few patrols moved jazzily across the sands, only a few footballs shot in the air occasionally like cannon-balls. But in the cooler late afternoon and early evening, when businesses closed, the armies returned in force.

A mile of tawny sand suddenly flamed with the myriad colours of flying knightly pennants—beach shorts in this case, of every hue and stripe and shape and brevity. The teams had no special members or even numbers and the players seemed to play first on one side and then on the other, depending entirely on whimsy. Old played and young played and flocks of lanky brown legs from holiday camps and orphanages played, frail, supple little things darting about the beach like rock-pool minnows. But mostly the adolescents and young men played, black heads and muscular brown bodies flashing and whizzing, weaving patterns dazzling to follow against the sand and the sky and the vivid clashes of colour from tents put up just for the day.

When I left the Hotel de France each morning the dignified elderly Frenchwoman who ran the hotel leaned over the stair-rail, wanting to know if I would be staying on for yet another night. El Jadida had become an addiction. Every time I thought about giving it up I took more.

'*Oui, Madame! Merci. Ce soir aussi!*'

Tonight also. But I knew a day was coming when it would not be tonight also, when tonight would be spent on the plane back to London. I was beginning to suffer withdrawal symptoms already. I stayed on at El Jadida instead of rushing on to yet another place because I wanted to engrave every line of it in my mind carefully, as on a copper plate, so that I could bring the mental engraving out in midwinter London and see this happy place again.

I stayed on also because I hurt my foot. The beach football games were not the deadly and serious affairs they are in English public parks. Anybody who stood to watch found themselves involved. Teams sometimes had as many as thirty a side. Half the side would, in any case, be taking quick plunges into the sea where the ball, often as not, was kicked or thrown deliberately. So I got myself involved. Although my feet had been well hardened in boyhood wheeling peat barefoot in the bogs of County Fermanagh, they were not up to Moroccan standards of camel-like horny hardness. But a limp was no excuse for the beach footballers and I still played, keeping mostly in the sea.

Such days could have gone on for ever. The knell was sounded when I detached my last traveller's cheque and this led with Doomsday finality to my last day on the golden sands of El Jadida. While families converged on the beach, the Frenchwoman leaned over the stair-well with her inquiry. I told her sadly that I would only need my room one more night because I was definitely leaving next day.

Women in billowing *haiks* paddled in the shallows, holding up ankle-length pantaloons discreetly to their calves. Children hunted crabs in the brown rock pools and collected cuttlefish for their caged birds. A string of miniature Berber villages, like those strange desert castles on the southern side of the High Atlas, had sprung up along the sea's edge, where children made sand kasbahs, surprisingly skilful replicas of those I had seen in the southern regions. I saw long chains scored in the sands, the links being hearts, leading right from the road down to the water. Old Arabs rode their horses along the beach and took them into the waves for a bath, which the animals seemed to enjoy. A huge Dalmatian hound came bounding amongst the footballers and chased the ball, followed by a crowd of fifty screaming, delighted children.

I wandered past the football and the picnicking families and the fashionable Marhaba Hotel, which had the largest colony of changing tents, in order to go along the bay to one of the rocky outcrops and a score of sandy coves beyond which were always deserted. But one old woman went there. Tattoos and deep crevices of age criss-crossed her face. She bent over the rock pools, washing sheep fleeces. Beyond, the wrinkled saltings bore the delicate, clear patterning of spoors from the little stints. The tiny, perky waders hurried along, looking for sandhoppers and small shellfish. I had one of the coves to myself until two women, fully clothed in *haiks* tried to get a young girl into the water. The sea was shallow there and the girl succeeded in soaking her veiled relations besides being ducked herself.

Her brothers laughed at the women's cries. They lived in the sea and came from a swim, shooting spurts of water with cupped hands, until everybody, including me, was soaked. I spent the rest of the day with the family. They were seaweed gatherers farther along the coast and had come, like so many hundreds of others, to spend Sunday on the beach at El Jadida. The two eldest brothers were like Parisian teenagers just returned from the Riviera. Their smart clothes had not been bought with the meagre profits of harvesting seaweed for agar-agar, but from the more lucrative oyster beds. But they were Moroccan boys, and having showed off their smart-cut clothes, were soon in bathing shorts and playing football in which once again I tried to forget my painful foot and half of my thirty-odd years.

As the sun rose to midday heights the salt atmosphere, the running about and the swimming produced roaring appetites, but my new friends would not hear of me going back into town for lunch. I suspect I deeply offended them by suggesting I should not join their picnic. The cups of buttermilk were not less refreshing than the bottle of beer I usually drank with my lunch. And by this time, in spite of Sam Weller's belief that poverty and oysters go together, I certainly could not have afforded such meaty oysters, which the boys had probably gathered from the farm pens earlier that morning.

The head of the house and father of all the children was small and dried-up like an old potato with curious pink patches in the pigmentation of his skin. But he wore authority with as much ease as he wore his fresh-laundered *djellaba* and turban. Over his right shoulder a curved, inlaid, silver dagger hung from a thick silken cord. It was a symbol of his dignity, the patriarchal dignity of old men which was the same everywhere in Morocco. He was no more than a seaweed gatherer, but he was a king in bearing, and talked of kings, and claimed blood ties with King Hassan II and descendancy from the Prophet. Two brothers I knew who owned a cinema in the Marrakesh *medina* had made similar claims. All three may have been right, for after all, one king alone, Moulay Ismail, produced eight hundred sons and untold multitudes of daughters. And Morocco was the Sherifian Empire of the Prophet's descendants.

In his prime of manhood the seaweed gatherer had been a sailor. He knew the world, or at least the coasts of Africa. Solemnly he tugged the thin wisp of white beard and looked out to sea, recalling high days before the mast. Even his sons in their Paris-cut slacks and pink silk shirts listened to the old man's meanderings, and said nothing except to translate for me.

Before I could understand what the old man was trying to say about Madagascar, a map of Africa had to be drawn in the sands. The pink blotches on his face were not unlike an old-fashioned map of the British Empire in Africa. His comments about the vastness of stone Pharaohs in Egypt were simple to understand. But only when going back to town for the last time along the beach did I realize what the old seaweed gatherer meant about the Queen of England getting her crown up a tree in a wild elephant jungle. This somewhat surrealistic conversation made sense when I remembered that Elizabeth II had come to the throne while in a Kenya tree-house watching elephants coming to drink in the moonlight.

But the old man questioned me about places I had seen in Morocco. What did I like and what did I not like. And, most important, had I seen the King riding to prayers on Friday in Rabat. I confessed I had not, though, I said hastily, I *had* seen him driving to his palace at Ifrane. But the old seaman did not think much of that. Before leaving Morocco, I *must* see the Sultan on his charger—*Insha' Allah*—God willing, he added with the phrase which spiced all talk in Morocco.

I stayed with the family all the afternoon, swimming and playing with the children, and listening to the old man. I was sorry when evening began to steal over the sky and they packed their things and went off along the coast, the old man riding a horse. The beaches began to thin out, the tents were coming down, the footballs were being dribbled back towards the shadowed Portuguese walls.

When I returned after supper the beaches were deserted. I could hear the little stints above the soft roar of breakers far out, and from trees beyond the sands the shrill trill of cicadas. On the moon-lacquered sands I saw the chains of hearts melting under the incoming tide. By morning when the sea was far out again the hearts would be gone. Then other lovers would come and make other chains. But invisible links held me. It would take more than tides to melt the chains which suddenly seemed so real and so heavy now that I was leaving. Of course, I still had the journey back to Tangier. But I bid good-bye to Morocco there at El Jadida, in the moonlight on the sands. It seemed right somehow. Moroccans call their country Maghreb el-Aksa—The Land of the Farthest West. El Jadida was the farthest west I would go during that journey.

Index

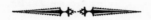

INDEX

INDEX

INDEX

INDEX

INDEX